Performance Design

Performan

ce Design

Edited by
Dorita Hannah
and Olav Harsløf

Museum Tusculanum Press
University of Copenhagen 2008

Dorita Hannah and Olav Harsløf (eds.):
Performance Design

© Museum Tusculanum Press and
the authors, 2008
Copy editor: Jordy Findanis
Layout and composition:
Pernille Sys Hansen
Cover: Pernille Sys Hansen
The book is set in Fresco sans and Taz
Printed in Denmark by Narayana Press,
www.narayanapress.dk
ISBN 978 87 635 0784 4

Image on the front cover: From *Under
the Surface – Looking into Springtime*,
Madeleine's Madteater. Photo: Annick
Boel. Image on the back cover: From *The
Memory Project*. Photo: Luca Ruzza

The book is published with
financial support from
Department of Communication,
Business and Information Technologies,
Roskilde University, Denmark

Museum Tusculanum Press
Njalsgade 126
DK–2300 Copenhagen S
www.mtp.dk

Contents

conSTRUCT

Preface Edward Scheer

This collection comes at a crucial time for scholars and artists in performance studies as Western theatre continues its post-dramatic turn and fuses ever more completely with the contemporary environment – where performances occur in a multiplicity of places and styles and where artists, scenographers and architects have all begun in different ways to consider the performative dimensions of their practices. The traditional skills and crafts of theatre have had a similar journey to undertake and cannot remain unchanged by this paradigm shift. As the editors say in their introduction, these essays chart the itinerary of scenography as it too "leaves the confines of the stage and begins to wander." The essays here do not centre on a particular kind of design or endorse a specific scenographic practice, but instead chart different migrations of design around the worlds of performance.

One significant, perhaps even central, question for the contributors to this collection is the problem of lighting. It is one which illuminates other aspects of the project as well since the essays return to this enigmatic correlation of light and performance design again and again. It becomes not simply a technical or operational issue, but a conceptual one which is connected to the very meaning and possibility of performative action.

None go quite as far as Paul Virilio's observation that drama itself is linked to the excessive desire for luminosity, which is surely one of the more enigmatic statements on performance and scenography. Perhaps this becomes clearer when expressed conversely, that the desire for drama is related to the hunger for light and its effects, the enhancement of the visible, the accentuation of the perceptible.[1] Light shining on faces and events. Light streaming from projectors and televisions.

In his manifesto "Theatre and the Plague," Antonin Artaud has a similar vision, noting that "in the theatre as in the plague there is a kind of strange sun, an unusually bright light by which the difficult, even the impossible, suddenly appears to be our natural medium."[2]

This is the light of revelation, of illumination as something more than the selection and emphasis of stage objects and action. Suddenly a door opens and the light pours in. The senses are flooded, space apprehended, and "the impossible" roused from its sleep.

The door in performance, Lilja Blumenfeld writes here, "is the Door, the Eros and the Thanatos ... the framing imaginary line that implicitly or explicitly keeps the performance and the spectator apart. The threshold of a door is a stage edge mirror 'in between'." The door becomes a signifier of liminality and the space of possibility.

A door opens and the light pours in.

In the opening essay, Arnold Aronson argues for a differential luminosity to the theatre, that "Live theatre requires ... an external source of light – originally the sun, then candles, oil lamps, gas, and electricity... But film and video projection and digital display *are* the light sources. In fact, their visibility – and thus the ability of the spectators to read them – depends upon the reduction or elimination of external light." Perhaps performance expresses the hunger for luminosity because it doesn't have its own. Some others seem to disagree.

For Fabrizio Crisafulli, "light is not a technical element 'projected' onto the production, but becomes a component of the relational 'place' itself: woven into the actions, time, spaces, forms, sounds and words that define themselves through their relationship with each other. In relation to these elements, light is both origin and consequence. From the beginning it is considered an active and formative factor." Here the desire for light closes the gap between theatre and film while in Rodrigo Tisi's *Plastic Forest* lighting becomes the substance of the work in another way with hundreds of light emitting diodes responding to "the presence of the participants ... in the heart of the plastic structure."

Lisa Munnelly points to another version of the question of illumination: "I would be struck by a sudden thought," she says, "rather than ideas emerging as though through a gradual awakening. The phenomena evoke Henri Poincaré's poetically phrased observation that 'thought is only a flash between two long nights, but this flash is everything'." Her fear of not experiencing this flash – "What if this flash of illumination fails to reach us?" – beautifully conveys the anxieties of the artist and the writer waiting for the flash of light and waiting sometimes in vain.

From the *Southern Lights* project of New Zealand artist Anne Noble to the deeps of the sea in Carol Brown and Mette Ramsgard Thomsen's *SeaUnSea* and Quarantine's *Geneva*, the lights show the way in this collection and draw the various places of the performances and projects described here together. For me, my own place of Sydney is connected to this publication in the most unlikely manner through the work of the Danish designer Poul Henningsen, whose lamps, Olav Harsløf imagines, inspired Jørn Utzon's iconic Sydney Opera House, a metonymic image of Sydney and a place where performance and design were imagined together from the very beginning.

Harsløf's chapter is perhaps typical of the fascinating connections the writers have made in these pages and testifies to the unique contribution this book is making to the contemporary debate about the changing places and practices of performance. These essays describe performances of design in ways that challenge the perception of scholars, artists and designers to make the journey from the familiarly visible objects of one's own place, whether in the theatre or elsewhere, to the illumination of new practices and discourses.

Edward Scheer is President of Performance Studies international, PSi

Notes

1 Paul Virilio, *The Aesthetics of Disappearance* (New York: Semiotext(e), 1991), p. 73.
2 Antonin Artaud, "Theatre and the Plague," in *The Theatre and Its Double*, trans. Victor Corti (Calder and Boyars, 1970), p. 21.

Introduction
Performative expressions across disciplines

Dorita Hannah and
Olav Harsløf

> Being an event rather than an object, performance is radically unstable
> in the meanings it generates and in the activities it engages.[1]
>
> Gay McAuley, *Space in Performance*

Performance is a complex socio-political phenomenon, which could be summed up as any public demonstration of actions, tasks and skills – consciously enacted and received – that encompasses dramatic expressivity, culturally codified behaviour and operational competency. However, this expanded notion of performance has tended to focus on human agency and expression, excluding the dynamic role played by seemingly inanimate places and things. As Marvin Carlson parenthetically notes in *Performance: A Critical Introduction*, "even in the theatre we do not speak of how well the scenery or costumes performed."[2] Yet design artefacts – whether objects, materials, occasions, environments, or still and moving images – are inextricably bound to performance through notions of embodiment, action and event. Within them stories are told, forces are harnessed and roles are played out.

This link to theatricality originated in Western modernity through scenography (*scenografia*), where design (*disegno*) as invention (*invenzione*) was celebrated as a mimetic practice that utilized the perspectival image to unify art, architecture and theatre. Although Aristotle referred to *skenographia* in *Poetics* as a "scenic writing" connected with stage painting, and Vitruvius described *scaenographia* as the art of perspective, it was the Renaissance architect Sebastiano Serlio who utilized *scenografia* as a means of integrating the science and craft of architecture, scenery and painting into a combined stage and auditorium,

11

which in turn influenced the planning of buildings, cities and landscapes.[3] As a theatrical phenomenon, design artifice came to permeate a range of fields from urban and architectural design to fine arts and public spectacle. However, over the next four centuries, a unified world picture was philosophically called into doubt, challenging and destabilizing the role of mimesis and the fixed spectator. Space and matter began to fracture and multiply as exemplified in twentieth-century modernism – particularly through its avant-garde – thereby creating a schism between dramatic form and other art forms. A distrust of representation and an emphasis on 'authenticity' demoted the role of the theatrical – commonly defined as 'false' or 'exaggerated' – in everyday life. Scenography, which once shaped both our real and imagined worlds, was relegated to the performing arts alone as the design of settings, costumes and lighting. Although Arnold Aronson (the first author in this anthology) defines scenography as the all-encompassing and transformative visio-spatial field of the stage,[4] the contemporary scenographer is generally expected to serve and supplement the theatre director's imagination rather than initiate projects or experiment with this spatial realm. But what happens when design leaves the confines of the stage and begins to wander?

Performance Studies with its interdisciplinary focus – or even its claim to be a "post-discipline of inclusions"[5] – has provided a more open discursive field that shifts the emphasis from theatricality's overtly orchestrated artifice to the dynamic and fluctuating forces of performativity, whereby the lived world is regarded as a complex construction of manifold macro and micro-performances capable of being isolated, framed and manipulated. As a phenomenon operating beyond the exclusive and often hermetically sealed realm of the stage, a performance paradigm provides the means of recuperating the more extensive role of the scenographer while also embracing the skills of other artists and designers who transform the public domain with fleeting, time-based interventions that comment on our contemporary condition. This opens up a new interdisciplinary design field within which to practice and theorize aesthetic, cultural and everyday experiences, where cultural artefacts are considered *performative* (active) rather then *constative* (descriptive).[6] Performance Design – as a porous, fluctuating term – works across a broad spectrum that embraces the theatrical, historical and quotidian. In this way, our places, things, gestures and imagery are rendered more mobile, dynamic and affective. If performance is, as Elin Diamond contends, "a risky and dangerous negotiation between a doing ... and a thing done,"[7] what can design effectively *do* as a practice (a doing) and as a production (a thing done)?

This question was put to a group of artists, architects, scenographers, performers and theorists who were invited to attend a weeklong international symposium on Performance Design at the Danish Institute of Rome in January 2005. Organized by two newly established university programmes in Performance Design (located at New Zealand's Massey University and Denmark's Roskilde University), the aim was to assemble a diverse cast of participants from around the globe to share *performative expressions across disciplines* through presentations, workshops and performance events. The contributors – made up of 24 invited academics and as many of their students – represented a cross-section of interested parties from the Czech Republic, Chile, Denmark, Estonia, Greece, Italy, New Zealand, the United Kingdom and the United States. A number of the research papers and projects presented that week have been developed further for this book. As the symposium progressed it became clear that the majority of the participants considered themselves to be *refugees* from their original disciplines, unwilling and unable to be contained by the singular nomenclatures of well-defined fields such as architecture, music, theatre, literature, linguistics, gastronomy, fashion, fine arts, film, media or choreography. However, all who gathered were prepared to explore common and uncommon ground through the fluid and emerging field called Performance Design. Like many working across art, architecture and performance in the early twentieth-century avant-garde, they were seeking to replace the static principle of the autonomous *art object* with the dynamic principle of *embodied spatio-temporal event*.

The Rome symposium also highlighted the impossible task of presenting creative work as a seamless coherence between practice and theory as well as the dilemma of representing performances that, as fleeting spatio-temporal acts, have long since disappeared. These perennial issues surrounding *presentation* and *representation* persist in the creation of a printed publication, which itself demands that *re-presentation* becomes a creative act. Like the symposium it followed, this book is structured around three thematic sections entitled *dis-PLAY, enCOUNTER* and *conSTRUCT*, investigating and re-presenting a range of

13

aesthetic, *cultural* and *technical* performances. However, all three themes necessarily intertwine, exposing their inseparability. In *Perform or Else: From Discipline to Performance*, Jon McKenzie (another contributor to this publication) establishes a similar matrix of aesthetic, organizational and technological performances, which are measured through efficacy, efficiency and effectiveness, respectively.[8] However, just as the modalities cannot be separated, neither can their performance criteria, which in this publication encompass the *efficacy* of public displays, the *affect* of socio-political encounters and the *effectiveness* of technological constructions. Despite inevitable overlaps, the three sections structure the discussion around the performative aspects of showing, interacting and generating. Acknowledging the oppositional (dis-), immersive (en-), and resistant (con-) prefixes of these three actions, the theoretical discussions (scholarly chapters) and realized projects (visual essays) negotiate between the political and private, dramatic and routine, material and immaterial. Rather than designing *for* performance these artists emphasize the performative nature of their creative work as both the speculative and projective act of *designing performance* and the embodied and ongoing practice of *performing design*.

To **disPLAY** is to self-consciously make a show of something, aware of the aesthetic charge elicited by an act of revelation. But this charge – predicated as much on what is withheld as on what is revealed – is also influenced by the relationship between the viewer and the viewed. Arnold Aronson's opening discussion on the "Power of Space in the Virtual World" utilizes the theatre as a site that calls into question both the materiality of the lived world and the immateriality of the event, reaffirming Elizabeth Grosz's contention that the real world has always been a space of virtuality – "saturated with spaces of projections, possibilities, and the new."[9] This saturation is made evident when theatrical performance is un-housed from the dark and disciplined confines of the traditional stage and auditorium, encountering sites and audiences with their own specific stories and characteristics. No longer held at a distance, the mimetic image is troubled, doubled, fragmented and destroyed – infusing the everyday with the mythic and reintroducing elements of danger and difficulty to both dramatic events and the built environment. Kathleen Irwin, whose scenographic practice taps into the immaterial qualities that haunt the material world, discusses the complex dynamics of site-specific performances in her essay "The Ambit of Performativity," where heterotopic spaces are created as hybrid worlds mindful of multiple histories and diverse occupants.[10] For fine artist Lisa Munnelly, drawing is both a specific site of exploration and an action that leads to spatial interventions which transform the image into performance. In "Drawing upon the Aesthetics of Immersion," the dynamic effects of Munnelly's mark-making are utilized to incorporate spectators within the performative presence of her work. This presencing through immersion is played out in Rodrigo Tisi's architectural intervention on a pier in the Chilean city of Valparaiso, which encourages active public participation. Tisi's *Plastic Forest*, created with students of architecture for a media festival, considers the construction, occupation and destruction of a temporary responsive structure as a time-based urban event. Fabrizio Crisafulli is another architect directly involved in performance, directing and designing his own site-specific productions. Considering "Light as Action," Crisafulli enlivens bodies, spaces and objects through the luminous poetics of his creative work. Massey University's Art Design Collective (ADC) re-enliven the traditionally sedate surroundings of an art gallery with their "Antarctic Shopping Party," a satellite event to Anne Noble's photographic exhibition, *Southern Lights*. By transforming the sublime image into a series of collectible objects, ADC not only test the distance required between artwork and visitor, but also comment on the consumption of the image. This emphasis on a fractured experience rather than a focused viewing is played out in Hotel Pro Forma's *jesus_c_odd_size* – a contemporary take on the medieval mystery play spearheaded by Kirsten Dehlholm. Avoiding the presentation of a fixed linear narrative to a stationary public, Dehlholm encouraged a mobile audience to re-construct familiar stories occurring simultaneously in a range of spaces. These aesthetic events – whether in the theatre, metropolis, art gallery or abandoned buildings – exposed the mythical in everyday life and challenged the visual primacy of design for performance, emphasizing its more sensory, experiential and virtual nature.

An **enCOUNTER** is a dynamic interaction that can result in confrontation, not only between performers and spectators but also between communities and their formations of knowledge. The performance event, as a cultural production, can be found in historic moments, daily occurrences and in environments both local and global, highlighting how the quotidian world is framed and stage-managed through sedimented social dramaturgy.[11] This troubles the relationship between performativity and normativity, exposing the multiple performances we are all compelled to take part in ... or else! Who better to open this section than Jon McKenzie, for whom performance design – as something we feel as much as we see – occurs on a global level. Focussing on "Global Feeling" and recent catastrophic events played out on the world stage, McKenzie suggests that these orchestrated spectacles of war and terror could be resisted and combated with "political love." Lilja Blumenfeld addresses similar universal issues of authority and the law in "Kafka's Door," where she aligns the framed proscenium stage to a portal we perpetually face and dare not enter in a life-long quest to meet the Other. For Blumenfeld, the scenographer maintains this fragile doorway, which separates and binds us to unknown worlds. Brandon LaBelle addresses the rupture of such delicate boundaries through sound – an often-overlooked design element that inherently resists containment – documenting "Street Noise" as a defiant force for political, social and cultural demonstration. Catherine Bagnall transports us from the raucous European and American streets of protestors, street fighters and marching bands to the New Zealand wilderness where she dons glittering gowns in extreme climates. In her "Encounters with Simple Pleasures," Bagnall regards 'feeling' as truly local rather than global: yet there is a universal quality to the images she takes of these solo performances enacted for an audience of one. While the fine artist encounters her pleasures in remote landscapes, architect Luca Ruzza encourages the public to actively engage with the fleeting and unstable nature of history. Ruzza's design for the "Memory Project" in Amsterdam houses an accumulating collection of multiple voices scored by composer Arnold Dreyblatt, which folds the past into the present and recognizes the archive as an interactive organism. This complex relationship with history is found in the site-specific performance *Her Topia* – a riff on *heterotopia* referring to Isadora Duncan's failed utopia – which was commissioned by the Isadora and Raymond Duncan Dance Research Centre in Athens. Designed by Dorita Hannah, this project (to be developed further in other sites) stages encounters between the slow performance of architecture's mute objectality and the fluctuating forces of the dancing body. Ephemeral interventions become the means of bridging between bodies and buildings and invoking 'other' places and persons. The section concludes with Simon Banham's presentation of Quarantine Theatre Company and its collaborative project *Coming and Going*, which, through inter-cultural dialogue, aims to address issues of the outsider as a body in-transit. These scholarly and visual essays exemplify how, in affective encounters with strangers, we become aware of the variations of sights, sounds, disturbances and spatio-temporal dimensions played out in the varying magnitudes of performance, and that these effects can be loud and spectacular or invisible, silent and subtle. As Banham contends, design provides the means of "tinkering with the familiar," and the results range from the pleasurable to the catastrophic.

To **conSTRUCT** is to fabricate from disparate parts, involving a technical performance – whether it be weaving, cooking, building or digital coding – which Heidegger referred to as a poetic "challenging forth."[12] However, through the immaterial nature of most contemporary technologies, what is challenged forth remains seductively out of reach, troubling events with an unsettling and otherworldly presence. Challenging forth therefore involves a *calling forth* of the virtual – technology's inherent condition of possibility. This phantasmatic extension of space and time is inherent to the stage that has always invoked "a world which is not determined, but is rather in the process of becoming."[13] Carol Brown and Mette Ramsgard Thomsen combine the processual tools of choreographer and architect to disturb spatial and temporal fixity in their collaborative performances, *Spawn*, *The Changing Room* and *SeaUnSea*. Their essay "Dancing-Drawing Fields of Presence in *SeaUnSea*" considers how inscriptions on stage and page challenge ideas of liveness and presence. Olav Harsløf calls forth the figure of Denmark's modernist architect Poul Henningsen in "PHantom of the Operas in Sydney and Copenhagen" in order to discuss the complexity of jazz improvization and its transcription to objects such as Henningsen's lamps, which Harsløf contends are further spatialized into buildings for performance. In "You are Here" John Di Stefano analyses an event he inadvertently videoed at Amsterdam's *Homomonument* to examine how performative elements disturb the constative nature of documentary filmmaking. The following chapter "Under the Surface – Looking into Springtime," documents Jan Krag Jacobsen's gastro-theatrical experience at Madeleine's Food Theatre in

Copenhagen, which utilized the performative elements of media to enhance the culinary event. Whilst the sensory act of eating binds the community in such multi-media performances, Omar Khan discusses how media can be a distancing device, despite our living in the age of global networked communications designed to bridge such distances. In "SEEN Fruits our Labor," Khan outlines how he and Osman Khan collaborated to give voice to invisible migrant workers in California's Silicon Valley, a global hub for networked communication. Khan reveals the voice of the invisible worker by way of a seemingly inscrutable urban object, which engages with members of the public through an intimate sharing of their personal viewing devices (digital cameras, phone cameras, DVcams, etc.). While the Khans' installation forms a spontaneous community out of the disparate passers-by, Joslin McKinney reminds us that the act of viewing performance involves a personal construction, which will always individualize the experience for each member of an audience. Through her project *Homesick*, McKinney explored how spectatorial reception involves a complexity of internal visual constructions that interpret, augment and play with those of scenography. This ability to shuttle between communal and individual experiences is confounded when the live presentation has to be represented in publishable form. The book concludes with Richard Downing's re-presentation of *The Water Banquet* – an ever-changing feast staged and re-staged on an immense flooded table, which reconfigures each space it occupies. Downing recuperates the archival image as a performative element (active rather than descriptive) by suggesting that the careful consideration of its placement, like scenography, provides a "'window' to an imaginative elsewhere." In this way, a publication such as this one allows performance designers – whether they operate in the performing, visual or tectonic arts – to call forth the disappearing acts they once orchestrated as something fresh, re-enlivened and discursive.

As a loose and inclusive term Performance Design asserts the role of artists/designers in the conception and realization of events, as well as their awareness of how design elements not only actively extend the performing body, but also perform without and in spite of the human body. This reinforces Jiri Veltrusky's claim that "even a lifeless object may be perceived as the performing subject, and a live human being may be perceived as an element completely without will."[14] Acknowledging that places and things precede action – as action – is critical to performance design as an aesthetic practice and an event-based phenomenon. In harnessing the dynamic forces inherent to environments and objects, and insisting on a co-creative audience as participatory players, it provides a critical tool to reflect, confront and realign worldviews.

Notes

1 Gay McAuley, *Space in Performance: Making Meaning in the Theatre* (Ann Arbor: University of Michigan Press, 1999), p. 16.

2 Marvin Carlson, *Performance: A Critical Introduction* (London and New York: Routledge, 1996), p. 3.

3 Aristotle, *Poetics*; Vitruvius, Book I.2 of *de Architectura*; and Sebastiano Serlio, Book II, *Architettura* (1545).

4 Arnold Aronson, *Looking into the Abyss: Essays on Scenography* (Ann Arbor: University of Michigan Press, 2005), p. 7.

5 Kirshenblatt-Gimblett, "Performance Studies," in *The Performance Studies Reader*, ed. Henry Bial (London and New York: Routledge, 2004), p. 43.

6 This references J.L. Austin's "performative" in *How to Do Things with Words* (Cambridge, Mass.: Harvard University Press, 1975), where "speech acts" expand language into action itself. Just as

statements can be active rather than descriptive, the material, spatial, and gestural elements that accompany them also contain a performative force, suggesting *How To Do Things With Gestures*, or *How To Say Things Without Words*, or even – *How Things Do*.

7 Elin Diamond, *Performance and Cultural Politics* (London and New York: Routledge, 1996), p. 5.

8 Jon McKenzie, *Perform or Else: From Discipline to Performance* (London: Routledge, 2001).

9 Elizabeth Grosz, *Architecture from the Outside: Essays on Virtual and Real Space* (Cambridge, Mass.: MIT Press, 2001), p. 78.

10 *Heterotopia* is a term coined by Michel Foucault to describe how certain localizable places are saturated with "other spaces," which contain an excess of meaning and integrate the mythical with the real. Michel Foucault, "Of Other Spaces: Utopias and Heterotopias," in *Rethinking Architecture: Reader in Cultural Theory*, ed.

Neil Leach (London: Routledge, 1997).

11 Theorists such as Erving Goffman, Michel de Certeau, Richard Schechner and Judith Butler have expounded this notion. The significance of their work in relation to performance theory is outlined in *Performance Studies: An Introduction*, ed. Richard Schechner (New York: Routledge, 2002) and *The Performance Studies Reader*, ed. Henry Bial (London and New York: Routledge, 2004).

12 Martin Heidegger, *The Question Concerning Technology* (New York: Harper and Row, 1977), pp. 14-15.

13 Michael Hays, *The Public and Performance: Essays in the History of French and German Theatre, 1871-1900* (Ann Arbor: UMI Research Press, 1981), p. 6.

14 Jiri Veltrusky, "Man and Object in the Theater," in *A Prague School Reader on Esthetics, Literary Structure, and Style*, ed. and trans. Paul Garvin (Washington: Georgetown Press, 1964), p. 84.

disPLAY

The Power of Space in a Virtual World

Arnold Aronson

> For several years scenic art has been on a path of evolution. [New forms] have violently shifted the earlier boundaries ... Hence some confusion: these days we hardly know the style appropriate to a particular play.
>
> Adolphe Appia, "Ideas on a Reform of Our *Mise en Scène*"

Swiss designer Adolphe Appia spoke the language of music, movement, light, and space. In fact, he was among the first theatre practitioners or theoreticians to talk about space and its effect on both performance and reception. Although the essay from which I have quoted above was written in 1902, the evolution of which Appia spoke is still in progress: the theatrical vocabulary is still in flux and scenography is perhaps less well-defined than it ever has been. And Appia's vision is still relevant – new forms *are* still violently shifting the earlier boundaries. In recent years, scenographic and performative borders have shifted in ways so profound as to call into question the very notion of theatre and performance as it has been understood for over 2,500 years. The old designations of theatre, auditorium, two- and three-dimensional images, physical framing, and real time and space, have been perforated, stretched, fractured, and dissolved. We are facing a crisis – albeit an exciting one – brought about by digital technology. There is a significant change occurring, a fundamental transformation of human consciousness akin to what occurred between the Middle Ages and the Renaissance in Western history.

Here, too, Appia seems prescient. These words, written in 1891 about the staging of Wagner's *Ring of the Nibelungs*, could, with no alteration, be applied to today's stage:

23

This art is still in its infancy, not, to be sure, because of the means available but because of the manner in which they are used ... The realization of the drama on the stage, difficult to begin with because of the numerous media required at present, is completely thwarted by the impossibility of bringing these diverse efforts together with even relative precision ... The impossibility of integrating those pieces derives from the disproportion of the intentions, not of the media. On the one hand, the means of expression are wantonly exhausted; on the other, we must be content with the worst in the visual field, which has been developed separately and on its own, and which has accustomed us to subtleties of its own.[1]

Appia was using the term *media* in its truest sense, of course, that is, "a means by which something is communicated." A century later we are still confronting the complications of "numerous media" and the "impossibility of [their] integration" into the existing scenographic vocabulary. For most of history, the scenographer's materials have been largely unchanging: wood, canvas, paint (or their equivalents such as metal, glass and various synthetic materials), and, of course, light and space. But it is also true that for most of history the theatre was the primary site for cultural exchange and the artistic investigation of society – the theatre itself was a medium, both a locus and a tool for conveying information. In order for it to serve as a site of communication, the stage had to be readable by its audience – the intended recipients of that information; and therefore it had to reflect the visual and, especially, the spatial constructs of the culture in which it existed. Today, however, as theatre's role as social arbiter has vastly diminished, the visual and spatial domain has shifted to other public forms, most obviously electronic and digital media and their multiple means of dissemination. Several generations have already grown up for whom the dominant visual motifs are neither the simulacra of the illusionistic stage nor the theatricality of the empty space of the self-conscious stage, but the constantly shifting images and flickering light of the television screen, and the virtual worlds of the computer monitor, both of which have utterly undermined industrial-age understandings of time and space. (Film, perhaps the dominant visual medium of the twentieth century, is now almost irrelevant in terms of reception, and thus in this discussion. Increasingly, films are viewed on flat-screen TV monitors, computers, and most recently on portable media players held in the palm of your hand. It has become merely one more form of digital distraction.)

It may no longer be a case of violently shifting boundaries, but rather that the boundaries have disappeared all together. If so, the whole concept of design will require a new vocabulary if it is to have meaning. With no border there is no locus for display, no vantage point from which to view.

The theatre has made mostly feeble and misguided attempts to adapt to these changes or to incorporate the new technologies with their new ontologies, and the results have generally been unsuccessful, even laughable. We are assaulted by productions uncomprehendingly employing video screens and digital projections in a misguided attempt at modernity. It would be as if carriage makers had placed pneumatic tires on their products in an attempt to compete with automobiles. It is a fundamental misunderstanding of the nature of the new forms, or as Appia said, "the impossibility of integrating those pieces derives from the disproportion of the intentions, not of the media."

■ ■ ■

If I am correct that the boundaries are evaporating, or have already disappeared, can we still properly talk about space? Space is defined by its boundaries, by its framing, so to speak. The framing determines the quality – the power – of a particular physical space. Many factors contribute to the power of a space: light, décor, juxtaposition, sound, temperature, etc. But in dealing with human constructions one starts with architecture; with natural spaces it is topography. Physical space produces tangible effects on the mind and body. But we can also talk about psychic space, metaphoric space, and, most relevant to this discussion, cyberspace. These so-called spaces can certainly be analyzed, and they most certainly produce real effects. But identifying them spatially is problematic. Whatever cyberspace is, it is not physical space. So if it has power – and I think it does – it is of a different order than that of physical space.

And yet these days people work in both realms – the physical and the 'cyber', the real and the virtual. Still, if these 'spaces' possess not only different qualities, but also radically different properties, is it possible for designers to work in both? The simple answer is, of course they can. There are, and always have been, many artists and designers who move fluidly among several or all these disciplines. Baroque architects, for example, designed churches, palaces, and theatres as well as the décor, furniture, and the performances and spectacles to be found in each. The early twentieth century witnessed a new *gesamtkunstwerk* in which artists designed houses, furniture, clothing, transportation, theatres, parks, and even entire utopian urban schemes. But whether we are talking about Giacomo Torelli or Norman Bel Geddes, and their brethren, we are talking about the design of concrete, physical space. Even the creation of illusionistic space is done with flats, drops, and other tangible elements. (In this regard we might also note that, until recently, architects and scenographers were confined by physical means – sketches, blueprints, renderings, for instance, all on actual paper; and, of course, three-dimensional models – in their creation of physical spaces. Now, however, much of the design is done on computers. There has long been software that can create 3D images, and, more recently, 'printers' that can convert such images into actual 3D models. While architects are ultimately creating physical constructions, scenographers can increasingly use computer-generated design to create scenery consisting only of ephemeral projections of digital images. One could argue that projected scenery – in the moment it is perceived – exists in real time and space, not unlike movies. But what possesses dimension is the projection *surface*, not the projection.)

Now Plato, in the *Ion Dialogue*, famously declared that someone can do only one thing well. He discusses categories that can be described as 'whole'. For instance, as he cleverly points out, all poetry is a whole and anyone who understands poetry should be able to discuss all of it equally. Accepting his argument for the moment, if we consider all theatre (in its historical and traditional meaning) as a whole, and if scenographers are part of the theatrical project, then scenographers should be able to design only for theatre. And if digital technology is another whole, then those who design for, say, the World Wide Web are of a different category. If I wished to be Platonic I could say that this has been true in part because theatre designers worked in material space, while others worked in two-dimensional space or in virtual space. But if we acknowledge that there are those who design equally well for a wide range of media, including both theatre and virtual space, then space cannot be the defining criteria and there must be some other category that includes scenography. There must be a different Platonic paradigm.

Is it possible to find a unifying theory of all the forms under discussion? Scenography today is not unlike the Poland that serves as the locale for Alfred Jarry's masterpiece *Ubu Roi* (which, coincidentally, was written in 1896, simultaneously with Appia's first writings). Jarry's stage direction declares, "the play takes place in Poland, that is to say, nowhere." Contemporary scenography, likewise, is virtual, liminal, conceptual, but only occasionally tangible. Unifying the virtual with the actual presents a challenge.

■ ■ ■

Aristotle famously observed that humans are the only animals that laugh. He might also have noted that we are the only animals that *decorate*. We transform our bodies with clothing and makeup; we design everything we use, from toilets to automobiles; we transform our environment with color, texture, and images. So strong is the decorative imperative in humankind that it is now built into the most basic computer programs. We have 'wallpaper' and screen savers, decorative templates for stationery, a variety of visual 'enhancements' for slide shows, etc. In all such cases, the content does not change; only the superficial aspects of the image have been transformed. But inevitably, by changing the visual context, the content is altered in some small way. The viewer will read the meaning differently depending on the decorative framing. Painters have always understood this. In the Renaissance and Baroque periods, artists created not only the painting, but also the incredibly ornate frame around it, not only to delimit the image and distinguish it from the surrounding environment, but to enhance the sense of grandeur – to contextualize it. Derrida, among others, explored the peculiar nature of the picture frame and its relation to both the image it contains as well as to what he calls the "general text" of the wall on which it hangs.[2] A generation ago, of course, Marshall McLuhan suggested that the medium is the message. In a sense, in our image-saturated culture, the meaning rests in the packaging.

Packaging – framing – is an essential aspect of art. It creates distance, the separation from daily life that allows us to distinguish the work of art from all that surrounds it. But in the case of performance, I think it is more than simple distancing that is at work – it is a form of signaling, of communication. Certain forms of performance trace their origins to ritual, and the purpose of ritual is to attract the attention of the gods. We pray for health, or rain, or good fortune. In order for our pleas to be heard, we must let the gods know that this is not ordinary speech or everyday behavior; we must grab their attention. So we put on masks, we transform pedestrian movement into dance, we change speech into incantation and song, and we create special buildings expressly for the purpose of communicating with the gods. Decoration, scenography, and architecture are the equivalent of a ringing telephone: Pay attention! Answer me! We are, like Antonin Artaud, "signaling through the flames." But if I may play with the telephone metaphor a bit more, look what has happened to that ringing! The archetypal sound of the twentieth century was the ringing phone – slightly different in each country, but recognizably repetitive and insistent. If a phone rang you were compelled to answer. The ring was loud and functional. But now, as phones are no longer anchored to architectural structures, their ringing has become decorative. On all sides we hear fragments of popular tunes, operas, rap music, vibrations or sounds sampled from industry or conversation. The sound has taken on a life of its own and become as important as the voice that it signals. As the broader notion of performance has become detached from real space, perhaps the scenography, too, has become separate from the performance it once supported. It is no longer a signal but a message in itself.

■ ■ ■

In recent years, linguists have noted the increasing prevalence of *retronyms* – the attachment of modifying words or prefixes to existing words in the face of changing usage – very often as a result of technology or commerce. For instance, we now distinguish 'tap water' (that is, water right out of the faucet) from bottled water. There is no longer such a thing as 'water'. Once upon a time there were telephones; now we have land lines, cordless phones, or mobile phones. Retronyms carry with them an air of nostalgia, a sentimental longing for a lost past. This feeling has been closely identified with the postmodern condition, a reaction to the deprivations of modernism as well as a response to globalized economies. There is an implication that the original or old-fashioned meaning denotes a closer connection to human or organic activity.

Theatre itself has become retronymed. Until recently, theatre would only be modified by genre: musical theatre, dramatic theatre, and so forth. But now we talk about 'live theatre' which implies another form that presumably does not require live presence. (Though fortunately it is not referred to by its logical opposite, 'dead theatre'). The opposite of live theatre is most often some form of mediatized performance or art – digital theatre, perhaps, or virtual theatre. But from theatre's very beginnings liveness has been an integral aspect of the definition – so fundamental that it seemed superfluous or redundant to even include it in the definition. Live theatre, of course, implies time and space, and this in turn implies scenography – traditional scenography is, in essence, the organization of space. But if there is something other than live theatre, if liveness is now reduced to a nostalgic condition, a vestige of an increasingly obsolete form, then discussion of space and therefore scenography is immediately problematized. Architect Bernard Tschumi has noted that we live in the age of "postmediation," in a time "after simulation."[3] Is it possible that we are also in a post-dimensional, post-spatial world in which scenographic concepts must be radically rethought? Can virtual space or non-dimensional space have power?

■ ■ ■

To return once more to Appia, whose foremost contribution was to reconceptualize the use of light on the stage, let me first consider the question of light for a moment. Live theatre requires illumination. The actors must be visible, and to one degree or another the stage and whatever scenic elements it contains must also be visible. Thus, from its inception, theatre has required an external source of light – originally the sun, then candles, oil lamps, gas, and electricity. Light emanated from its source, reflected off the actors and the stage, and was received by the spectators. The same was true for all the visual arts. And given the limited ability to control these light sources until the latter part of the nineteenth century, the audience was also illuminated, sometimes more brightly than the stage itself. But film and video projection and digital display *are* the light sources. In fact, their visibility – and thus the ability of the spectators to read them – depends upon the reduction or elimination of external light. This has several implications, but I will start with a simple, mechanical one.

Since at least the 1920s and the work of German director Erwin Piscator, there have been attempts to include projected imagery on the live stage. More recently, of course, digital display has been incorporated as well. The problem is that the people who are attempting this amalgamation of live theatre and projected imagery are usually theatre people. They are proceeding from a fundamentally theatrical vocabulary which for the past century has been basically an Appian vocabulary of sculptural space and the centrality of the actor to the three-dimensional image. Film, video, and digital projection work with a different vocabulary and a different mode of reception. Time and space in relation to the viewer are fundamentally different in electronic media and live theatre, not to mention the psychological and physiological effects of the viewing environment and the relationship of the spectator to the image. These differences inevitably lead to a clash of language systems and an inability to communicate.[4] In the present-day theatre, on the most basic level, we are currently fighting technical problems over control of stage illumination – how to make both the actor and the projection fully visible at the same time. Increasingly sophisticated projection systems and lighting control are eliminating or at least significantly reducing the problem, but I am not sure we can ever fully resolve the epistemological question regarding a mode of performance in which one element emanates light and another depends on reflected light. Perhaps this can serve as an Aristotelian mode of classification of designers – those who create objects to reflect light, and those who create objects that emit light or are composed of light.

Designers for the stage are organizing and sculpting space and may be creating three-dimensional objects for that space, and also creating two-dimensional images that nonetheless will be exhibited in real time and space. Designers for film and television are doing something similar in terms of the space in which the performers operate, but the entire creation – both design and performance – is then captured and re-transmitted to be viewed on a screen. Of course, this has been problematized of late with the creation of digital scenery so that performers are working in empty space – the captured image of the performers are then merged with the virtual imagery of the designer which consists of nothing more than computer codes and pixels. And this does not even begin to address questions of technology relating to the capture and projection of images and the different textures, qualities, and sizes that result, not to mention the differing technological modes of reception. (We are now entering a period in which the iPod and its equivalents are the media for watching films. What happens to films created for the large screens of movie palaces when reduced to less than five centimeters, often viewed in a multi-sensory and distracting environment?) And, finally, there are designers for digital and computer technologies who are creating the virtual environments and often virtual performers with whom we interact almost every time we access the Web, use our mobile phones, use guidance systems in our automobiles, take money out of the bank, etc. If liveness is removed from the equation, and if the traditional boundaries separating theatre performance from media are increasingly eradicated or breached, is there any way of re-categorizing the scenographers who work across these media?

French philosopher Alain Badiou describes *evental sites*, which, at the risk of oversimplification, may be described as nodes or sites in which a particular action or actions – events – occur, or, to use another term of Badiou's, a "truth process" occurs. In other words, an event that leads to the revelation of a truth. Writing about the nature of the event in the work of Deleuze, Badiou says, "An event does not make a composite unity of what is. There is, to the contrary, a decomposition of worlds by multiple evental sites. Just as it performs a separation of times, the event is separated from other events. Truths are multiple, and multiform. They are exceptions in their worlds and not the One which makes them converge."[5] I think Badiou may be providing a means of addressing the seemingly cross-disciplinary activity of scenographers and, incidentally, answering Plato. Like Plato, we tend to think of theatre as a 'whole', that is to say, an *event* in Badiou's terms. But, in fact, an event such as theatre is actually comprised of multiple events, including the scenographic. And the event we think of as theatre may not necessarily unify all the events contained within it. Postmodern theatre actually tends to valorize the fragmentation of the event into multiple, juxtapositional, contradictory processes. Let me then define the visio-spatial activity of performance as a scenographic event. If we choose to limit the scenographic event to the material space of the stage and perhaps the auditorium, we are, of course, restricted to the world of live theatre. But if we relinquish the idea of theatre as whole in the Platonic sense, and view it instead as a form or place for multiple, even disparate evental sites, we can begin to re-order or reformulate our notion of acting, design, sound, and so forth. Scenography (or whatever one wants to call the visio-spatial construct) can be seen as an evental site (a whole) that is not limited to live theatre, but encompasses the design of space in any medium, including the virtual. All such sites are visual and thus convey certain kinds of information or truths. Live events contain space; virtual events may not, although they may imply or simulate space. There is, however, one constant: the human observer who must exist in time and space. The reception of the performative or visual event occurs in the time and space of the observer. Since, for most of human history, it was the event that was located in a particular space, it was necessary for the observers to gather in that time and space to experience the event. Now, of course, that particular formulation no longer holds true in all cases.

Architectural critic and geographer Edward Soja, building upon the work of Henri Lefebvre, has proposed three categories of spatiality that provide another means of organization: Perceived, Conceived, and Lived, or what he calls Firstspace, Secondspace, Thirdspace. The first two are fairly easily defined. Soja describes Firstspace as "the directly-experienced world of empirically measurable and mappable phenomena."[6] Secondspace is "more concerned with images and representations of spatiality ... [I]t concentrates on and explores more cognitive, conceptual, and symbolic worlds."[7] Thirdspace is less well defined but suggests something that exists outside the dichotomous limitations of the first two. It is neither descriptive nor process-oriented but experiential and an attempt to understand human space through the body. We might say that traditional theatrical scenography is a form of conceived space, which is based on perceived space. But lived space in the digital age – the post-dimensional world – is something different. If that which is conceived is no longer based upon the empirically measurable and mappable, then old vocabularies, old systems of representation, will no longer suffice.

■ ■ ■

This raises the question of meaning and thus of communication. Communication requires, at the very least, a sender and a receiver. But most theories of communication require a true exchange, a two-way movement of information, signs, ideas, etc. Theatre is one of the great embodiments of the dialectical process; it encompasses a series of binaries, most notably performer-spectator and stage-auditorium. Meaning (synthesis) is produced at the intersection of these opposing forces.

This dialectic of the stage and theatron leads us inevitably to the notion of the gaze, a topic addressed, of course, by Sartre and Lacan. The questions that always arise in relation to the gaze are: who is looking and who (or what) is being seen? And of particular importance to the discussion of theatre and media: does the object of the gaze look back? In Section 3 of *Being and Nothingness* ("The Existence of Others"), Sartre articulates the scopic regime of being alone in a park and describes the objects in his line of sight: "those things in my universe; grouped and synthesized *from my point of view* into instrumental complexes."[8] Sartre's gaze is absolute; he is at the center of the universe or, more properly, the center of the visual field, which amounts to the same thing in this case. He is, in a sense, the embodiment of Descartes' *cogito*, the self as universal center. The spectator in the Baroque theatre, for instance, looking through the metaphoric window embodied by the proscenium was not unlike Sartre in the park with a god-like, self-centered view. But in a theatre such as that of ancient Greece or much of the theatre of today which emphasizes the three-dimensionality of the scenic space and, by implication, the cubic volume in which the spectators exist, it is more difficult to have such a self-centered view. This encourages multiple perspectives or multiple gazes, as it were. There emerges the possibility that as spectators we are also the subject of another spectator's gaze. Sartre addresses this disruption of the gaze in his scenario as well. Into this public park comes a second individual. And because this is a person and not an inanimate object, Sartre is no longer the master of the gaze, an omnipotent observer, but becomes an object of another's gaze. And furthermore, this Other disrupts the lines of vision. No longer do all lines of sight connect the first observer equally with the horizon and all objects in the park; the intruder becomes the focal point from whom all lines of sight emanate. "The distance," Sartre declares, "*is unfolded starting from* the man whom I see ... Instead of a grouping *toward me* of the objects, there is now an orientation *which flees from me*."[9] Modernist scenography can be read as the introduction of an Other into the frame which thereby destabilizes the frame in relation to the viewer. The self-centered gaze is disrupted, the singular, unchanging objectification of vision is destroyed. Modern, i.e. post-Renaissance, theatre was based upon the controlled, unifying vision of the frame, which implied a singular or unified spectator and a mono-directed gaze. Just as Sartre's second park denizen disrupts the notion of a frame by interrogating the position of the viewer, so too does the modernist project, through its attempts to alter or eliminate the frame, throwing the whole notion of theatre into question. Something is being seen.[10]

Lacan, though calling Sartre's paradigm brilliant, nonetheless questions Sartre. "The gaze sees itself," says Lacan. "[T]o be precise, the gaze of which Sartre speaks, [is] the gaze that surprises me and reduces me to shame, since this is the feeling he regards as the most dominant. The gaze I encounter ... is, not a seen gaze, but a gaze imagined by me in the field of the Other."[11] Lacan continues: "This is the function that is found at the heart of the institution of the subject in the visible. What determines me, at the most profound level, in the visible, is the gaze that is outside. It is through the gaze that I enter light and it is from the gaze that I receive its effects. Hence it comes about that the gaze is the instrument through which light is embodied and through which ... I am *photo-graphed*."[12]

In discussing scenography in the age of digital media, is liveness perhaps no longer the *truth process*, to use Badiou's term again, but, rather, the return of the gaze? As Nietzsche proclaimed, "When you look long into an abyss, the abyss also looks back into you." To what degree are we implicated in the gaze of any visio-spatial form? Can certain forms even be said to truly possess a gaze?

Without going through a detailed analysis of each genre and each period in theatre history, I think it is safe to say that most forms of live theatre at least hold the potential to gaze back. The audience observes the performers and, by implication, the physical visio-spatial environment in which they exist. The stage is capable of returning the gaze – certainly the actors implicitly or explicitly challenge us – but the scenographic elements also reflect our world back to us. In doing so, do we, as spectators, lose our privileged position? To the extent that the performers look at each other and at the scenography, should they be considered extensions or substitutes for our gaze, or do they encounter us, and if so, as character or performer?

An interesting turning point came with the productions by Richard Wagner at Bayreuth. By doing away with audience boxes and introducing 'democratic' seating which dominates theatres to the present day, and, more significantly, by dimming the auditorium lights he attempted to obliterate the individuality of the spectator and asked the spectator to project him or herself onto the ideal world of the stage – a world which was, of course, created through scenographic means. In so doing, the dialectic that had defined theatrical exchange since the dawn of human performance was dissolved; the material space of the auditorium was eradicated. There could be no dialectic process and, arguably, no communication. In Wagner's theatre, the gaze could no longer be returned because, in a sense, the gazer – the spectator – existed only as a conceptual idea. Several recent scholarly studies have traced a line from Wagner to virtual reality.[13] If the virtual image is the logical end point of the Wagnerian revolution, it would seem to suggest that there can be no returned gaze in such forms. But I think perhaps something else has happened. The direction of the gaze has been reversed. In this last part I want to show how the image, dimensional or not, theatrical or digital, gazes at the individuated spectator, and how we have been trained to respond.

■ ■ ■

We have all attended performances at which the revelation of a beautiful or astonishing bit of scenery evokes applause or audible gasps from the spectators. In 2004-05 Andrew Lloyd Webber's *The Woman in White*, designed by William Dudley, ran in London and briefly on Broadway. From a technical standpoint, this was a landmark production – all the scenery was created by the projection of digital images. At least on Broadway the scenography elicited little or no reaction from the audience, though they clearly were enamored of Webber's musical. When the show began, and throughout numerous scene changes, there was none of the usual appreciative applause; and during intermission there were few of the usual conversations about the design. I think that instead of surprising the audience, the images fulfilled their expectations. The spectators saw something that looked like their particular experience of performative scenography; they saw something that in texture and tone was very familiar – a reflection of lived space. They saw a visual world that looked remarkably like the environments found in computer gaming or in many Websites.

Every medium requires an act of translation, what Coleridge famously called "the willing suspension of disbelief." Although we are fond of believing that a clever illusion is indistinguishable from reality, this is a mere conceit on our part. On some level we will always be aware of the difference between illusion and the experiential world. In every generation some artist creates a work that strikes the viewers (or in the case of sound, the listeners) as more realistic – which really means more illusionistic – than anything that existed previously. The spectators and auditors, perhaps to justify being fooled, claim that the illusion is so complete they cannot tell the difference between reality and its simulacrum. So, in ancient Rome we are told by Pliny of a fresco on which grapes were painted so realistically that it fooled the crows who tried to pick the fruit off the vines. Illusion is whatever combination of conventions we accept at a particular point in time. A painted, candle-lit scene was acceptable in the Renaissance, today it is computer-generated graphics. It is, in fact, the techniques of illusion that shape our view of reality, not the other way round. When the so-called real world matches our depictions of it, we take enormous delight.

In many parts of the world going to live theatre is an increasingly rare experience. Audiences, therefore, have little experience of scenography and thus they have poorly developed criteria with which to analyze and respond. Ironically, it is for this very reason, I believe, that many of them respond so enthusiastically to highly decorative design – it is outside their realm of experience and therefore startling and delightful. What these audiences *have* experienced, however, is digital imagery. The increasing ubiquity of the World Wide Web and its particular visual aesthetic is what most spectators associate with performative imagery. Performance means television, DVDs, Web images, and computer graphics. The quality of the images in English designer William Dudley's graphics, combined with the suggestion of movement through space, is neither theatrical nor cinematic – it is cybernetical (to coin a term); it is the contemporary visual language of computer gaming. It conforms to the visual environment through which denizens of a technological society pass on a daily basis. So, an audience whose sense of performance and entertainment, and, in a certain sense, of reality, is shaped by such cybernetic forces expects all scenography to look like this. Because Dudley's scenery for *The Woman in White* met their expectations, there was no reason to applaud.

We are at the fourth level of Baudrillard's hierarchy of simulacra – the creation of a copy for which there is no original. On a daily basis we experience simulations of space or references to space for which there is no existing model in the experiential world. For spectators for whom such simulacra are part of quotidian life, the distinction between live and virtual becomes increasingly less significant. For designers, the fact of moving among several media encompassing both the real and the virtual is not only acceptable, but also unremarkable. The boundaries that previously existed have disappeared. What is not yet entirely clear is whether there will be new bodies to encompass a new embodiment of the scenographic project.

Notes

1 Adolphe Appia, "Ideas on a Reform of Our *Mise en Scène*," in *Adolphe Appia: Essays, Scenarios, and Designs*, ed. Richard C. Beacham, trans. Walther R. Volbach (Ann Arbor: UMI Research Press, 1989), p. 89.

2 Jacques Derrida, *The Truth in Painting*, trans. Geoff Bennington and Ian McLeod (Chicago: University of Chicago Press, 1987), p. 61.

3 Bernard Tschumi, "Six Concepts," in *Architecturally Speaking: Practices of Art, Architecture and the Everyday*, ed. Alan Read (New York: Routledge, 2000), p. 156.

4 See Arnold Aronson, "Can Theater and Media Speak the Same Language?," in *Looking into the Abyss: Essays on Scenography* (Ann Arbor: University of Michigan Press, 2005), pp. 86–96.

5 Alain Badiou, "The Event in Deleuze," *Parrhesia* 2 (2007), p. 40.

6 Edward W. Soja, "Thirdspace: expanding the scope of the geographical imagination," in *Architecturally Speaking: Practices of Art, Architecture and the Everyday*, ed. Alan Read (New York: Routledge, 2000), p. 17.

7 Ibid., p. 18.

8 Jean-Paul Sartre, *Being and Nothingness: A Phenomenological Essay on Ontology*, trans. Hazel E. Barnes (New York: Washington Square Press, 1956), p. 341, italics in original.

9 Ibid., p. 342.

10 See Arnold Aronson, "Avant-Garde Scenography and the Frames of Theatre," in *Against Theatre: Creative Destructions on the Modernist Stage*, ed. Alan Ackerman and Martin Puchner (New York: Palgrave, 2006), pp. 21–38.

11 Jacques Lacan, *The Four Fundamental Concepts of Psycho-Analysis*, ed. Jacques-Alain Miller, trans. Alan Sheridan (New York: W.W. Norton & Company, 1981), p. 84.

12 Ibid., p. 106.

13 See Matthew Wilson Smith, *The Total Work Of Art: From Bayreuth To Cyberspace* (New York: Routledge, 2007).

The Ambit of Performativity
How site makes meaning in site-specific performance

Scenography inscribes space in performance and has, for the better part of the twentieth century, implied the aesthetic and spatial organization of a theatrical text in a stage space to support the philosophical and ideological themes of both play and production. But what can be said of scenographic strategies deployed in site-specific circumstances that suggest a hybrid form of presentation that takes its impulse from the material world? How is meaning constituted in a context that, while dramatic, embraces a variety of physical circumstances that are not overtly theatrical? What is the nature of the complex exchange between the performance, the spectator and the place in which meanings are made?

I will attempt to answer these questions by addressing how site-specific representation differs from conventional practice and how site may be considered as heterotopic in its proliferation of meaning. Finally, I will discuss how these processes are mediated through a scenographic discourse. In particular, this argument employs performativity, in both its critical and non-critical deployments, to discuss spatial engagement. It looks, as well, at the notion of *excess* and how it might be used to illuminate this simple set of questions.

In its most essentialist meaning, the performative stands in for the theatrical. However, Judith Butler's argument that identity (specifically gender) is iterative and citational, a thing defined only in the performing of itself and held under a kind of Derridean erasure, is productive in developing the notion of spatial performativity as a way of reading topographies and structures of power in built environments. Spatial performativity, as argued here, presumes a potentiality, an excess or efficiency of meaning rendered strongly present in places framed by performance.

The terms I take up in this writing represent an attempt to mediate the practical considerations of site-specific production by adapting theoretical language typically found in performance analysis. I find this language of considerable use in understanding my role as scenographer occupied in devising performance in non-conventional sites. Through my affiliation with the Theatre Department at the University of Regina, my research allows me the opportunity to produce large scale, site-specific events in culturally, socially and historically marked sites in Southern Saskatchewan, Canada.[1] While these events are neither described nor analyzed here, as practice-based research, they inform my understanding of scenographic practice in found environments, as do the discursive works of other site-specific theatre-makers, particularly the wave of UK-based artists during the 1980s and 90s whose practice of performing outside traditional venues exhibited a social engagement and a relationship with community markedly different from the gestural, site-related experiments that characterized much of the neo avant-garde. The defining characteristic of their work was that it considered the physical site as a representational and discursive field, profoundly influencing a generation of artists who address issues relevant to specific constituencies while reflecting a wider perspective of the human condition. While the artists mentioned do not represent an exhaustive chronology, they will provide, for those interested, a point from which to begin a more thorough investigation.

Fundamental to any discussion of site-related performance is that of the Wales-based company Brith Gof. From 1981 to 2004, when they ceased to produce,[2] their work defined a unique dramaturgical approach to the mapping of specific locations through performance. Producing events in culturally and politically charged sites where place, community and performance became interlocked, Brith Gof was internationally recognized for its intense and innovative engagement with site and its local contingencies. Under the leadership of Mike Pearson, the company worked at all scales, from small solo works of storytelling to large epic works staged in locations such as disused factories, sand quarries, ice hockey stadiums, railway stations, abandoned farmhouses and deep in the forest.

Concurrent with Brith Gof, poet Fiona Templeton and theatre artists Deborah Warner and Hildegard Betchler, through a series of unique performance-based events, mined the urban environment for resonant metaphors that implicated spectators in the experience of the location. In one of the earliest examples, *You – the City* (New York, 1988), described by Templeton as "an intimate Manhattan-wide play for an audience of one,"[3] the performance was structured to provide individual spectators with a sequence of encounters in Times Square and Hell's Kitchen. In this work, Templeton focused strongly on the notion of subjectivity, urban habitation, and on the spatial relationship of the spectator to the city – the way individuals trace their own routes through the urban landscape. *You – the City* led the way for the *St Pancras Project: A Fantastical Walk* (1995),[4] a public performance produced by the team of director Warner and designer Betchler on the site of the abandoned Grand Midland Hotel in the heart of London. As in *You – the City*, individual spectators were admitted at prescribed intervals to an hour-long and ostensibly unguided tour of the ornate but dilapidated Edwardian building in order to draw public attention to rampant urban redevelopment. In this performance, the building itself was the central performer.

More recently, the potent intersection of art and architecture is exemplified by the Almeida Theatre Company's use of the defunct Gainsborough Studios to stage their 2000 season of Shakespeare's history plays *Richard II* and *Coriolanus*. This re-occupation of the deteriorating industrial site showed how the performance space interacted with the venue's previous functions and with the surrounding City of London, the historical presence of which impinged palpably on the performances. This concise survey suggests that the practical strategy of rejecting conventional venues and embracing the contingencies of found spaces questions the finality of monolithic narratives, and valorizes multiple subjectivities and local perspectives in ways that make dense the theatrical event.

Historically, scenography addresses the production and reception of the visual text of a staged performance; this activity is fully integrated with the physical site of the performance and how the spectator functions within that frame. As a kind of visual dramaturge, the scenographer's practice embraces aesthetic, theoretical and practical considerations. While scenography is certainly a function of text-centered performance in traditional venues, it is also comfortable in relation to performance in found space, where the material site is equal to, or privileged over, the predetermined text. The absence or devaluation of a textual armature necessitates working from the site's physical contingencies and histories, both real and putative. Here the scenographer conveys a unique experience of the site by demarcating or differentiating the space using only minimal interventions such as may impede or enhance the position of the spectator, thereby allowing the site's intangibles (socio-political context, received history, accreted myths and legends, personal memory and so on) to play a defining role in the generation of meaning.

In *One Place After Another: Site-Specific Art and Locational Identity*, art historian Miwon Kwon states that, over the past forty years, there has been an etiolation of the term *site specific* as the phenomenon has fragmented into new directions; these manifestations have little in common with original practices of early 1960s and '70s minimalism (frequently identified as the wellspring of site-specificity) which recognized the physical conditions of a particular location as integral to the production, presentation and reception of art. The uncritical adoption of the term, however, has provoked a rethinking of the word and alternative formulations have been offered to address the nuances that differentiate practices; these include site-determined, site-oriented, site-referenced, site-conscious, site-responsive, site-related, context-specific, debate-specific, audience-specific, community-specific and project-based. As Kwon points out, the refining of the terminology helps to clarify the particularities of a term that, by now, appears to be ubiquitous in art and performance practice to denote (accurately or not) "criticality or progressivity." Not withstanding the tendency for these terms to mesh with one another, they "collectively signal an attempt to forge more complex and fluid possibilities for the art-site relationship."[5] In the hyphen space between all these terms, however, the site speaks out as the central creative impulse and organizing principal.

The Breach between Theatre Design and Scenography

The introduction of gesturality and site-specificity affected experimental practices in all disciplines. The result was a drift from indiscriminate, non-institutionalized sites of exhibition and performance to specific found sites absolutely integral to and integrated with the work itself. The relationality of the performing and spectating body became absolutely defining.

The inclination away from prescribed stage space and towards found space profoundly altered the way that scenography understood and mediated performance space. Historically, when darkened and emptied of painted decoration, the status of the theatre stage has been considered unmarked, neutral – a tabula rasa. Onto this blank canvas was layered the scenic painter or scenographer's interpretive strategy, which left its mark on a production alongside that of the actors and managers, and, more recently, that of the director, lighting and sound designers, etc.

This practice came under scrutiny in the early decades of the twentieth century when theatre artists in Europe and North America engaged in the widespread debate surrounding the margins and boundaries of artistic conventions and the material site of performance was reconsidered and reconfigured as already replete with meaning and signification. Such a debate challenged the fixed conventions of the proscenium stage and the style of realism from which the majority of plays derived or for which plays of an earlier period were adapted.[6]

The ensuing revisioning of scenographic practice frequently ignored the proscenium, gravitated increasingly to found space circumstances and embraced an ever widening range of practices that referenced everything from in situ spectacle, to performance art, to political demonstration. Under the rubric of 'devised' performance, these practices came to represent hybrid genres generated from a range of impulses and situated ambiguously on the border of installation, theatre, performance art, and intermedia practice. Throughout the volatile decades of the 1960s and '70s, challenges to dominant ideologies by a politically engaged arts community manifested a trend towards self-reflexivity and a questioning of the assumptions that grounded the methods and boundaries of heretofore discrete disciplines.

In an era of vibrant social debate surrounding hierarchies of power, scenography, in so far as it could be analytically removed from the general *mise en scène*, was not content to remain in the background. Scenographers mapped out new positions as discussion grounded in semiotics, reception, representation, mimesis and performativity vied with burgeoning technologies and as scenographers drew from the experience of other disciplines.

The impulse to experiment with found space redefined the scenographic function; the scenographer's focus shifted from interpreting text within a prescribed stage space to deconstructing found space within a critical context.

In general terms, the theoretical consideration of space in performance developed out of the experimental practices engaged over the twentieth century and the critical analysis of performance systems and relationalities based in the semiotic investigations of the Prague School in the 1930s.[7] This analysis hypothesized the use of space as neither casual nor merely functional but representing a semiotically loaded choice, subject to rules which generated a range of connotative cultural units. These, according to American anthropologist Edward T. Hall, were explicit and determined. His theory of proxemics described the relative relationships that include the fixed feature space of the theatre itself and the formal dimensions of stage and auditorium; the semi-fixed features including the set and the 'movables'; and the shifting relationship between individuals, i.e. the interplay between actors, between actor and spectator, and between spectators.

Released from the physical confines of the stage into 'real-lived' environments, the range of possible proxemic relationships and semiotic significations multiply and collide in ways that subvert conventional representational codes. Thus split apart, relationships become open and ambiguous. Playfully disordered, they create a space, as Andrew Houston writes, "where anything might and even should happen."[8] Such spaces may be said to be theatrical heterotopias: potent, dense and replete with potentiality.

In practical terms, the aesthetic that governs the scenographic engagement with found space is best described as fragmented or collage-like. It represents an approach that examines the activities and rituals of everyday life attributable to a given location and an acknowledgement of the location's sensuous materiality, saturated with lived experience and memory. The scenographer is instrumental in apprehending and negotiating the site's materialities towards a performative conclusion in which the spatial dynamic of the site takes focus. Rather than the fixed proxemic boundaries of the stage and auditorium, as described by Hall, the relationship of the body to the site is determined by its unique materialities. Unfettered by the conventions of fixed seating and proscenium arch, a blurring occurs in found space between the categories of actor and spectator, between those elements considered theatrical and those con-

sidered real. The experience of found site is thus highly theatricalized or heightened by the demands placed on the spectator to identify, make meaning of, and
recognize his/her own place in relationship to the site.

The blurring of the theatrical and non-theatrical enfolds the spectator into
a collage event, what David Harvey calls a "stitched together collage of equi-
important and simultaneously existing phenomena" that posit a spectator who
"shares the perception of history as an endless reserve of equal events."[9] There
is an implicit invitation to the individual to encounter the performance on the
basis of all the other events experienced and to read it "as a series of texts
intersecting with other texts, producing more texts." Harvey describes this way
of interacting with the world as intertextual; it offers a reading that has a life
of its own, which spirals out into an infinite number of potential meanings.[10]
This collage view provides a way of coming to terms with, identifying with, and
making meaning from the performance through an apprehension of the local
contingencies and related histories, legends, myths and memories that the site
embodies.

In *Constructing Postmodernism*, Brian McHale suggests that an intertextual way of being in the world represents an overlapping and intersecting cor-
pora of constructions, which, while not necessarily mutually contradictory, are
not fully integrated, or perhaps even integrable.[11] In the context of performance,
this implies a rather productive collision between theatrical and extra-theatri-
cal, with the result that a spectator may simultaneously realize the potential of
both codes; such engagement realizes an 'excess of meaning' or a heightened
state of knowing that extends beyond either a semiotic or a phenomenological
reading. Houston emphasizes the importance of 'potential' here, writing that
"in terms of energy, potential means potent and powerful"; in quantum theory since Heisenberg, potential "introduces something standing in the middle
between the idea of an event and the actual event, a strange kind of physical
reality just in the middle between possibility and reality."[12]

According to Patrice Pavis, proscenium-based scenography elaborates a
site of scopic signs that encodes the topography of stage space and decodes
the dramatic text. The system of signs that makes up the scenographic text,
the visual metaphors, oppositions and contrasts, alternately support and contest the written text, constituting a parallel text or sub-text. Due, perhaps, to an

evermore sophisticated and media-heavy environment, visual signs are becoming more pervasive, playful, irresolute; the visual language of the stage more self-reflexive, multi-layered, full of potential.

Appropriating semiotic devices situates the scenographic function within the linguistic or textual analogy pervasive in the 1970s and '80s. However, the linguistic models and semiotic theories that derived from Saussure, Peirce and Jakobson's notion of the sign were rigid, restrictive and demonstrated a crisis in the "closure of representation" on the proscenium's emblematic stage. Indeed, Keir Elam suggests that the use of a semiotic model to account for all possible meanings in the environment of the stage is an "all-but-boundless enterprise since the entire gamut of social and cultural constraints is potentially involved."[13] While semiotic models may be productive (albeit problematic) in decoding scenographic signs within the closed circuit of the proscenium, in site-specific situations, where theatrical and non-theatrical signs intermingle, the attempt to secure a relationship between signifier and signified is rather more precarious. Instead, Pavis suggests that considering a sign vector, pinpointing the starting and ending points and the network of energy between them, is more helpful.[14] In this interval between the intention and the understanding occurs a fruitful slippage in which signs are read and misread, meanings lost, rediscovered, overturned and uprighted. The chaotic nature of found space exploits this indeterminacy and sets up a situation where the full ludic potential of the site is explored.

In the latter decades of the twentieth century, linguistic and semiotic models have been interrogated and displaced by other forms of performance analysis which, partially in response to experimentation in site-specific engagement, have focused frequently on identity construction; in this model the spatial has implied the social. Despite the shift in theoretical approaches, "the linguistic performative" remains a productive lexical term; engaging queer theory and performance studies along the way, it is employed to a number of ends.

Within the ambit of the stage, in its most reductive sense, the 'performative' refers to, stands in for and replaces the 'theatrical'.[15] Pavis suggests that the performative refers, somewhat simplistically, to that which "concerns the stage."[16] Beyond this use, the performative has accrued meanings, paradoxes and nuances that help make a case for its use in theorizing a critical framework for found performance space and its generative function. The following argument will attempt to justify the use of the spatial performative as a term and a concept that will productively open up this discussion.

A Case for the Spatial Performative

Being "marked by cross-purposes," Elin Diamond writes that the term performativity slips and slides through several discourses before it rests, for a while, within performance analysis where it has become a useful and ubiquitous tool. Identifying it as a "crucial critical trope" of postmodernism's rejection of totalizing notions of gender, race and national identity, she links performativity with the enunciation of subjective identity when gender and race are without true substance. In the absence of a stable identity there is no such external representation of an internal truth; there is only performance that counts in the making and receiving of meaning. She writes, "as soon as performativity comes to rest on performance, questions of embodiment, of social relations, of ideological interpolations, of emotional and political effects, all become discussible."[17] Here Diamond illustrates the relatedness between performance and performativity and suggests how the term has accreted meaning beyond that of a word for which it frequently stands in – theatricality.[18]

So efficient and so widely used is the term performative that Jon McKenzie, in "Genre Trouble: (The) Butler Did It," even suggests that performativity may, indeed, be *the* postmodern condition.[19] In this spiral of meanings, a case will be made here for the consideration of found space as a site of performativity (not merely of theatricality) and an argument extended for the recognition of a spatial performative to represent the potentiality of a site used for performance. In this construct, the site is recognized, as Heidegger writes, not as a bounded entity "at which something stops but ... from which something begins its presencing."[20] Anthropologist Victor Turner characterizes such a state as liminal. He argues that certain spaces, specifically those marked off by performance, are potent, defined by a condition of "being-on-the-threshold" or "betwixt-and-between the normal tension that exists between the normal, day-to-day cultural and social states and processes."[21]

Judith Butler employs the performative, as critical theorist, to open up the term's linguistic capacity and introduce it into the area of performance, focusing on the performative naming and performance of gender: an act that not only names a social subject but constructs a subject in the naming. She writes that "the acts by which gender is constituted bear similarities to performative acts within theatrical contexts" in which repetition establishes both a veracity and an accretion of meaning over time.[22] Jon McKenzie supports this by writing that "subjects do not expressively perform their genders; rather, gendered subjectivity is itself constituted through compulsory performances of social norms. Through repeated performances, these norms become sedimented as (and not in) gendered bodies."[23]

Butler focuses on the reiterative nature of social action to show how theories of ritual may be generalized to understand gender construction and its normative or transgressive performance. In doing so, she employs Turner's definition of performative sites or situations as limens where social norms are broken apart, turned upside down and played with. Her theory of normative performance challenges the distinction between appearance and reality, suggesting that performance happens in the liminal zone where the possibility of a variation exists and where the normative can be troubled and destabilized.

How do Butler and McKenzie's sense of performativity support the notion of a spatial performative that comprehends found space as a generative adjunct in performance? While Butler, of course, is exploring the embodied performance of gender, it is possible to extrapolate from her argument a model that considers space/place in the conjunction of performance and performativity. Her claim that the body is not figured as passively scripted and prior to discourse, but rather as a reenactment of a set of norms already socially established that at the same time conceals its interiority and dissimulates the conventions of which it is a repetition, is helpful here to understand how particular places signify in covert, complex and paradoxical ways.[24] Her statement illuminates a circumstance where the materiality of a specific location is able to be read both normatively and transgressively in relationship to that which is displaced, hidden, buried, erased, and absent, existing only as a palimpsest. Seen in this way, the site experiences resignification or *queering* as a disruption of the normative, expressing instead whatever is at odds with the normal, the legitimate, the dominant.

To co-opt Butler's language, site-specific performance interrupts a land-scape, like a conversation, that "has been going on long before one arrived," a landscape that is emblematic of a range of established social norms rein-forced by its reiteration or ongoingness. Indeed, landscape is neither a mute nor a passive surface on which cultural meanings are inscribed and fixed. Rather, it reflects a myriad of reenactments, "a sedimented stratum of performance always already repeated for the nth time."[25] Defined by variable and permeable boundaries, landscape is an open and reversible construction, capable of being subverted and transgressed through performance.

Butler writes that "performativity describes this relation of being impli-cated in that which one opposes, the turning of power against itself to produce alternative modalities of power, to establish a kind of political contestation."[26] This assertion allows performativity to sidestep into the discourse of site-specif-icity. Cannot a site, designated for performance, be considered a performative field, generating both normative and transgressive readings in relationship to gestures or activities (space-acts) that cannot be imagined as separate from the place in which it originates?

In her own unpacking of gender performance, Butler's claim that power is made normative through reenactment further supports the argument for a spatial performative. As gender is socially enacted on a body, dominant nar-ratives are similarly enacted and reenacted through architectural language in constructed environments and public spaces. This symbology simultaneously reaffirms, reinforces and subverts the social systems and historical norms embodied and embedded in the material surfaces. Where buildings and pub-lic spaces are used for performance, the site performs citationally; it is always already quoting itself, summoning its own authority and reaffirming its pres-ence. Abandoned places, sites with gaps or absences, reiterate and reaffirm their authenticity by performing a function that suggests that their pasts are vividly present, while at the same time confirming their absence. The site sum-mons its own ghosts and counter narratives that trouble its emblematic façade. Histories are never recovered wholesale nor restored; rather, the engagement embodies half-remembered behaviours and attenuated rituals. This performa-tive function of site represents what Houston calls a symbolic potentiality: an ability to offer an excess of meaning.

Performance Heterotopias: Sites of Excess

In approaching a conclusion, I would like to relate my argument to Michel Foucault's consideration of space in his seminal essay "Of Other Spaces." The impulse to consider particular places in performative terms emerges in an elaboration of Foucault's heterotopia, a notion that recognizes certain places as complexly layered, superimpositions of all other real sites within a socio-cultural paradigm.

Foucault illustrates the idea of heterotopia in regards to specific places that are, he suggests, dense with meanings. He writes: "we do not live in a homogeneous and empty space, but in a space that is saturated with qualities, and that may even be pervaded by a spectral aura."[27] He considers two kinds of sites that exemplify this paradigm: utopias (perfected spaces with no real jurisdiction) and heterotopias (spaces of excessive meaning that are located in identifiable places):

> There also exist, and this is probably true for all cultures and all civilizations, real and effective spaces ... which constitute a sort of counter-arrangement, of effectively realized utopia, in which ... all the real arrangements that can be found within society ... are at once and the same time represented, challenged and overturned: a sort of place that lies outside all place and yet is actually localizable. In contrast to the utopias, these places ... might be described as heterotopias.[28]

Foucault's theory asserts that certain places (theatres, gardens, museums, libraries, cemeteries, ships) are semiotically loaded. These are capable of simultaneously representing, in a single real place, other spaces that enact historical, political and social moments which contest and invert normative expectations and behaviours. Such sites operate in performance as a means to posit a multiplicity of narrative fragments and illustrate a postmodern perspective that recognizes space as replete with many meanings, ambiguities, excesses, erasures, and already-present potentiality. This plurality includes narratives that are contradictory, unintended and undesirable. Hence the meaning of the work is undecidable; this is, in fact, an intrinsic property of the work itself.

The idea of 'excess of meaning' or 'supplement' assumes certain conditions in the communication of meaning. In his essay "Nolo Contendere," Jeffrey

Kipnis suggests that an endless network of meanings fans out from a given entity or signifier:

> In order for there to be meaning at all, one entity must refer to another, a signifier must refer to the signified. ... Yet every entity – a word, an object, a building and so on – can both refer to other entities and be referred to by other entities.[29]

Jacques Derrida notably addresses the notion that something "in excess" always exists as residual meaning within all truth claims or narratives:

> ... no element can function as a sign without referring to another element which itself is not simply present. This interweaving results in each "element" ... being constituted on the basis of the trace within it of the other elements of the chain or system. This interweaving, this textile, is the *text* produced only in the transformation of another text. Nothing, neither among the elements nor within the system, is anywhere ever simply present or absent. There are only, everywhere, differences and traces of traces.[30]

Derrida argues this through the notion of mimetic reproduction and its binary opposite, claiming that the structure of a signifier is determined by a trace or shadow of the other reality which, under this binary opposition is absent or partially erased. In "Structure, Sign and Play in the Discourse of the Human Sciences," he writes:

> One cannot determine the centre and exhaust totalization because the sign, which replaces the centre, which supplements it, taking the centre's place in its absence – this sign is added, occurs as a supplement. The movement of signification adds something, which results in the fact there is always more ...[31]

Although the notion of supplemental meaning was first employed to critique a literary field, the spread of linguistic analysis into other disciplines opened up performance to semiotization, thereby allowing the concept of excess to shed light on how meaning is made in a variety of performance situations, specifically in site-specific performance where the juxtaposition of 'real' and 'theatrical' generates paradoxes, citations and erasures. A good example of this is Brith Gof's 1988 collaboration with Test Dept. on *Gododdin*, a performance presented in the machine shop of a disused Rover car factory in Cardiff's docklands, itself a potent symbol of economic decline and industrial decay in Thatcherite Britain. The scale of the site's found elements (hundreds of tons of sand, dozens of trees, wrecked cars, and thousands of gallons of water which flooded the performing area during the performance) resisted any kind of formal resolution between real and fabricated elements in the event; the site maintained an identity of its own and its assertion into the performance problematized the relationship of reality and performance. Andrew Houston cites an interview with scenographer Clifford McLucas:

> Pieces of work like <u>Gododdin</u> are operating within architectures that are not backdrops. They're not kind of 'at the service of' in any sense of being seemly towards the performer or the story or something like that [sic]. They've got a parallel identity of their own. They're real places, you know. <u>Gododdin</u> had real trees, real oil drums, real cars and I think that introduces, into the heart of the theatrical discourse, a whole array of questions about reality and pretence ...[32]

In *Gododdin* the use of found objects marked an excess in theatrical representation as the real emerged as an indeterminate but forceful 'presence' in the theatre event. In this manner of working, the challenge is thereby thrown to the spectator to negotiate meaning through frames that intermittently reference a way of being that is and is not theatrical – is and is not reality – where gaps and spaces allow for subjective interpolations.

In broad terms, designated or found performance sites operate as complex social and cultural signifiers, what Harvey calls "incommensurable spaces that are juxtaposed or superimposed upon each other."[33] Exhibiting the traces of recent and not so recent tenancies, such sites, in the words of Thomas Docherty, exemplify a world that resonates with meanings; such a world, he writes, "in the wake of Roland Barthes ... became an extremely 'noisy' place: [where] signs everywhere announced their presence and demanded to be decoded."[34] Such heterotopic sites, simultaneously utopian and dystopian, contain the familiar but dissimilar narratives of those who participate in their social structure and those who are occluded from them. As cultural geographer Doreen Massey writes, "space is by its very nature full of power and symbolism, a complex web of relations of domination and subordination, of solidarity and co-operation."[35] In Foucauldian terms, a heterotopia is not merely spatially and socially constituted; it is also a heterochrony, a "slice in time" revealing its past and signifying its present in a series of moments and discontinuities. Exhibiting ambivalence to the interconnectivity of space/time that this view suggests, Fredric Jameson writes of "the horror of multiplicity" of "all the web threads flung out beyond my 'situation' into the unimaginable synchronicity of other people." A recuperation of Jameson's "vertiginous terror," Massey suggests, may be realized through an understanding of how complex social relationships are implicit in the spatial and vice versa. She suggests the need to conceptualize space as constructed out of interrelationships, as the simultaneous coexistence of social interrelations and interactions at all spatial scales, from the most local to the most global.[36]

Conceptually, Kristin Ross has suggested, narrative and history, characterized by "intentionality, vitality, and human motivation," have had a dynamic appeal as an organizational paradigm while spatiality connotes "stasis, neutrality, vitality and passivity."[37] However, Massey writes, "seeing space as a moment in the intersection of configured social relations ... means that it cannot be seen as static."[38] Art historian Lucy R. Lippard agrees with this. She writes that space, specifically certain places (viewed through the lens of performance or art making) represent potent, multi-centred loci of hybridity and desire; they are places through which one can gain an understanding of difference, of otherness.[39]

Scenography and Community

In conclusion I will return to my own practice-based research in order to answer the questions set out in the opening paragraph. In my own scenographic work I seek out institutional and industrial sites that resonate through their palpable material presence as well as their abject state of abandonment. Examples of this include a disused mental hospital in a community still affected by its stigma (*The Weyburn Project*, 2002),[40] and a decaying brick plant situated on top of aboriginal spiritual land, now maintained as a heritage site commemorating only its colonial and industrial past (*Crossfiring / Mama Wetotan*, 2006).[41] A viable site typically exhibits a balance of line, form, colour and texture, hints at a dense and contested past and reveals itself, within its own landscape and social context, as a universal metaphor for broader humanitarian considerations. Recognizing the full potential of the site necessitates an activity that, when successful, represents the adage "think globally, act locally."[42] It is also a way of working that, as Lippard claims, lies "buried in social energies not yet recognized as art ... the idea ... [being] to look at what was already in the world and transform it into art by the process of seeing – naming and pointing out – rather than producing."[43] Such a strategy is effective when it succeeds in gathering an audience into a rich experiential event that engages the senses and both confirms and disturbs a preordained perception of a given place. Connecting specific places with the interlocking social networks through creative acts is potentially recuperative – a way of giving back places to people and restoring, however temporarily, a sense of the reciprocal relationship between who we are and where we are.

How does the scenographer function in this? Suzanne Lacy writes that "engaging in site-specific work enables the artist to enter the territory of the other and ... becomes a conduit for [collective and individual] experiences. Their work becomes a metaphor for a relationship – which has a healing power."[44] Giving each person a voice is what builds community and makes art socially responsive. How does my own work function in this modality? Speaking from my experience, my role as scenographer fuses the creative process with a theoretical analysis that recognizes the unity of the site/spectator/performance triad. *The Weyburn Project*, for example, served to interrogate a dominating representation of the mental hospital as a spent and impotent architectural symbol among community stakeholders at odds over the building's future. Through the provisional recovery of the building by means of the performance, lost narratives of patients, hospital workers and families were reconstituted. The event required a consideration of other symbolic orders and practices that challenged not only received or authorized history, but ways of telling that history and the uses made of that history in fashioning community outcomes.

In the case of *Crossfiring / Mama Wetotan*, the event explored the layers that enacted the real and putative histories of aboriginal and non-aboriginal inhabitations on the site of the Claybank Brick Plant. The event attempted to open up the discourse around this particular site, asking those responsible for its public presentation and commodification to consider the complexities of cultural representation and to imagine its future as an-other kind of identity space that is inclusive of multiple perspectives.

Working through these issues is a constant challenge for the site-specific scenographer. Fundamentally, this role embraces an ever-expanding portfolio – one that includes the role of theorist, producer, and community liaison. Using the properties, qualities, and meanings inherent in a specific place, the scenographer reveals the layers that symbolically and emphatically attest to, confirm and unsettle the complex and ongoing relationship between our physical environment and ourselves.

Where site itself is the dominant signifier, what is the role of the scenographer? While not emphatically eschewing conventional design strategies, a scenographer who works in this way recognizes the intrinsic aesthetic value of a location where the patina of life is seductive but does not obscure the presence of individuals who have invested in it over time. The implicit relationship with the community becomes the starting-point for work that is inseparable from the site itself. Where a stage designer uses scale, rhythm, balance, light and shadow to develop a visual language within the proscenium, a site-specific scenographer delineates a site and, using an overlay of myth, memory, personal narrative and contemporary detail, frames a place within a local and global context. In this way, an open, ambiguous work is created that allows the embedded narratives to fragment, proliferate and reveal the interpenetration and interaction of people/place/time: their histories, their desires, and their identities.

1. *The Weyburn Project*: Ensemble.

2. *The Weyburn Project*:
Trenna Keating.

3. *The Weyburn Project*: Before the Performance.

4. *Crossfiring / Mama Wetotan*: (left to right) Derek
Lindeman, Michael Kolodziej, Dave W. Ouellette.

Notes

1 These sites include the Weyburn Mental Hospital, a building that encapsulates 75 years of mental health practice spanning the better part of the last century; the Claybank Brick Plant National Historic Site, a pristine example of turn of the twentieth-century industry erected on Aboriginal spiritual land; and (in planning for 2008) the town of Ponteix, an historic community and a bastion of nineteenth-century French language and culture in the Canadian prairies.

2 Founding member Clifford McLucas died in 2001 of a brain tumour. Michael Shanks took over as Company Director in 1997. The Brith Gof company closed down in 2004.

3 Described on Fiona Templeton's website <http://www.fionatempleton.org/>.

4 Mel Gussow in the *New York Times* (August 14, 1995), and accessed online at <http://query.nytimes.com/gst/fullpage.html?res=990CE5DA103BF937A2575BC0A963958260>.

5 Miwon Kwon addresses this in *One Place After Another: Site-Specific Art and Locational Identity* (Cambridge, Mass. and London: MIT Press, 2004), pp. 1–2.

6 Through the work of Meyerhold, Reinhardt, Appia, Craig, among others, Christopher Baugh thoroughly addresses the revisioning of theatre space in the early twentieth century from a scenographic perspective in *Theatre, Performance and Technology: The Development of Scenography in the Twentieth Century* (Basingstoke and New York: Palgrave Macmillan, 2005).

7 Keir Elam engages the earlier work of the Prague Structuralists Otakar Zich, Jan Mukařovský and Jiři Veltruský in *The Semiotics of Theatre and Drama* (London and New York: Routledge, 1980), pp. 5–10.

8 Andrew Houston discusses the liminal space of potency, potential and play in Brith Gof's work in "Postmodernism: A Construction of Reality and the Limit of Representation" (diss., University of Kent, Canterbury, 1994), chapter 5, p. 2.

9 As discussed by David Harvey in *The Condition of Postmodernity: An Enquiry into the Origins of Cultural Change* (London and Cambridge, Mass.: Blackwell, 1989), p. 1.

10 Ibid., p. 49.

11 Brian McHale, *Constructing Postmodernism* (London and New York: Routledge, 1992), p. 3.

12 Werner Heisenberg, *Physics and Philosophy: The Revolution in Modern Science* (London: George Allen & Unwin, 1959), p. 42, and cited by David E. R. George in "Quantum Theatre: Potential Theatre: a New Paradigm?," *New Theatre Quarterly* 5.18 (May 1989), p. 178.

13 As discussed in Elam, *The Semiotics of Theatre and Drama*, p. 33.

14 See "Towards an Integrated Semiology," in Patrice Pavis, *Dictionary of the Theatre: Terms, Concepts, and Analysis* (Toronto, Buffalo, and London: University of Toronto Press, 1998), pp. 331–2.

15 Andrew Parker and Eve Kosofsky Sedgwick, eds., *Performativity and Performance* (New York: Routledge, 1995), p. 2.

16 Pavis, *Dictionary of the Theatre*, p. 394. This use of "performative" is frequently heard in performance art practice where the gesture, action or implied presence of the artist marks the piece as both embodied and somehow more "like theatre."

17 As discussed by Elin Diamond, ed., *Performance and Cultural Politics* (London and New York: Routledge, 1996), pp. 2–5.

18 Although, what is needed here is a great deal more than a side-bar to discuss "theatricality," it is here taken to reference a certain visual quality that lends itself to stage presentation or scenographic treatment, a density of signs and sensations: "theatre-minus-text." Patrice Pavis's point that "theatricality," in the Artaudian sense, is "opposed to literature, to the theatre of text, to written means, to dialogues and even at times to the narrativity and 'dramacity' of a logically constructed story" is certainly of relevance to the question of performativity and the indeterminacy of site-specific performance, *Dictionary of the Theatre*, p. 395.

19 As discussed by Jon McKenzie in "Genre Trouble: (The) Butler Did It," in *The Ends of Performance*, ed. Peggy Phelan and Jill Lane (New York and London: New York University Press, 1998), pp. 217–35.

20 Martin Heidegger as cited by Homi K. Bhabha in *The Location of Culture* (London and New York: Routledge, 1994), p. 1.

21 Victor Turner, "Frame, Flow and Reflection: Ritual and Drama as Public Liminality," in *Performance in Postmodern Culture*, ed. Michel Benamou and Charles

Caramello (Madison, Wisconsin: Coda Press, 1977), p. 33.

22 Judith Butler, "Performative Acts and Gender Constitution: An Essay in Phenomenology and Feminist Theory," in *Performing Feminisms: Feminist Critical Theory and Theatre*, ed. Sue-Ellen Case (Baltimore: Johns Hopkins University Press, 1990), pp. 270–82.

23 Jon McKenzie, "Genre Trouble: (The) Butler Did It," in *The Ends of* Performance, p. 221.

24 Sue-Ellen Case, *Performing Feminisms: Feminist Critical Theory and Theatre* (Baltimore: Johns Hopkins University Press, 1990), p. 278, 282.

25 See Phelan and Lane, *The Ends of Performance*, p. 228.

26 As discussed by Judith Butler in *Bodies that Matter: On the Discursive Limits of "Sex"* (New York: Routledge, 1993), p. 241.

27 Michel Foucault, "Of Other Spaces: Utopias and Heterotopias," in *Rethinking Architecture*, ed. Neil Leach, trans. Charles Siebert (London: Routledge, 1997), p. 351.

28 Ibid. p. 352.

29 Jeffrey Kipnis, "Nolo Contendere," *Assemblage* 11 (1990), p. 1.

30 As discussed by Jacques Derrida in *Positions*, trans. Alan Bass (Chicago: University of Chicago Press, 1981), p. 26.

31 As discussed by Jacques Derrida in *Writing and Difference* (Chicago: University of Chicago Press, 1978), p. 289.

32 See Houston, "Postmodernism," p. 23.

33 David Harvey, *The Condition of Postmodernity*, p. 48.

34 As discussed by Thomas Docherty, ed., *Postmodernism: A Reader* (New York: Columbia University Press, 1993), p. 9.

35 Doreen Massey, *Space, Place and Gender* (Minneapolis: University of Minnesota Press, 1994), p. 265.

36 Doreen Massey, *Space, Place and Gender*, p. 259. She quotes Frederic Jameson's *Postmodernism, or, The Cultural Logic of Late Capitalism* (Durham, N.C.: Duke University Press, 1991), pp. 363, 362.

37 Quoted in Massey, *Space, Place and Gender*, p. 259.

38 Ibid., p. 265.

39 Lucy R. Lippard in *The Lure of the Local: Senses of Place in a Multicentered Society* (New York: New Press, 1997), pp. 4–6.

40 See also *The Weyburn Project*, ed. Richard Diener and Kathleen Irwin, 2002, University of Regina, Saskatchewan, <http://uregina.ca/weyburn_project/>.

41 See also *Crossfiring: The Claybank Project*, ed. Kathleen Irwin, 2006, University of Regina, Saskatchewan <http://crossfiring2006.ca/>.

42 Hazel Henderson cited by Lucy R. Lippard in *The Lure of the Local*, p. 114.

43 As discussed by Lucy R. Lippard in "Looking Around: Where We Are, Where We Could Be," in *Mapping the Terrain: New Genre Public Art*, ed. Suzanne Lacy (Seattle: Bay Press, 1995), p. 126.

44 As discussed by Suzanne Lacy in "Debated Territory: Toward a Critical Language for Public Art," in *Mapping the Terrain*, p. 174.

Credits

1, 2, 3.
Performance: *The Weyburn Project*
Location: The Weyburn Mental Hospital, Weyburn, Saskatchewan
Date: September 2002
Producer: Knowhere Productions Inc.
Scenographer and Producer: Kathleen Irwin
Director: Andrew Houston

4.
Performance: *Crossfiring / Mama Wetotan*
Location: The Claybank Brick Plant National Historic Site, Claybank, Saskatchewan
Date: September 2006
Producer: Knowhere Productions Inc.
Scenographer and Producer: Kathleen Irwin
Director: Andrew Houston

Drawing upon the Aesthetics of Immersion

Lisa Munnelly

This essay documents the intimate and unfolding nature of a conversation that occurs between the drawer and her work through a retrospective examination of a multi-media installation created in 2005, titled *The Aesthetics of Immersion*. Focusing on a wall drawing (*The Mother-Board*) and two video pieces (*The Fullness of Emptiness* and *Sweeping Vistas*), this text continues the dialogue between transience/immanence, materiality/immateriality, emptiness/fullness, and stasis/movement.

Relegated to a warm-up role, drawing has traditionally found itself subordinated in favour of the 'real event', whether it is painting, sculpture or architecture. However, in today's climate, in which genre boundaries are blurred to the point where we can talk of painting as sculpture, sculpture as architecture and architecture as performance, it is hardly surprising to find this newfound porosity permeating the definition of drawing.

In the current cross-disciplinary environment, with its shifting grounds and unstable borders, the increase in books devoted to the re-examination of drawing signifies a search for firm ground. In the preface to *What is Drawing?*[1] Michael Ginsborg typifies this trend when he states that the conditions under which a drawing is made and shown are, in common with other forms of art, "newly complex." He cites three factors for this complexity: the relationship drawing maintains with its "earliest material forms and processes," the experimental quality of the discipline and the role it played in instigating and consolidating changes in visual art in the late nineteenth and most of the twentieth century, and the development of an expanded multi-disciplinary understanding and application of drawing.[2]

In order to engage with Ginsborg's three points, I intend to employ a personal account of the evolution of *The Aesthetics of Immersion*. Beginning with figurative sketches, the work shifted to large-scale abstract wall drawings, and expanded to incorporate digital video and sound works. In response to the question "what is drawing?" this text asserts that any explanation must utilise an extended definition – one that includes matter, movement and dialogue.

Background

Drawing has a long and rich history that informs contemporary fine arts practice. Yet one can wonder whether today's artists regard themselves as heirs to a centuries old drawing tradition, or if they feel adrift from it, being "participants in, or competitors with, a wholly immediate image world that includes billboards, videogames, magazine ads, pornography, instructional diagrams, television and an infinite number of other things ..."[3]

The impetus for *The Aesthetics of Immersion* emerged after I found myself asking that same question when attending a multi-media group exhibition several years ago. What struck me with this show was the way in which the large digitally looped projections completely overwhelmed the neighbouring static drawings. Later that evening, watching a televised preview of another exhibition, I was struck by the mode of documentation as the camera swooped, spun, jerked and ducked, synchronised to a superimposed techno soundtrack. The clip seemed more inspired by the music than the work itself, which hung on the wall impassively, helpless to arrest the darting gaze of the camera. At the time, these observations brought to mind André Girard's lament that "I would not be surprised if, fifty years from now, almost no one would pay attention to paintings, whose subjects remain *still* in their always too-narrow frames."[4] The television item seemed to affirm Walter Benjamin's assertion that "the masses seek distraction whereas art demands concentration from the viewer."[5]

Studies of visual perception show that of all stimuli, motion appeals most strongly to our senses. As someone whose practice was dependent upon materials and processes that resulted in static work, I wanted to investigate how drawings could compete against the innate attraction of the moving image. A body of work that focused on exploring the effect of duration on both the artist and the viewer began to emerge as *The Aesthetics of Immersion*.

Mihaly Csikszentmihalyi and Rick Robinson argue that time is a crucial factor when engaging with artworks, in that "it's not a blast, it's a dialogue ... if you just walk by a painting you're not going to get anything out of it, anything at all, seeing takes time."[6] The temporal aspect of the relationship between artwork and audience has been documented extensively, whereas critical analysis concerning the effect of temporality on the artist proves more elusive.

Time Embodied

To ascertain what effect time had on the psyche of the artist, on the type of line produced, and on the final drawn outcome, I set about executing a series of timed figure sketches. These ranged in duration from one to forty minutes, all depicting the same subject, holding the same pose. The one-minute sketch was straight forward, involving pure action, accompanied by little or no dilemma. As the duration increased, the marks became tighter, less expressive, more homogenous, and over the course of forty minutes, the drawing started to appear overworked. An attempt to rectify this by erasing marks failed as the charcoal-impregnated surface of the paper could not be restored to its initial state. Although these figurative time-trials were an effective tool in gauging the effect of time upon my drawing, I found the representation of the nude figure to be too encumbered with issues concerning the body. Issues of gender, the gaze, and the politics of representation threatened to derail the primary focus, that of exploring the temporal potential of drawing.

The answer to my new dilemma, how to present time without resorting to figurative means, lay in the very work I was struggling with. From the thwarted attempts to erase areas of the charcoal-impregnated drawing, a new awareness of surface and saturation emerged, generating a fresh investigative imperative: exactly how much charcoal could be loaded onto the paper? To answer this question I set about covering a large sheet of matte board with compressed charcoal. In pursuit of the desire to completely cover the surface the gestural sweeps and dashes of the life drawings were abandoned, replaced by a field of small, firm marks.

About eight hours and twelve charcoal sticks later my desire was realized. The outcome was fairly predictable: a large flat black board. However, the unexpected material nuances generated by the process now fired my imagination anew. What I was faced with was not a featureless black board as expected, but a velvety, deep expanse. The endpoint of each meticulous mark seemed to catch the light like the wing of some great black moth. I retrospectively titled the large charcoal wall drawing *The Mother-Board*, due both to its capacity to relay information (the mother-board in a computer is a circuit board through which all signals are directed) and its generative properties: it was from this work that all subsequent works (which were to form the exhibition *The Aesthetics of Immersion* in November 2003) came into being.

Dialogue

The marks of *The Mother-Board*, though tight and seemingly mute in themselves, told a story, a performative narrative. The confines imposed by the scale of the work meant that I had to constantly rearrange my body. I was continually changing hands and angles when fatigue set in, and this had imposed an unforseen structure on the work.

The artist Robert Morris, discussing the responsiveness of materials, observed that the black velvet of the powdered graphite read "less as a trace or imprint of the hand's passage, than as a mirror surface for touch itself – the drawing touching back the artist's hands."[7] In parallelling the "touching back" that Morris attributed to the drawing surface, and the exchange that occurs in conversation, one could speak of the act of drawing as developing a dialogue, drawing one into a conversation and inciting a response.

The notion that art comprises a dialogical event, that "[c]onversations can bring things ... into play which the participants of an exchange would not have anticipated prior to their exchange" emerges in the writing of Hans-Georg

Lisa Munnelly, *The Mother-Board* (detail), 2003. Compressed charcoal, matte board, 3 × 1.5 metres.

Gadamer.[8] The unforeseen qualities that surfaced from my application of charcoal parallel the way language operates. As with a conversation, one cannot be sure of the direction the work will take, or be secure in its final outcome. Gadamer, when talking about art, preferred the term "presentation" to that of "representation," arguing that "[r]epresentationalists hypostasize an external or transcendent reality as a primary truth which, in being prior to art, is esteemed as the proper object of art."[9] This, he reasoned, subordinated art in favour of an "original truth" and restricted it to a mere facsimile of that truth. In contrast, presentation speaks of a coming forth of a subject, supporting the idea that "[a]rt is no longer subordinate to its conceptual subject but becomes a vehicle of its sensual appearance."[10]

Immersion

To think of art as a vehicle reflects Rupert Thomson's musings on travel and the nature of the journey to be undertaken:

> The feeling of a ship or train or a bus beneath me, each with its different rituals, its different rhythms. A destination was useful because it was a substitute for purpose; it answered any question I was likely to be asked. Movement became my reason for being, my excuse. Movement for its own sake. I forgot who it was who wrote about the importance of doing nothing, how the art of doing nothing is one that most people seem to have forgotten. Well, I decided to resurrect the art. In doing nothing, I would be reduced to what I was moving through. I would, quite literally, become part of the scenery. I would blend, immerse, dissolve.[11]

Thomson's assertion that each mode of travel has its own "rituals and rhythms" finds a parallel in the terrain of visual art, where pencil, chalk, acrylic, oil and video are themselves carriers of ritual and rhythm. His celebration of movement for movement's sake provided a rationale for the large scale of my drawings. When the dimensions of my charcoal wall pieces were questioned, I responded that in dealing with time, a lengthy duration was best suited, hence the large scale. When countered with "Why not a brief duration?," it dawned on me that in effect what I had been doing was *inhabiting* the work through exertion and extended duration, and the larger the scale the longer I occupied it. I had been depending upon an immersion in time and matter to facilitate the emergence of thoughts/ideas. Thomson's reflection that "I would be reduced to what I was moving through. I would, quite literally, become part of the scenery. I would blend, immerse. Dissolve" resonated strongly with me, and the title *The Aesthetics of Immersion*[12] arose from my engagement with this notion.

Getting Lost

The terms *blend*, *immerse* and *dissolve* capture the hypnotic state induced in the traveler by the landscape as it hurtles past the window of the vehicle, where the passenger, bodily bound, is committed to the journey, absolved of responsibility and freed from demands of decision making. In effect the same phenomenon was experienced during the execution of the large charcoal wall drawings. Once underway I too became a passenger, as all of the decisions were made prior to execution: the size of the area to be filled in, the media employed to fill it, the types of marks executed in the filling, all being pre-determined before disembarking. The mesmerizing effect of travel was invoked by the repetitive nature of the marks employed in these drawings. Graham Gussin captures the mantra-like effect of monotony multiplied when he writes:

> If all is the same, over and over, then nothing is distinguishable; deprived of the means to measure, of the ability to tell one from another, one point from the next, we slip, merge into an enveloping sameness and lose our place.[13]

This strategic daydreaming in which one *intentionally* loses oneself, and where getting lost is a creative and generative tactic, lies in stark contrast to the loss of direction I had suffered in the figure studies. In the figurative work, the pressure exerted by the forty-minute drawing process produced a feeling of being physically lost, with increased awareness of oneself and of one's surroundings, and a constant return to known landmarks for re-orientation.

Economy and Excess

Yet there is something appealing in the draftsmanship that life drawing demands. Unforgiving, the line's weight, direction, angle, position and speed is, ideally, captured in one attempt. Sometimes the line is fluent, the path to be followed clearly visible, whilst at other times the hand hovers tremulously, and the sketch behaves more like a house of cards. A poorly placed line could bring the whole teetering construction crashing down.

Another satisfying aspect of making figure studies is the economy of mark. Many of my best drawings have been some of the most spare in terms of marks laid down upon paper. In life drawing, the economy of line gains utmost importance as an expression of observation, measurement and control. Experience has taught that less is often more. In contrast to the life drawing, where I seek to find the most eloquent and economical means to capture the form in front of me, the wall drawings seem excessive, consuming vast quantities of time and charcoal in their execution.

Perhaps the rationale for such excess can be found in the German philosopher Hegel's rumination on the transformation of quantity to quality:

> It has been said that there are no sudden leaps in nature, and it is a common notion that things have their origin through gradual increase or decrease. But there is also such a thing as sudden transformation from quantity to quality. For example, water does not become gradually hard on cooling, becoming first pulpy and ultimately attaining a rigidity of ice, but turns hard at once. If temperature be lowered to a certain degree, the water is suddenly changed into ice, i.e., the quantity – the number of degrees of temperature – is transformed into quality – a change in the nature of the thing.[14]

Although Hegel's line of thinking applies to both figurative and process-based drawing and, as already discussed, while the *quantity* of time set for the figurative studies had an immediate effect on the *quality* of mark, it was the process-based drawings that elicited a *conscious* desire to transform quantity into quality. The decision to apply the charcoal in such small tight marks exaggerated the large scale; in effect, the drawing became an event – consciously designed so as to demand an intimate face to face engagement with the picture surface, drawn out over an extended period of time. In such habitation of the artwork I was dependent upon thoughts about the work to emerge by way of my own bodily immersion in time and matter.

Perhaps the term "emerge" is a misleading one as it suggests a slow burgeoning of awareness, which one might assume happens when involved in such protracted processes. Yet, despite adopting such strategies, I would be struck by a sudden thought, rather than ideas emerging as though through a gradual awakening. The phenomena evoke Henri Poincaré's poetically phrased observation that "thought is only a flash between two long nights, but this flash is everything."[15]

Illumination

What if this flash of illumination fails to reach us? As always in the "long nights" of Poincaré's prose there looms what Jean-François Lyotard posits as

> ... the possibility of nothing happening, of words, colours, forms or sounds not coming; of this sentence being the last, of bread not coming daily. This is the misery that the painter faces with a plastic surface, of the musician with the acoustic surface, the misery the thinker faces in the desert of thought and so on.[16]

I personally encountered the misery of which Lyotard speaks when I was swamped by the initial crisis of how to visually represent time.

In shifting from a figurative to a process-based approach, the work is in line with Asger Jorn's assertion that action art reduces art to an act in itself, that the work of art is a mere trace in which there is no more communication with the audience: "this is the attitude of the pure creator who does nothing but fulfil himself through the materials for his own pleasure."[17] Thus the charcoal wall drawings, where I laboured with my back to the world and face inches away from the picture plane, were made solely for my own benefit. The work comprised a 'working through' the predicament of *what* to show – to *present* further questions rather than *represent* an answer. I was not asking of my work the sorts of questions that required hard and fast answers, all I wanted was a prompt, a promise, a glimmer of light (to stave off those long nights), a yet to be realised 'something' to chase. As Jean Dubuffet declared, "chances are, quite rightly, the game the artist hunts, which he constantly calls out to, watches and traps."[18] To use Dubuffet's analogy, in the large wall drawings, after the borders were staked out and defined, a vantage point secured and the ground constantly surveyed, it was (hopefully) just a matter of time before my quarry revealed itself. And my efforts were rewarded when I discovered that this large charcoal covered board and I were engaging in some kind of dialogue, the drawing emitting/performing a distinctive compressed charcoal dialect.

Dust and Dialect

Besides the emergence of patterns of fatigue already discussed, another unforeseen outcome of the drawing activity was the beauty of the falling charcoal – a fine stream of exhausted dust accompanying each small stroke. Also not anticipated was the double-time of the drawing, where the paper laid out at the foot of the wall as a groundsheet to capture falling dust became the ground of a second work, with my footprints forming a diagrammatic depiction of time and movement, unwittingly created in the process of executing the wall drawing.

The work responded in a language specific to its material – in billowing, embracing, velvety, dusty and dirty words, exemplifying Henri Focillon's statement that "all different kinds of matter are subject to a certain destiny."[19] Focillon's warning that matter must not be seen as passive, "for it is plainly observable how matter imposes its own form upon form,"[20] highlights the fact that matter, far from being mute, exerts its own set of criteria on any conversation; the media used is always a prevailing factor in the form of the work.

These new encounters with the work meant that, while drawing, my focus was now fractured in three ways: on the vertical surface being drawn upon, on the patina of marks accumulating at my feet, and on the cascade of dust falling to the floor. Evidence of the first two elements would remain after completion, whereas the dust's descent was limited to the act of drawing itself as an event. Hence the decision arose to record, using digital video, the passage of dust as it submitted to gravity in its fall to the floor.

Falling

Video opened up a whole new world of vision where, looking through the lens, the charcoal dust took on a particularly mesmerizing quality. Dust, I discovered, does not 'fly', but sets its own pace; the smallest specks eerily hovered, the middle-sized particles lazily descended whilst the larger chips of charcoal crashed like boulders to the floor. Through the camera's ability to isolate and enlarge, I was able to focus in on what is normally overlooked: the byproduct or detritus of drawing. The nineteenth-century essayist and poet Ralph Waldo Emerson believed that it was the "responsibility" of the artist to call to attention the overlooked, stating that "[t]he virtue of art lies in this detachment, in sequestering one object from the embarrassing variety. Until one thing comes from the connection of things, there can be enjoyment, contemplation, but no thought."[21] Given the rather narrow confines of the lens, the camera has an innate ability to detach its subject from the "embarrassing variety" of everything else. But it also functions to detach on another level: the camera detaches whoever is behind the lens from whatever, or whoever, appears in front of it. This distancing function inevitably found its way into the work, with me stepping back from a very intimate face-to-face engagement with the picture surface to reposition myself behind the camera.

With this shift into video, am I not forgetting the initial question: how can static works compete against the innate attraction of the moving image? Let me first respond by explaining that as it has evolved, my practice has complicated the general assumption of what drawing is. The initial question assumed that all drawings are by nature static, which in retrospect seems far too narrow a definition. Much more liberating is Tony Godfrey's assertion that drawings are everywhere, created whenever two objects or two materials touch and evidence of their meeting is left behind.[22] Godfrey illustrates this with examples ranging from a child running a stick along a fence, to spilt coffee, to the skid marks made by a car desperately breaking. If stick and rail, liquid and earth, rubber and tarmac, constitute drawing materials, then so too do light and celluloid, pixels and memory, as well as a myriad of other things. Widening the terrain of what constitutes drawing to include video leads to an interesting response to how the static object can compete in relation to the dynamics of the moving image. In an environment saturated by sound bites and snappy editing, the artist, through invoking sparseness and slowness, has the opportunity to utilize, or rather frustrate, the viewer's expectations. This of course is heightened when one employs media that the audience associates with happenings or events (such as video). As David Hockney commented, "the media we use finds it easier to show Rome being burnt than being built."[23]

Pause

Artists working in a range of genres have enjoyed and exploited the beauty of the pause. For example, electronica musician and producer Brian Eno's interest in film soundtracks emerged in response to the tendency of commercial media to cram space with as many images and sounds as possible. Speaking of film music as music with its centre missing (because the film itself is the music's centre), Eno maintains that

> If you just listen to the music alone without seeing the film, you have something that has a tremendous amount of space in it, and that space is important, because it's the space that invites you as the listener into the music. It sucks me in, that kind of space.[24]

So amidst a glut of visual information, a cacophony of sounds, colours and moving images all clamouring for our attention, we find artists drawing the viewer in through quietness, stillness and emptiness. The void has become a device for capturing and holding the attention of the audience.

The Fullness of Emptiness

Curiosity can be characterised as a desire to extricate oneself from waiting. This desire was explored in *The Fullness of Emptiness*, a video work inspired by the falling dust (residue) of my drawing process. The video employed long takes showing little or no action, utilizing the potential of expectation, frustration and curiosity. The footage presents an empty white space accompanied by out-of-frame people discussing the placement of cameras and lighting supports in relation to the space, alerting the viewer to the fact that what they are witnessing is not a paused image, but a real-time feed. This reveals what is normally denied to the viewer: feedback from others, how equipment is deployed, and the true time of setting up. Whilst it could be argued that I am concerned with the element of truth, the entire setup is paradoxically one of staging. It is theatrical. I am in effect directing, and the materials have become my performers. The materials in this case consist of: one empty white room, video cameras, and a large amount of charcoal dust that is (eventually) dropped into the white space from up high and out of view. The script demands that the dust should initially fall with a gestural sweep, like the first bold mark on the white surface of the paper, then expand and lose definition like the intentional smudge one adds in drawing to suggest weight and mass. This expansion should continue until it permeates the entire page/space, creating an ambiguity whereby what is full appears empty. A slow settling, a quiet fade out, closes the sequence, leaving the main character lying inert on the floor. In re-viewing the *The Fullness of Emptiness* it became apparent that the pressure I felt in response to watching the footage of empty and eventless space paralleled the pressure I felt when faced with a blank page during figure drawing, for even when the subject stands right in front of the artist, tension created by the possibility of *nothing* coming to fill the page is exacerbated by the blank materiality of the paper.

Lisa Munnelly,
The Fullness of Emptiness, 2003.
DVD sequence.

The artist knows that the act of drawing a line on a blank piece of paper activates the spatial qualities of the paper, an awareness articulated by John Berger, who writes:

> I now began to see the white surface of the paper on which I was going to draw in a different way. From being a clean flat page it became an empty space. Its whiteness became an area of limitless opaque light, possible to move through but not to see through. I knew that when I drew a line on it – or through it – I should have to control the line, not like the driver of a car, on one plane: but like a pilot in the air, movement in all three dimensions being possible. Yet when I made a mark, the nature of the page changed again, the area of opaque light suddenly ceased to be limitless. The whole page was changed by what I had just drawn just as the water in a tank is changed immediately you put a fish in it. It is then only the fish you look at, the water merely becomes the condition of its life and the area in which it can swim.[25]

In titling the video work *The Fullness of Emptiness*, I paid homage to the void's potential to operate both positively and negatively, either enhancing or impeding creativity. Within the work, the expansion of the black dust, to the point where it completely filled and transformed the white room into a black void, made what is full appear empty. Gaston Bachelard deploys a spatial analogy to collapse the ostensible opposition between 'full' and 'empty' when he observes that "... to great dreamers of corners and holes nothing is ever empty, the dialectics of full and empty only correspond to two geometrical non-realities. The function of inhabiting constitutes the link between full and empty."[26]

In swapping the gestural, intuitive and idiosyncratic marks that I had made in the figure drawings for repetitive, non-hierarchical and mechanical marks two things arose: firstly, the psychological emptying out that took place during the repetitive mark-making process made room for the unforseen. Secondly, by using marks that anybody could have made, what I was in effect doing was challenging traditional art world assumptions concerning truth, beauty, skill and form.

Repartee

The second video in *The Aesthetics of Immersion*, *Sweeping Vistas*, documents the act of sweeping up the fallen charcoal dust after the first act of its release. The resultant marks are visually reminiscent of Abstract Expressionist Mark Rothko's work, with its darkness and horizontal divisions suggestive of landscape. The title alludes to how the forms in the filmed floor drawing evoked the movement's fascination with the sublime, transcendence, and majestic mountaintops.

When Gadamer spoke of art as a dialogical event he was not so much talking about the reflexivity between artist and materials (discussed here in depth), nor was he focusing on the dialogue between artwork and viewer (a topic extensively covered by many others); rather, he was concerned more with "the inherited presuppositions (traditions) which structure an artist's pre-understanding of his or her chosen theme."[27] In characterising the entire art historical tradition as an ever-evolving conversation, he stressed its participatory nature. What is so liberating about Gadamer's philosophy is the opportunity it creates for the artist to participate in historical conversations, that closure on a conversation, a body of work, or even an artistic movement is never final. It can be revisited. No one, no movement, no era can ever claim to have had the last word.

For example, *Sweeping Vistas* can be apprehended through a feminist critique of the Abstract Expressionist references, and read as a challenge to the male dominated terrain of Abstract Expressionism through the replacement of the trademark tool of artistic genius (the paintbrush) with one of domesticity (the household broom). In this conversation, *Sweeping Vistas* signals the conspicuous absence of female artists from the movement's *his*-story and the lack of value accorded 'women's work'. Alternately, another conversation might foreground the role of labour in the work and find beauty in the banality of the everyday.

The ability of the individual artist to pick up on previous conversations is likened by Rebecca Schneider to the way a solo is indicated in jazz or blues, where an artist makes a call and another responds, stating:

> Solos, in jazz, cite each other, bleed into each other, react to each other, re-enact each other, and perform an entire cross-hatch of work in which the "solo" quality of any one action becomes profoundly

riddled with the echoes of precedence *and* the fore-cast echoes of future response ...[28]

Schneider goes on to elucidate how the title of "solo artist" or "auteur" is given to those who have abandoned the primacy or authority of the text – those whose practice runs counter to, or "un-becomes," sedimented practices of genre or media distinctions:

> [A]rtists become agents or *actors* (the emphasis on the active) by deploying gestures that seem to resist ... the very media through which they emerge and, often, by or through which they are recorded. In this way, act-based art makes itself available to *become* in a *different* form, to be retold. This becoming different *as retelling* is key.[29]

It is clear how such media distinctions (i.e. drawing as lines, pictures or plans made by using pencils, pens or crayons on paper) in the traditional definition of drawing fail to take into account the spatial, dialogical and performative aspects inherent in the act of making marks. Yet, I maintain that it is the very *limitation*, the very *narrowness* of drawing's traditional definition, that opens up a space for the artist of today to react, retell, resist and re-engage.

In retrospect, my initial assertion that any definition of drawing must take into account matter, movement and dialogue needs re-examining. The term "definition" itself seems to have become questionable, its certainty and author-ity seemingly untenable in an environment where things set in stone have a tendency to erode, where rules and boundaries generate creativity through deconstruction. Paradoxically, acknowledging the impossibility of presenting a definitive statement as to *what* drawing is brings us closer to it. A vehicle of its own sensuous experience, an event particular to its time of address, drawing is a unique and unpredictable affair, reflecting the indeterminacy of existence which "means tolerating a world in which the things (subject matters) which concern us – meaningfulness, goodness, love – remain uncertain in nature and outcome."[30]

Notes

1 Angela Kingston et al., *What is drawing?* (London and New York: Black Dog Publishing, 2003). *What is Drawing?* examines the new ways in which artists have been using drawing in their work. The book explores the tactile drawings of Claude Heath's practice, Lucy Gunning's video works, and Rae Smith's theatre designs.

2 Michael Ginsborg in Kingston et al., p. 11.

3 Barry Schwabsky, "Painting in the Interrogative Mode," in *Vitamin B: New Perspectives in Painting* (Oxford: Phaidon Press, 2002), p. 7.

4 Cited by Marshall McLuhan in *Understanding Media: The Extensions of Man* (London and New York: Routledge, 1995), p. 128.

5 Walter Benjamin, "The Work of Art in the Age of Mechanical Reproduction," in *Illuminations* (London: Jonathon Cape, 1970), p. 241.

6 Mihaly Csikszentmihalyi and Rick E. Robinson, *The Art of Seeing: An Interpretation of the Aesthetic Encounter* (California: Getty Trust Collections, 1990), p. 144.

7 Cited in Cornelia H. Butler, *AfterImage: Drawing Through Process* (Los Angeles: Museum of Contemporary Art; Cambridge, Mass.: MIT Press, 1999), p. 85.

8 Nicholas Davey, "Hans-Georg Gadamer," in *Key Writers on Art: The Twentieth Century*, ed. Chris Murray (London and New York: Routledge, 2003), p. 133.

9 Ibid., p. 131.

10 Ibid.

11 Cited by Francis McKee in "From Zero to Nothing in No Time," in *Nothing*, ed. Graham Gussin and Ele Carpenter (Sunderland: August and Northern Gallery for Contemporary Art, 2001), p. 20.

12 Lisa Munnelly, *The Aesthetics of Immersion: Time Process and Performance in Practice* (Wellington: Massey University School of Fine Arts, 2003).

13 Gussin, "Out of It," in *Nothing*, p. 11.

14 Hegel, "The law of Quantity into Quality (and vice-versa)," cited by Rob Sewell in *What is Dialectical Materialism*, accessed online at <www.marxist.com> on 7 August 2003.

15 Cited by Avis Newman in "The Marks, Traces, and Gestures of Drawing," in *The Stage of Drawing: Gesture and Act. Selected from the Tate Collectiontion*, ed. Catherine de Zegher (New York: Tate Publishing and The Drawing Center, 2003), p. 68.

16 Jean-Francois Lyotard, "The Sublime and the Avant-Garde," in *The Continental Aesthetics Reader*, ed. Clive Cazeaux (London and New York: Routledge, 2000), p. 454.

17 Asger Jorn (1914-73). Artist involved in the early stages of the Situationist International. Quote originally from *On the Passage of a Few People Through a Rather Brief Moment in Time: The Situationist International 1957-72* (Cambridge, Mass.: MIT Press 1991). Sourced from Charles Harrison and Paul Wood, eds., *Art in Theory 1900-2000: An Anthology of Changing Ideas* (Oxford: Blackwell Publishing, 2003), p. 709.

18 Ibid., p. 604.

19 Henri Focillon (1881-1943). Original work published as *La Vie des Forms* in 1934. Henri Focillon, *The Life of Forms in Art* (New York: Zone Books, 1989), p. 97.

20 Ibid.

21 In *Emerson's Literary Criticism*, ed. Eric W. Carlson. (Lincoln: University of Nebraska Press), p. 17.

22 Tony Godfrey, *Drawing Today* (Oxford: Phaidon Press, 1990), p. 9.

23 In Paul Joyce, *Hockney on Photography: Conversations with Paul Joyce* (London: Jonathon Cape, 1988), p. 169.

24 Brian Eno, *Paul Mertons Hour of Silence Interview*, accessed online at <www.nwu.edu/music/eno/thursaft-2.html> on 17 October 2000.

25 John Berger, "Drawing," in *Selected Essays and Articles: The Look of Things* (Harmondsworth: Penguin, 1972), p. 167.

26 Gaston Bachelard, *The Poetics of Space* (Boston: Beacon Press, 1969), p. 140.

27 Gadamer in Davey, p. 131.

28 Rebecca Schneider, "Solo Solo Solo," in *After Criticism: New Responses to Art and Performance*, ed. Gavin Butt (Malden, Mass: Blackwell Publishing, 2005), p. 37.

29 Ibid., p. 41.

30 Gadamer in Davey, p. 132.

Lisa Munnelly, *Sweeping Vistas*, 2003. Charcoal dust, broom, Digital Video.

Plastic Forest
An interactive structure
for Mutek 2005

Rodrigo Tisi

Plastic Forest was an interactive architectural installation that was produced in Chile and designed for Mutek 2005, an international festival of music, sound and new technologies.

The design process for this installation explored ideas of performance and performativity as two crucial aspects that shape public space and its experience. With constraints imposed by site and festival on one hand and those of economy and materiality on the other, we decided to *build*, to *experience* and to *destroy* a site-specific interactive structure as three embodied actions generated by the project in a day-long spatial event.

The artificial landscape we constructed was the main visual attraction of the Mutek event that took place between the Chilean cities of Santiago and Valparaíso during 2005. Based in Montreal, Mutek is recognized for its promotion of new forms of digital media, including acoustic and visual art forms (Djs and Vjs), providing a necessary exploratory platform for artists working in these emerging fields.

The interactive structure was located on the pier promenade of Muelle Barón, in the port of Valparaíso. It was designed and developed by the advanced studio Spaces of / for Performance that was conducted over fifteen weeks in the School of Architecture at Universidad Técnica Federico Santa María. The brief was to create a performative structure that took into account notions of the event as a site-specific spatiotemporal phenomenon, enacting its own forces as well as provoking actions from the public. The piece was sited on a ramp connecting varying levels of the pier and constructed of 850 orange plastic pipes placed in a grid of 30 × 30 cm units. A system of colored LEDs was embedded in the flexible industrial tubing that activated the circulation space of this ramp through which the public had to move to access the pier, thus transforming the *Plastic Forest* into an interactive corridor for all the participants of Mutek.

Three types of lighting were utilized. Three hundred flashing red LEDs appeared and disappeared at 15 cm from the ramp level, resembling from a distance an airport runway. Two hundred and forty white LEDs, aligned with the 40 pipes located in the perimeter of the main oval space at the center of the structure, were installed with electronic movement sensors that were activated by the presence of the participants. The white light registered the presence of people participating in the heart of the plastic structure. Finally, allocated microphones in the base of the structure recorded on-site sounds and two oscilloscopes projected the acoustic curves of light as moving waves. The low-tech technology used in the installation captured both the acoustics of the music performed by musicians and the detailed sonic ambience of the circulating crowd. The result of the installation was a landscape of movement, sound, color and lighting produced by all the participants – musicians and visitors – performing with, and in response to, the dynamic construction. From a distance, the display of the moving orange structure reminded some people of Valparaíso of the old lighthouses once typical in this South American port.

Because this structure was designed for an interactive event that lasted a single day and night, the design considered the intervention's own progressive creation and destruction throughout the time of its occupation. The growing dynamics of the crowd during the night led to a performative transformation of the forest, generating new paths and landscapes by dawn at the end of Mutek 2005.

Credits

Performance/Project: *Plastic Forest*
Location: Muelle Barón, Valparaíso, Chile
Date: December 2005
Producer: Universidad Técnica Federico Santa María and Mutek
Designers/Directors/Choreographers: Rodrigo Tisi, Roberto Barria and Pablo Silva as well as the students of the advanced studio Spaces of / for Performance at Universidad Técnica Federico Santa María, Valparaíso, Chile
Photographs and Digital images: Professors and students of the advanced studio Spaces of / for Performance at UTFSM, Valparaíso, Chile. Special thanks to Jose Vega, Marcela Godoy and Hans Vidaurre

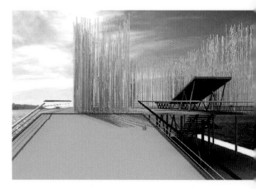

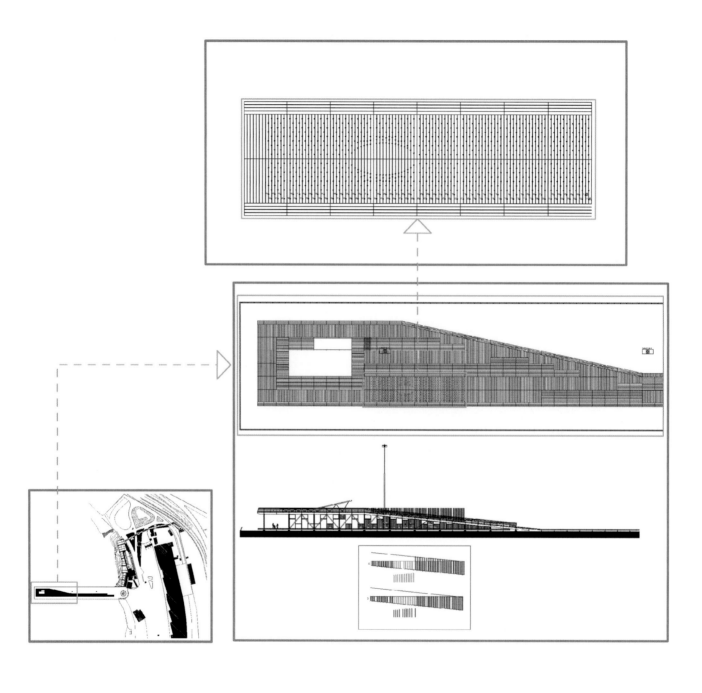

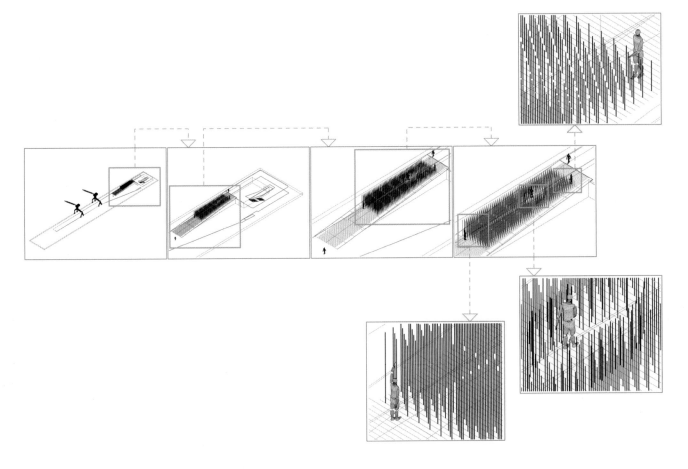

Magnetico, theatre performance, 2004. Photo: Milka Panayotova.

Architettura mobile, installation work, Museo Laboratorio d'Arte Contemporanea, Rome, 2004. Photo: Domenico Scudero.

Light as Action | Fabrizio Crisafulli

In my theatre work, I seek to entrust light with a role similar to that which it occupies in the natural world. Not by imitating it, but by considering light as a vital substance – an essential, primal and emergent element – and thereby liberating it from its secondary role as a tool for *effect* or *staging* to which it is often relegated. I believe that light does not belong only to the technical or visual domain. Its fundamental functions are to shape time and space, to become a dramatic structure, and serve as a means of unfolding or producing 'actions'.

In my work these ideas are part of a mode of creating productions based on what I call "real relations." With this, I encourage participants to immerse themselves in a given situation, with precise parameters, deriving from an initial engagement with a theme or a text; or with the poetics of an author; or from a concrete relationship (physical, spatial, or visual). The situation might also be derived from a real site, as it is in the case of projects I call "Theatre of Places." The participant's reactions and suggestions form additional variations on the initial situation during the embryonic stage of the production, modifying its relations. In rehearsal, a *place* is created: a realm of evolving relationships.

This process is crucial for determining the role of light, which, even though it differs from production to production, remains an integral and evolving element within the entire set of relations. In other words, light is not a technical element 'projected' onto the production, but becomes a component of the relational place itself: woven into the actions, time, spaces, forms, sounds and words that define themselves through their relationship with each other. In relation to these elements, light is both origin and consequence. From the beginning it is considered an active and formative factor.

For the "Theatre of Places" (a project adopting the real site as the central text of each performance), light also acknowledges the pre-existing physicality of the site. It does therefore not intervene purely as 'illumination' but seeks an exploration of the site's essence in order to both adhere to the original identity

Le addormentate, site-specific performance, Sala 1 Gallery, Rome, 1995. In the top (left to right): Lucia Riccelli, Daria Deflorian. In the bottom: Daria Deflorian.

of the site while transforming it. Light is 'born' from the objects, from the architecture and from the landscape – shaping itself from these. At the same time, from this light emerge entirely new situations. I also try to manifest this in my installations. In some cases, I establish a reciprocal exchange between the projection and the object, between the digital realm and the material world.

One problem occurring with projections in general is that they are – technically and symbolically – an element separate from space, body, and matter. Moving images, primarily video projections, are often used today to parallel or juxtapose other actions. My intention is to utilize projections as a means of bringing the digital image and the object into the same sphere of relations. Consequently, I do not use pre-recorded material. Instead, I sculpt the projection's beam in the space, based on all of the information provided by the object, onto which the projector is directed from the beginning. The object thus becomes the matrix of the digital image from which I create a moving composition on the computer, based on the variable interplay between the form of light and the form of the object. In the end, the projection makes the object 'move' and 'perform'. Such an encounter between digital image and matter opens up a new dimension – empty, mysterious, suspended – that is difficult to attribute to a solely digital sphere.

Translated by Nina Heine and John Di Stefano

Battito, naso, lungo, installation work, Sala 1 Gallery, Rome, 2002. Photo: Stefano Fontebasso De Martino.

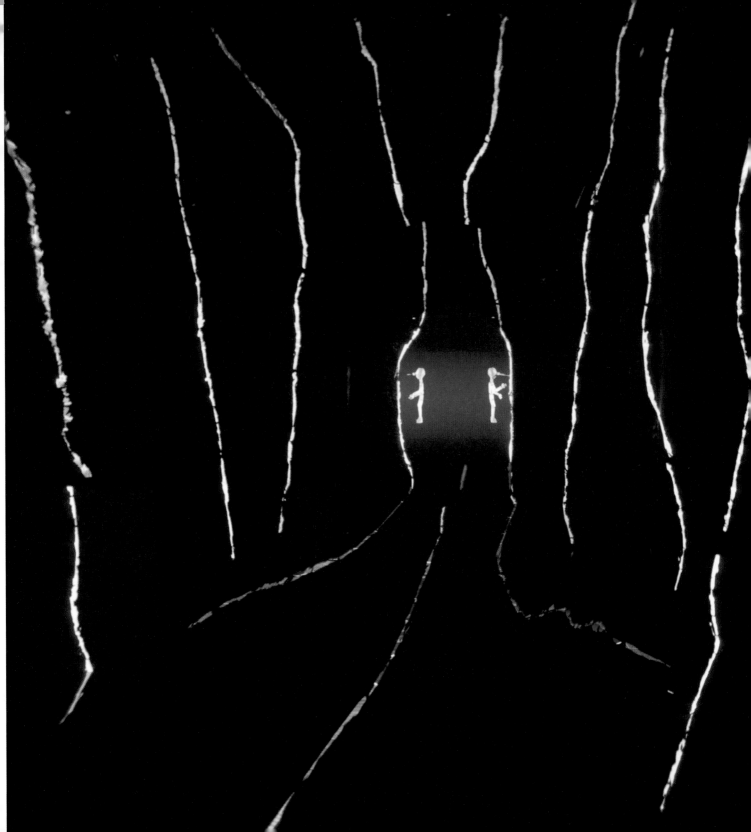

Et molto meravigliosi da vedere, site-specific installation, Ponte Milvio, Rome, 2003.

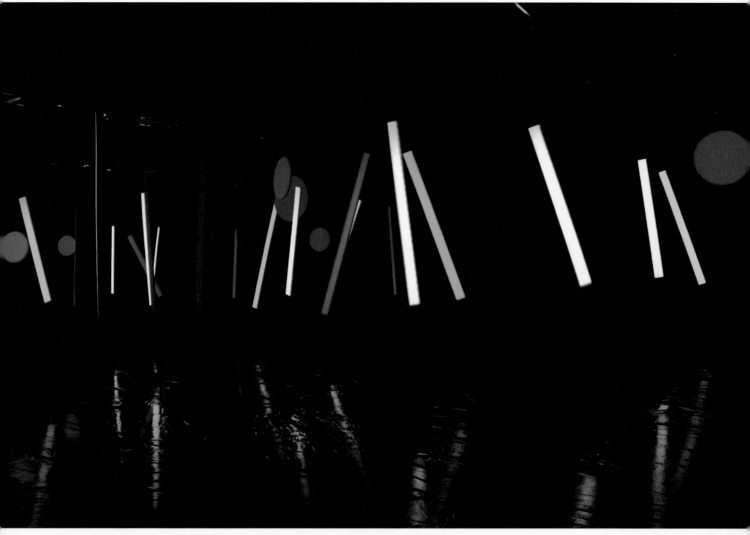

Forest, installation, Muzej 25 Maj, Belgrade (Serbia), 2005. Photo: Stefano Felicetti.

Senti, theatre performance, 2003. In the picture: Carmen López Luna. Photo: Fabio Marino.

Lingua stellare, theatre performance, 2000. In the picture: Carmen López Luna. Photo: Marta Orlik Gaillard.

Senti, theatre performance, 2003. On the opposite page (left to right): Carmen López Luna, Giuseppe Asaro, Alessandra Cristiani. Photo: Serafino Amato. Above (left to right): Carmen López Luna, Giuseppe Asaro, Alessandra Cristiani. Photo: Fabio Marino.

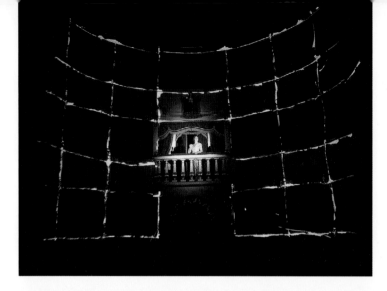

Teatro dei luoghi: Pomarance, site-specific performance, Teatro dei Coraggiosi, Pomarance, 1998.

Centro e ali, theatre performance, 1996. In the picture (left to right): Anne Line Redtrøen, Giovanna Summo, Carmen López Luna. Photo: Serafino Amato.

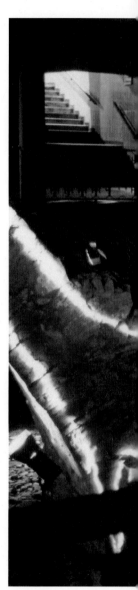

Sul posto, site-specific installation, Ponte romano, Parma, 1998.

Antarctic Shopping Party
Southern Lights – Antarctic Collectibles

ADC Art Design Collective:
Anne Noble
Sven Mehzoud
Lee Jensen

There are a network of social and commercial relationships implicit within the practice of landscape photography. Whether as trope of virgin wilderness or backdrop for human drama, the Antarctic landscape photograph is a manufactured cultural product that defines Antarctica and locates it as a place within the cultural imagination.[1]

Although Antarctica is a remote continent which most of us have never visited, it remains a landscape that many people connect with at some level. How are its images, stories and memories generated and comprehended? How do we travel to these places in our minds and imaginations? Such questions of distance and representation are encountered when designing exhibitions, revealing a dilemma for the designer, whose role is often to evoke that which is absent. Attempts at fixing place through visual representation can also erase temporality, the fundamental element of experiencing space.

Southern Lights – Antarctic Collectibles, and the *Antarctic Shopping Party* that launched this exhibition, were conceived by New Zealand artist Anne Noble to interrogate landscape practices and the role of photography and design in the construction of visual knowledge and understanding of Antarctica. In this art event the visitor encountered the translation of sublime landscape photography from a photographic image into commercial products in the form of a series of limited edition collectible items. These were raffled or offered for sale and consumption in the context of a commercial dealer gallery that had been transformed into a shop trading in these items, which were derived from one large photograph on the wall. The objects included Antarctic biscuits, Antarctic cookie cutters, Antarctic jigsaw puzzles and postcards.

The Art Design Collective was formed to draw attention to the role of both art and design in the creation, construction, sale and consumption of the photographic landscape image. Integral to the success of the event was the heightened visibility of design, branding and marketing within the gallery context. A series of light boxes displayed the objects and, suggesting luminous ice shelves, visually referenced the mythos of Antarctica. This evocation of the sub-zero sublime was extended to the semi transparent packaging that encased the artefacts in translucent plastic scored with abstract cartographer's grids. The brand was designed with reference to the kitsch qualities of popular and romantic narratives and included a brochure outlining the product range and prices in the style of a hypermarket catalogue.

Through the aestheticisation of a series of commercial transactions, the sublime art moment was relocated from photographic object to shopping experience, an aesthetic moment that included the gallery visitors as performers and participants. Their involvement also highlighted a series of spatial, cultural and social practices apparently at odds with the contemporary dealer gallery environment, yet familiar to the ubiquitous merchandising space now associated with public galleries and art museums. As habituated consumers the visitors viewed, rummaged and picked up the displayed items. They scrutinized the products, made purchases and ate a Christmas cake baked in the shape of the frozen continent, all the while encountering their own desire and longing related to the referenced imagery, symbols and myths. This embodied engagement emphasized the viewer's active role in interpreting displayed work within a gallery environment by framing the exhibition as a deliberately spatiotemporal event:

> Landscape implies an act of passage, a rite of passage. Perhaps the ultimate landscape is the one that always maintains a distance, that does not admit of representation, that resists rhetorical transmogrification, that demands perpetual journey.[2]

Visitors who journeyed through the *Antarctic Shopping Party* event consumed images of and information on Antarctica, but remained unable to fully comprehend, conquer or possess the terrain. This visitor experience brought limitations of engaging with 'other' places through representation into sharp focus and used the ineffectual nature of consumerism to suggest the eternal inscrutability of the Antarctic landscape. Perhaps, representations of landscapes such as Antarctica can only set us on a journeying towards it, but never allow us to arrive at the place itself.

Credits

Project: *Antarctic Shopping Party: Southern Lights – Antarctic Collectibles* was a satellite event following the opening of Anne Noble's exhibition *Southern Lights*, Christchurch Art Gallery, December 2005 – July 2006
Location: Jonathan Smart Gallery, Christchurch, New Zealand
Dates: December 2005 – January 2006
Installation Concept, Photographs and Artefacts: Anne Noble
Exhibition and Packaging Design: Sven Mehzoud
Graphic Design: Lee Jensen
Installation Photography: Anne Noble and Alastair McAra
Sponsors: Jonathan Smart and Massey University, Wellington, New Zealand
Assistants: Alistair McAra, Louise Menzies and Jane Apthorp

Notes

1 Anne Noble, artist's statement, *Southern Lights*, Christchurch Art Gallery/Jonathan Smart Gallery, 2005-2006.
2 Allen S. Weiss, *The Wind and the Source: In the Shadow of Mount Ventoux* (Albany: State University of New York Press, 2005), p. 40.

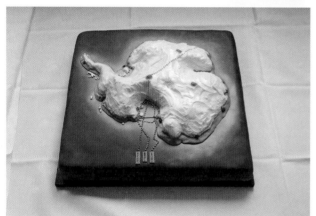

SOUTHERN
LIGHTS
ANTARCTIC
COLLECTIBLES

RAFFLE
1 / 100

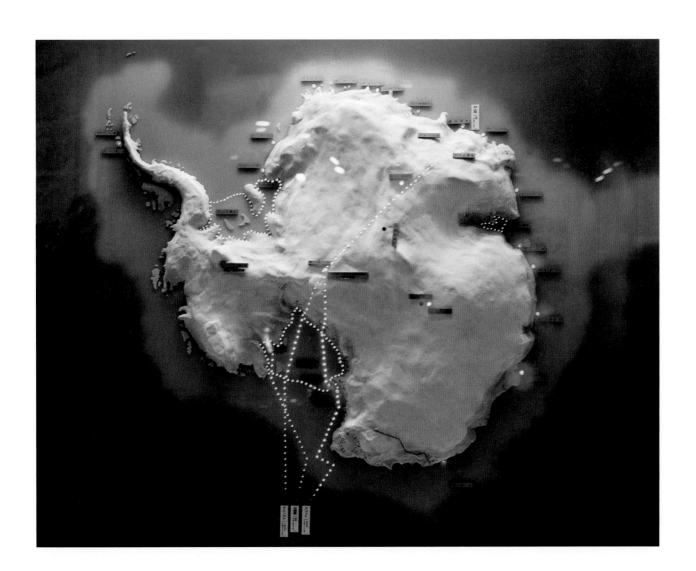

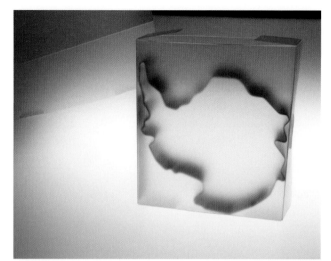

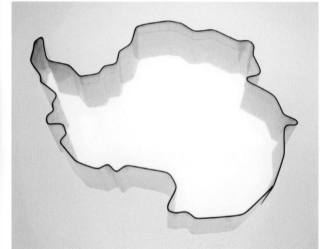

Golgotha. Photo: Roberto Fortuna.

jesus_c_odd_size Kirsten Dehlholm

jesus_c_odd_size is a site-specific performance created for a former church, now an art center, in the middle of Copenhagen. The audience wanders through the rooms encountering staged scenarios and exhibited objects. The architecture, spirit, and tradition of the venue frame the entire work, intensifying its themes and expression. Each spectator creates his or her own narrative according to the individually chosen path, resulting in an experience that slides between multiple layers of fact and fiction.

The title *jesus_c_odd_size* is a reference to present day websites, where all of us become superstars in the electronic firmament, while – like Jesus Christ – we walk around more or less misplaced in our time. Jesus is the odd figure and the common reference we bring with us into the performance space where well-known legends and stories are being investigated and updated.

jesus_c_odd_size is a performance and an exhibition in which installation art, tableaux vivant, live performance, conversation, film, lecture, sermon, interactive digital confessional, coffee room, sound art, and organ music take part. Fifty-five performers from several countries participate – all typecast and chosen according to their life story, their knowledge and experience. They meet the spectator face to face. They are unique, but disguised as ordinary people. They are people of our time.

The spectator enters like an unknowing guest who moves around exploring the world of a quietly buzzing, biblical market square. You cannot hide and are required to participate, being just as exposed as the people you look at; as the leprous girls on small boards with wheels who ride among the audience while singing very loudly; as the disciples' grandmothers who invite you for coffee while they talk about their grandchildren.

The performers are simultaneously themselves and characters. They perform as mythic figures, but their personal stories appear in the same web as that of the myths. Both spectators and those observed drift in indeterminable space, occupying a tension between the personal and the mythical. Because of your personal participation in these meetings, the peculiar feature of many of the performers never becomes subjected to voyeurism. They are there. You are there. And that is it.

The Jesus-figure appears as several characters, as many acts, as detail and whole, as form and content. But always hidden and disguised in the most visible, the most concrete. There is the secret, just in front of everyone.

jesus_c_odd_size reveals the frailty of mankind that appears in an objective ceremony of reality. Without background music, smooth surfaces and trendy light. Without the aesthetics with which you are used to having 'reality' presented. jesus_c_odd_size is the consequence of reality as a theatre of distance. If reality has become theatre, then the theatre should become real in order to remind us that reality – as it appears in the optics of theatrical distance – is not true. That theatre has to become real does not mean it should become 'realistic', i.e. represent reality through well known categories. To get real means to let something appear which exceeds worn explanations. To leave reality alone.

Credits

Performance: jesus_c_odd_size
Location: Nikolaj Copenhagen
Contemporary Art Center, Denmark
Dates: 2002
Production: Hotel Pro Forma
Concept: Kirsten Dehlholm, artistic director
of Hotel Pro Forma, Denmark;
Gritt Uldall-Jessen, playwright, Denmark;
Lawrence Malstaf, visual artist, Belgium
Direction: Kirsten Dehlholm

The venue, three disciples, the Virgin Mary, the angel, spectators. Photo: Richard Sandler.

Spectators, two disciples, Jesus, the lepers. Photo: Richard Sandler.

The Last Supper, the disciples, Jesus, Judas, spectators. Photo: Richard Sandler.

Mary Magdalene 1, Mary Magdalene 2, the leper, the army chaplain, spectators. Photo: Richard Sandler.

The grandmothers of the disciples, two disciples, spectators. Photo: Richard Sandler.

Jesus, Virgin Mary, one disciple, Judas, the little Lord, the angel. Photo: Richard Sandler.

Golgotha, the Virgin Mary, the woman possessed by demons, spectators. Photo: Richard Sandler.

The angel, the disciples, the leper, spectators. Photo: Richard Sandler.

enCOUNTER

Global Feeling
(Almost) all you need is love

Jon McKenzie

An experiential preface. My experience as a designer has four elements. These are, in chronological order, my mother, who taught art in elementary and high schools; my Bachelor's degree in fine arts, which included classes in color theory and two- and three-dimensional design; my industry work as a graphic designer and information architect, the latter in a web design firm; and my academic positions, where I have taught interface design and experience in departments of multimedia art, performance studies, and English. Each element has comprised a unique design encounter within different sociotechnical environments: family, university, business, and university again, but this time as both practitioner and theorist.

Significantly, right in the middle, between my BFA and my first design job, I worked toward a doctoral degree in performance studies, and though I did not focus on design per se, this training profoundly affected my ideas about design. In a nutshell: I went from seeing design in primarily – even exclusively – visual terms to feeling design in performative terms, by which I mean an open, synesthetic, and processual approach to design, one that includes all the senses and, as important, the temporal *and* the spatial dimension. Brenda Laurel's *Computers as Theatre* was the first eye opener for me – or perhaps I should say eye closer, for my experience teaching interface design soon revealed to what extent the visual had dominated the discourse of design.[1] This dominance has long marginalized issues of interactivity, and actual engagement with designed objects and environments had fallen under such clunky terms as "human factors" and "usability." Interactivity and usability have often been taken as issues assigned to the purview of industrial engineers or market researchers. It was as if design and use, aesthetics and practicality were opposed, despite the much-lauded modernist mantra "form follows function." By contrast, Henry Petroski, a

127

design historian trained in civil engineering, argues that *form follows failure*, that impracticality guides design as much as aesthetics, since flawed designs feed back and shape subsequent design decisions.[2]

The visual dominance of design may well be ending, an end brought about by many factors, including the rise of gadget culture with its insistent drive for innovative interactive features and the related emergence of user-oriented design approaches that put end users up front, at, or near the beginning of the design process. The emerging field of performance design may be another crucial factor. By providing designers with new concepts, models, and practices for approaching design in performative terms, performance design may help bridge aesthetics and functionality by providing a common language for designers, engineers, and others involved in the creative process, including those others called consumers, audiences, and users.

In addition, for cultural theorists performance design provides a critical discourse for understanding how the world has become a designed environment in which an array of global performances unfold – for better and for worse. What does it mean to design performances on a global scale? Who – or what – does the designing? For whom and to what ends?

On 25 June 1967, the Beatles performed a new song, "All You Need is Love," before an intimate yet immense audience, one numbering approximately 350 million people – an audience composed of dozens of invited celebrities and guests sitting around the band in a London BBC studio, and the millions upon millions of TV viewers watching from sites around the world. The performance was part of the BBC show *Our World*, considered by some to have been the first global television program.

One might approach the performance of "All You Need is Love" using Philip Auslander's concept of *liveness*, which entails seeing the contemporary stress on live performance as itself an effect of hypermediation.[3] John Lennon sang the song live while listening to taped tracks the band had recorded days earlier at Abbey Road Studios, tapes also listened to through headphones by Paul, George and Ringo, as well as the half-dozen classical musicians also sitting-in that day. One might also approach the performance through at least four paradigms of performance research: the cultural performance of rock music, the technological performance of satellite television, the organizational performance of the British Broadcasting Corporation and Capitol Records, and, lastly, the financial performance of these two entities, as well as that of the Fab Four themselves.[4] (Significantly, when "All You Need You is Love" was released shortly afterwards as a 45 single in more than a dozen countries, the B-side selection was the song "Baby, You're A Rich Man," as seen on the sleeve of the Yugoslavian release.)

I will consider "All You Need is Love" from another angle, however – that of *global feeling*. Though there has been much discussion about the political, economic, and cultural dimensions of globalization over the past decade, less attention has been given to the dimension of feeling. A few scholars have addressed it: anthropologist Arjun Appadurai has analyzed the complex "structures of feeling" that globalization entails, while literary scholar Bruce Robbins has begun theorizing a hypothetical, posthumanist way of *feeling global*.[5] I wish to approach this affective dimension in terms of performance in order to begin thinking about global feeling.

By global feeling, I mean at least two things. First, the possibility that affects and emotions can be transmitted globally in unprecedented ways. Much of this possibility has to do with profound changes in migration, tourism, transportation, international trade and communication technologies. Even if not felt by everyone on the planet, feelings can be communicated and shared around the world in ways that were never before possible, at least not with such immediacy and intensity. I am not arguing that everyone feels the same thing or that they interpret shared feelings in the same way. This first sense of the term global feeling simply refers to the possibility of affects and emotions being transmitted around the world.

Second, by global feeling I also mean the sense of *feeling global*, feeling a/part of and from global events, both local and distant. By this I do not mean "we are the world," much less "I am the world." Rather, I want to stress this pun "a/part": global feeling means both feeling a part of the world and feeling apart from it at the same time. Feeling global is feeling a/part: it is feeling both localized and globalized, situated and detached, a sort of passion or pathos at a distance: *telepathos*. It is not necessarily feeling the same thing, but it is feeling connected – and thus also disconnected. In some ways, this second sense of global feeling entails an awareness of the first sense; it's a feeling that one *is* feeling something with others around the world. The 1967 performance of "All You Need is Love," I want to suggest, can be approached as an instance of global feeling.

But let me offer a more recent and very different performance of global feeling, one whose repercussions are still with us today, though we may feel them in different ways.

The terrorist attacks of September 11 have been analyzed and discussed from many perspectives. In terms of global feeling, the crash of four airliners into the World Trade Center, the Pentagon and a field in Pennsylvania sent out a wave of shock around the world, a shock transmitted by television, radio and Internet, as well as word of mouth and frantic telephone calls. Though I was in Manhattan when the planes struck the towers, I first heard about it from my mother who telephoned me from Florida.

Now this global wave of shock was itself complex, and it produced a wide variety of feelings in a very short period of time. Many people in the US felt intense fear and confusion, others revulsion, sadness, anger – or some mix of these emotions. We know that such feelings were felt around the world, as the United States received many messages of sympathy from abroad. We also know, however, that for some people, the initial wave of shock produced very different feelings: feelings of joy and amazement, of triumph and satisfaction. The attacks were obviously carefully planned and executed in order to produce widespread impact.

If we can think of September 11 in terms of global feeling, can we also think of it in terms of performance? In his book *Terror in the Mind of God: The Global Rise of Religious Violence*, sociologist Mark Juergensmeyer analyzes an extensive set of case studies, including terrorist acts by Christian, Zionist, Islamic, Hindu, and Buddhist groups. Significantly, he uses performance as an analytical lens to identify patterns of religious violence. In a chapter titled "Theater of Terror," he stresses that such violence strives to be spectacular:

> At center stage are the acts of violence themselves – stunning, abnormal, and outrageous murders carried out in a way that graphically displays the awful power of violence – set within grand scenarios of

conflict and proclamation... By their demonstrative nature, they elicit feelings of revulsion and anger in those who witness them.[6]

Significantly, Juergensmeyer calls such theatrical forms of terrorism "performance violence." Terrorist acts, he argues, function as both performance events and performative speech acts. Performance violence makes dramatic, symbolic statements and also attempts to change things. The setting and timing of performance violence may themselves be symbolic. The Pentagon and World Trade Center, for instance, were potent symbols of the US military and international trade and finance. In terms of timing, Christopher Hitchens suggested in *The Guardian* a few days after the attack that September 11 marks a significant date in European and Islamic history: "It was on September 11, 1683 that the conquering armies of Islam were met, held, and thrown back at the gates of Vienna."[7] This military reversal, by the way, was soon followed by what, until recently, has been called the last Christian crusade against Islam.

Juergensmeyer also argues that performance violence usually has multiple audiences and that its perpetrators are often very media savvy. Using television and other media they may seek to strike terror into a general public, while at the same signaling strength and determination to a narrower audience. Following Juergensmeyer's line of inquiry, the attacks of September 11 can be understood as a performance designed to produce a specific set of global feelings: feelings of terror and revulsion for a wide, general audience, and feelings of triumph and determination for another audience whose size would surprise most Americans. One of the most striking things about the attacks on the World Trade Center was that they were recorded by helicopters capturing images of the city for broadcast on the morning news shows. These cameras produced broadcast quality images of the attacks that were quickly transmitted around the world. It was largely through such images that the world felt the shock and awe of September 11, 2001.

I use this term "shock and awe" here because it takes me to another closely related example of global feeling: the US "shock and awe" bombing of Baghdad. I am not equating the September 11 attacks and the March 21 bombing of the Iraqi capital. But I do think that the latter's coordinated, even choreographed, missile strikes can be understood as a direct response to the spectacle of the

World Trade Center attacks. The US military campaign produced carefully targeted, large-scale explosions in a major metropolitan area, explosions captured and transmitted by broadcast quality media to a worldwide audience. As the name indicates, this campaign was explicitly designed to create a specific set of feelings: shock and awe.

Many, if not most, Americans would not like to think of the shock and awe campaign in terms of terrorism; it was, after all, portrayed at the time by the US media as a turning point in America's triumph over the Iraqi army and Saddam Hussein's government. But though its stated goal was to shock, awe and confuse the Iraqi leadership, there is little doubt that the campaign also produced terror in the population. One might also consider both the effects and affects it produced elsewhere: in other Middle East countries, in Asia, Africa, Europe and also in the Western hemisphere. One thing is evident today: the war against Iraq has cost the US government and the American people the global feelings of sympathy and support that were expressed immediately after September 11. In the wake of the torture scandal at Abu Ghraib prison, the assault on Fallujah, and the continued violence elsewhere in Iraq, one wonders when, if ever, such feelings will return to displace the anger and suspicions now felt around the world towards the United States.

Though I have been discussing the global feelings associated with terror and war, I want to return to the Beatles' performance of "All You Need is Love." Today, almost forty years later, the televised performance and the song's sentiment may seem naïve, fanciful, even quaint and old-fashioned. Confronted with the complexities of contemporary globalization, American imperialism, and the two-headed monster of terrorism and the "global war on terror," surely we need something more than love:

> There's nothing you can do that can't be done
> Nothing you can sing that can't be sung
> Nothing you can say but you can learn how to play the game
> It's easy
>
> Nothing you can make that can't be made
> No one you can save that can't be saved

Nothing you can do but you can learn how to be you in time
It's easy

All you need is love
All you need is love
All you need is love, love
Love is all you need[8]

Almost. One also needs to consider *what sort of love* is needed. Lennon's notion of love was not restricted to commonplace understandings of this emotion. The song was written especially for the broadcast of *Our World*, with its intimate and immense audience. While we can and should critique the commercialism associated with the Beatles – and rock music generally – we should recognize that the band not only used musical instruments and magnetic tape as creative media, they also used Capitol Records and the BBC in a similar manner – and not only as creative media but also as *political* media. For "All You Need is Love" was a political anthem, a song sung worldwide during that summer of 1967, a season actively promoted as the Summer of Love from hippie-central San Francisco. Lennon's love was precisely a political love.

I am not being nostalgic here. Rather, I want to suggest that a resistant performativity cannot do without a global feeling of political love. In their book, *Multitude: War and Democracy in the Age of Empire*, Hardt and Negri write:

> People today seem unable to understand love as a political concept, but a concept of love is just what we need to grasp the constituent power of the multitude. The modern concept of love is almost exclusively limited to the bourgeois couple and the claustrophobic confines of the nuclear family. Love has become a strictly private affair. We need a more generous and more unrestrained conception of love. We need to recuperate the public and political conception of love common to premodern traditions.[9]

Because they argue that the multitude consists of singular desires, singular bodies, singular situations and struggles, Hardt and Negri contend that what is needed is a *common language of singularities*. The global feeling of love or, more accurately, multiple global feelings of love constitute an affective medium for creating such a language.

What other sort of performances might be relevant to creating these global feelings of political love? Though Hardt and Negri suggest that the political concept of love is difficult for many people to understand, the twentieth century contained several well-known embodiments of such love. They can be found in the legacy of modern civil disobedience practiced in countries around the world. Though there are a wide range of emotions associated with the practice of civil disobedience articulated by Thoreau and developed by Gandhi, King and so many others, perhaps no emotion is more important than love.

Love was crucial for Gandhi, whose term for nonviolence was *ahimsa*, which he defined in both negative and positive terms. Negatively, it means not injuring any living being; positively, it means "the largest love, the greatest charity," even towards one's opponents.[10] Thus for Gandhi, nonviolence, *ahimsa*, was closely related to love. Martin Luther King likewise stressed the overriding value of love, and he drew upon the Greeks to define it. King stressed not *eros* or sensual love, nor *philia*, the reciprocal love between friends. Instead, King valorized *agape*, which he defined as "understanding, creative, redemptive good will for all men.... It is the type of love that stands at the center of the movement we are trying to carry on in the Southland."[11] Of course, for Gandhi and King these practices of love resonated with their respective Hindu and Christian beliefs, and though they both preached love, it was a confrontational love that they taught and practiced.

A more secular version of such confrontational love can be found in the political protests of ACT-UP, the AIDS Coalition to Unleash Power, one of the most visible and effective American activist groups to emerge during the Reagan era. Before his death in 1993, AIDS activist Jon Greenberg wrote that although ACT-UP is united in anger, its protests function as primal scream therapy, getting the anger out so as to "open up to love, knowledge and power."[12] And it is striking in this context that the 1997 collection of essays devoted to ACT-UP founder Larry Kramer, often seen as the angriest of AIDS activists, is titled *We Must Love One Another or Die*.[13]

If love has been a crucial emotion for traditional forms of civil disobedience, what role might it have for more contemporary global forms?

I have been teaching courses on civil disobedience for several years, focusing especially on the emergence of electronic civil obedience and 'hacktivism'. In contrast to more traditional forms of activism, electronic civil disobedience is not limited to local actions undertaken by long-standing communities. Its campaigns often work through global networks, bringing together short-term coalitions from around the world for direct actions against the web sites of multinational corporations and transnational entities such as the International Monetary Fund (IMF) and the World Trade Organization (WTO). Such protests, however, are usually coordinated with actions on the ground, in the streets, and, in the case of the 2003 protests against the WTO, on the shores of Cancun, Mexico, where nude protestors used their bodies to write "NO WTO" on the white sandy beach.

The possibility of creating performances that elicit global feelings of political love faces many challenges in getting beyond private, familial, and bourgeois notions of love. What is a love that is both intimate and immense, both personal and public, both proximate and distant? Such a love, while drawing on premodern traditions (Hardt and Negri cite Christian and Jewish love – oddly leaving out Islam – but, again, there are obviously many other forms of love), involves creating truly postmodern structures of feeling, and here I do not limit the postmodern to aesthetics but include the very problematic economic and technological dimensions of postmodernity.

This brings me to another type of performance that may help us think – indeed feel – this global feeling. Counter-intuitively, I refer here to organizational performance, the performance of workers, managers and entire organizations. In *Perform or Else: From Discipline to Performance*, I argue that this performance paradigm is highly normative, both formally and politically, yet that it also contains mutant and potentially transgressive forces as well.

In *Multitude*, Hardt and Negri explicitly connect up with this mutant dimension of organizational performance, affirming its creative and productive potential. Indeed, such performance is for them crucial for the re-creation of "the common," that material realm held in common, beyond private property, which Hardt and Negri contend can connect the multitude's singularities of difference without universalizing or transcending them. In contrast to habit, which Hardt and Negri argue is the common produced alongside the material labor of industrial, Fordist economies, performance is the common produced by immaterial labor, which characterizes today's service and information economies. They write that

> post-Fordism and the immaterial paradigm adopt performativity, communication, and collaboration as central characteristics. Performance has been put to work. Every form of labor that produces an immaterial good, such as a relationship or an affect, solving problems or providing information, from sales work to financial services, is fundamentally a performance: the product is the act itself. The economic context makes clear that all of these discussions of habit and performance have to be given the sense of doing or making, linking them to the creative capacity of the laboring subject.[14]

I must stress here that the material labor found in mines and factories, the labor theorized by Marx and Engels, still obviously exists, especially in offshore sites in Asia and Latin America. Yet such labor – and the hard wares or commodities it produces – is now wrapped in 'soft wares', in flows of information and finance, in the flexible accumulation of capital described by David Harvey.[15] Indeed, the offshore manufacturing of hard wares presupposes the 'soft wares' of contemporary communication, finance and management. But, again, my main point here is that Hardt and Negri emphasize not the normative dimension of organizational performance but its accompanying creative and transformational dimension.

The cultural performances that performance scholars know and love are not as distant from these organizational performances as we may like to think. One place they mix and intermingle is in "experience design," the crafting and eliciting of affective and social experiences in such spaces as museums and retail stores, private homes and public spaces, video games and websites. Indeed, experience design may be a key form of immaterial labor. Brenda Laurel helped articulate the practice of experience design in her book *Computers as Theatre*, using Aristotle's *Poetics* to write her own poetics of human-computer interaction. I have long argued that contemporary forms of theater and cultural performance might offer more appropriate models for experience design, something my new media students have experimented with.[16]

Others, too, have explored alternative forms of performance, while at the same time moving from the intimacies of experience design to the larger structural complexities of the experience economy. B. Joseph Pine and James H. Gilmore are authors of a book published by the Harvard Business School called *The Experience Economy: Work Is Theatre & Every Business a Stage*. If Laurel theorizes human-computer interactions as theater, Pine and Gilmore theorize *all* economic activity in terms of theater and, like Laurel, they focus on designing experiences. Though they concentrate on the experience of consumers, such as those drinking coffee in Starbucks cafes or vacationing at Disney World, they also discuss designing the experiences of workers, managers and top executives.[17]

Significantly, to explain how "work is theater and every business a stage," Pine and Gilmore turn to Schechner's theory of enactments. Schechner proposes a nested structure: at the core is *drama* or the underlying scenario; surrounding this is the *script*, the basic code of events that interprets the drama; surrounding both drama and script is *theatre*, the actual enactment of the script by the actors; finally, surrounding them all is *performance*, which for Schechner includes the whole constellation of events that passes between actors and audience. In Pine and Gilmore's theory of experience economy, the central drama becomes the core business strategy; the script becomes the production process; the theater becomes the work that carries out these processes; and, finally, the surrounding performance becomes what Pine and Gilmore call the *offering*, that is, "the economic values [that] businesses create for customers."[18] Thus, in *The Experience Economy*, business performance is equated with theatrical performance, and customers with participatory audiences.

While one can critique business' appropriation of theater and cultural performance through experience design, one can also 'design back', ex-appropriating or refunctioning corporate experience design in order to produce different effects. Let me give you an example. One of the most famous TV ads ever sought to evoke a global feeling: I refer to a 1971 Coca-Cola ad – often referred to as "I'd Like to Teach the World to Sing." Produced by the advertising firm McCann-Erickson, it featured several hundred young people on a sunny Italian hilltop singing a jingle that ended: "Coca-Cola – it's the real thing." The song became a worldwide hit (minus the Coke reference) for a band called The New Seekers, and it reached #7 on the US charts and #1 in the UK.

Thirty-two years later, on a London hillside, I saw not the real thing, but a really surreal thing: a giant can of Mecca-Cola. In many ways, this can brings together a number of elements: experience design, performance, political philosophy and global feeling. The day I saw the big Mecca Cola was February 15, 2003, and I was surrounded not by hundreds of people, but by hundreds of thousands, indeed over 1.7 million people, all of them protesting the impending war on Iraq. The protest event had numerous sponsors and planners, and its overall experience design was emergent, distributed and immanent to the event itself. Nonetheless, using Schechner's notion of enactments, we can read the experience design thus: at the core was the unfolding drama of the war protest, surrounded by the scripts or plans for the protest event; this script was embodied in the theater of everyday life by the protestors themselves, while the performance passed not only from the stage to the audience, but from one site to many others.

Although it was located in Hyde Park, the protest was a networked, global event: not only did it concern an international crisis, and not only were there speakers from different nations and cultures, but we were also connected via satellite television to millions of other protestors around the world: in Australia, Germany, Italy, South Korea, Spain, Turkey and the United States. As a number of these protests began appearing on the large projection screens in Hyde Park, there was a palpable feeling that a wave of sentiment was circling the globe and that we were experiencing it live, in mediation. The complex of feelings differed in different places: festive and laid-back in London, tense and violent in New York.

A truly global feeling would entail a post-human love, a sentiment of care and affection that is not restricted to family and friends, or to communities and nations, or even to the human species. I have in mind an ecology of love, one that extends to animals and plant-life, to flocks and herds and forests and plains. A love that even includes the inorganic, an amorous feeling that swells up to the height of mountains, that follows the bends of a river, that's carried on and on by an ocean breeze or the sound of falling rain. Perhaps such a sense

beckons even from the stars, the black holes, the deep void of the cosmos. Thus beyond global feeling: a schizo, cosmocraving.

And yet, remaining earthly, perhaps the most challenging aspect of a global feeling of political love is, finally, initially, all too human. For Gandhi's *ahimsa* entailed a love for the British colonial officials he so opposed, while King's *agape* involved loving the Southern sheriffs who beat and arrested him and his fellow civil rights activists. Who, today, can imagine taking such feelings global – and thus learning to love Shell Oil or IMF officials, George W. Bush and Osama bin Laden? These are things perhaps even Lennon would have a hard time imagining – or perhaps not.

In the spirit of two dreamers – John Lennon and Martin Luther King – who in a sense both died for their dreams and live on in ours, I will finish sketching a performative poetics of global feeling. As I suggest elsewhere, resistant performativity involves 'scaling up' Butler's strategy of resignifying or queering normative discourses and practices. How does one queer a war machine, a terror network, a fascist regime?

Butler herself provides a clue, for she connects resignification to Brecht's tactic of refunctioning.[19] But while Butler's resignification targets discrete words and gestures, Brecht's refunctioning targets social and technical apparatuses. Moreover, refunctioning works at a different level than signification or semantics, for it involves the pragmatic transformation of concrete structures *and* processes, and here we are considering structures and processes of feeling. And yet, while Brecht sought to refunction the apparatus of German theater, the perfumance I have in mind must not limit itself to cultural institutions but instead seek to displace a much wider range of performance systems: corporate, technological, financial, educational, medical, governmental – indeed any sociotechnical system dominated by performance measures and incentives, by normative demands to perform – or else.

In a broader sense, I refer here to what Marcuse called the *performance principle*. In 1973, almost twenty years after he first introduced this concept, Marcuse wrote:

> According to this principle, everyone has to earn his living in alienating but socially necessary performances, and one's reward, one's status in society will be determined by this performance (the work-income relation). The rejection of the Performance Principle also rejects the notion of progress which has up to now characterized the development of Western civilization, namely, progress as increasingly productive exploitation and mastery of nature, external and human, a progress which has turned out to be self-propelling destruction and domination.[20]

I am the first to admit that the feelings which such performance systems usually evoke in me are not love and affection; quite the opposite: they are the feelings of alienation and disaffection which Marcuse associates with the performance principle. And yet, such performance systems are nonetheless lined with desires, passions, and, yes, even love at times. Anyone who has worked in them – and that would certainly include students and professors, artists and curators, activists and advocates – has very likely *felt* such love from time to time, even if she or he has trouble articulating or even admitting it. I have also seen – and felt – it among workers on the assembly line and in the small retail store, as well as in the large accounting and new media firms where I have worked during my life.

The challenge, then, is not only to elicit such emotions, but to sustain and interconnect them with the feelings of people in different institutions and other, far-distant places, not only places in the margins of societies and cultures, but also in the more centralized nodes of high performance sociotechnical systems. Since love has traditionally been conceived in terms of immediacy, proximity and presence, one must imagine a global feeling of political love that is also mediated, distant and marked by absence. Referring back again to Auslander's notion of *liveness*, perhaps we need to give some thought to 'loveness'. But I will let Marcuse have the last word, for where did he locate the most promising resistance to the performance principle, that reality principle of postindustrial societies? Here, there, in *Eros*. All you need is Eros. Almost.

Notes

1 See Brenda Laurel, *Computers as Theatre* (Reading, Mass.: Addison-Wesley, 1993).

2 Henry Petroski, *The Evolution of Useful Things: How Everyday Artifacts-From Forks and Pins to Paper Clips and Zippers-Came to be as They are* (New York: Vintage Books, 1994).

3 See Philip Auslander's *Liveness: Performance in a Mediatized Culture* (London: Routledge, 1999).

4 See my book *Perform or Else: From Discipline to Performance* (London: Routledge, 2001), as well as my essay "High Performance Schooling," *Parallax* 31 (April–June 2004), pp. 50-62.

5 For more on these concepts see Appadurai's *Modernity at Large: Cultural Dimensions of Globalization* (Minneapolis: University of Minnesota Press, 1996) and Robbins' *Feeling Global: Internationalism in Distress* (New York: New York University Press, 1999).

6 Mark Juergensmeyer, *Terror in the Mind of God: The Global Rise of Religious Violence* (Berkeley: University of California Press, 2000), p. 122.

7 Christopher Hitchens, "Why the suicide killers chose September 11," *The Guardian* (October 3, 2001).

8 The Beatles, "All You Need is Love / Baby You're a Rich Man," Parlophone (1967).

9 Michael Hardt and Antonio Negri, *Multitude: War and Democracy in the Age of Empire* (New York: The Penguin Press, 2004), p. 351.

10 M.K. Gandhi, "On Ahimsa," in *The Penguin Gandhi Reader*, ed. Rudrangshu Mukherjee (New York: Penguin Books, 1993), pp. 95-6.

11 Martin Luther King, Jr., "Facing the Challenge of a New Age," in *I Have a Dream: Writings and Speeches that Changed the World* (San Francisco: HarperCollins, 1992), pp. 22-23.

12 Jon Greenberg, "ACT-UP Explained" (1992), accessed online at <http://www.actupny.org/documents/greenbergAU.html> on January 28, 2005.

13 See Larry Kramer's *We Must Love One Another or Die: The Life and Legacies of Larry Kramer*, ed. Lawrence D. Mass (New York: St. Martin's Press, 1997).

14 Hardt and Negri, *Multitude*, pp. 200-201.

15 See David Harvey, *The Condition of Postmodernity: An Enquiry into the Origins of Cultural Change* (Oxford: Basil Blackwell, 1989).

16 See Laurel, *Computers as Theatre*.

17 See B. Joseph Pine and James H. Gilmore, *The Experience Economy: Work is Theater & Every Business a Stage* (Cambridge, Mass.: Harvard Business School, 1999).

18 Pine and Gilmore, *The Experience Economy*, p. 109.

19 See Judith Butler, *Bodies that Matter: On the Discursive Limits of "Sex"* (New York: Routledge, 1993).

20 Herbert Marcuse, "A Revolution in Values," in *Towards a Critical Theory of Society* (London: Routledge, 2001), p. 197.

Kafka's Door
Seeking to meet the Other

Lilja Blumenfeld

Before the law stands a door-keeper. A man from the country comes to this door-keeper and asks for entry into the law. But the door-keeper says that he cannot grant him entry now. The man considers and then asks if that means he will be allowed to enter later. "It is possible," says the door-keeper, "but not now." Since the door to the law stands open, as it always does, and the door-keeper steps to one side, the man bends to look through the door at the interior. When the door-keeper notices this, he laughs and says: "If you are so tempted, just try to enter in spite of my prohibition. But take note: I am powerful. And I am only the lowest door-keeper. But from room to room stand door-keepers each more powerful than the last. The mere aspect of the third is more than even I can endure." Such difficulties had not been expected by the man from the country; the law is supposed to be accessible to everyone and at all times, he thinks, but as he now looks more closely at the door-keeper in his coat of fur, at his great pointed nose and his long and straggly black Tartar's beard, he decides it would be better to wait until he gets permission to enter. The door-keeper gives him a stool and lets him sit to one side of the door. There he sits for days and years. He makes many attempts to be allowed in and wearies the door-keeper out with his entreaties. The door-keeper occasionally subjects him to brief interrogation, asks about his home and many other things, but these are the kind of apathetic questions great lords ask and in the end he tells him each time that he cannot allow him to enter yet. The man, who has equipped himself well for his journey, gives everything he has, no matter how valuable, to bribe the door-keeper. The latter indeed accepts everything, but as he does, he says, "I accept this only so that you may not think you have neglected anything." During these many years the man keeps watch on the door-keeper almost without a pause. He forgets the other door-keepers, and this first door-keeper seems to him the only obstacle to his entry into the law. He curses this unfortunate chance, loudly in the first years and later, as he grows old, he merely mumbles to himself. He becomes infantile, and as in the many years spent watching the door-keeper he has come to know even the fleas in his fur collar, he begs the fleas themselves to come to his aid and persuade the door-keeper to change his mind. Finally his sight grows weak and he does not know if it is really getting darker round him or if his eyes are deceiving him. But he does manage to distinguish in the dark a radiance which breaks out imperishably from the door to the law. He does not live much longer. Before his death, everything he has experienced during this time converges in his mind into the one question he has not yet put to the door-keeper. He beckons him, as he can no longer raise his stiffening body. The door-keeper has to bend down low to him, for the difference in size between them has changed, very much to the disadvantage of the man from the country. "What else do you still want to know?" asks the door-keeper. "You are insatiable." "But everybody strives for the law," says the man. "How is it that in all these years nobody except myself has asked for admittance?" The door-keeper realizes the man has reached the end of his life and, to penetrate his imperfect hearing, he roars at him: "Nobody else could gain admittance here, this entrance was meant only for you. I shall now go and close it."

Kafka, "Before the Law"[1]

Law

Kafka's tale is a tale of "a man from the country" who comes to a certain door in order to meet the law and is confronted by the mysterious door-keeper. The man from the country has arrived in the city where the law usually nests; there seems to be no possibility of approaching the law in the village where the man comes from. Besides, the law in the country is either simply a different one or utterly useless to the man. The door to the law is open, "as always," but the door-keeper who represents the law does not allow the man to enter. Just like the man from the country, he too stands before that same law. "The man only makes his way to the law [while] the door-keeper is already there."[2]

Both men seem to be equal from the perspective of the law, yet there is an invisible line that always draws them apart, constituting a difference and seemingly making the man subordinate to the door-keeper, who backs the law with his whole body while facing the man from the country. The door-keeper and the law do not refuse the man entirely, but only postpone the desired interview. What kind of law it is the story does not reveal, and thus it obtains a Messianic dimension. It is not just *a* law, but *the* Law.

The man from the country bends over in order to peep into the half open door – the image itself reminding us of the spellbound spectator in front of the picture frame of theatre. The door-keeper suggests that the man should defer his visit with the warning that he is "powerful," and after him other door-keepers will emerge who are even more so. With the wild description of a series of doors and door-keepers, proliferating and growing in scale, the door-keeper evokes a phantasmagoria within the imagination of the man whose mind is overwhelmed and confused because the operating law behind the door does not quite seem to coincide with the law without. The imagery escalating in scale throws the man from the country back to the very bottom of the line of subordination. Like an opaque mirror that bounces back the gaze, the invisible eye of the Law constitutes an impasse and keeps the man under surveillance; into that mirror the man looks as if through the glass darkly.

The view open to the man from the country waiting patiently in front of the door is a restricted one. The door-keeper partly blocks it, just as a column sometimes does in a theatre auditorium. In his mind's eye, the man sees multiple guards as the obstacles to his immediate access to the desired law – that maintains an almost supernatural quality. The abysmal image of the infinity of doors and door-keepers constitutes a kind of *mise en abîme*, a structure that operates according to laws of its own. The repressed desires of the man are projected to that same door and the potential transgression that lurks behind its threshold. These desires seem to be reciprocal with the law that holds the door invitingly open yet stops the man from entering. There is a great power hidden within the very absence of the mysterious law from the immediate visual field.

The man is kept away from the door by powerful images, each potentially more monstrous and violent. The door-keeper is a good man. He gives a stool to the man, who takes a seat in front of the door and becomes deeply immersed just like a fascinated theatre spectator watching a play. Why would the man/

145

spectator wish to meet the law in the first place? What sort of law is this, and what makes this *rendez-vous* so desirable? Why is he stopped? Why doesn't the man use another door? Is there just one door to the Law, or are there other doors and other laws? Could it be that the man is so blind that he cannot see through the charade and thus cannot see that behind the door there may be nothing at all. Does he not suspect that the fact of standing (and later sitting) before the Law marks him as an outlaw? If so, the door-keeper seems to be out of the Law as well. As Jacques Derrida has noted, it looks as if the Law, which manifests its presence through its absence from the scene, itself seems to have no essence. The Law does not appear in person, but sends a door-keeper to represent it; it does not refuse the man an interview, but only postpones it to the end of time. Moreover, Derrida interrogates the very existence of the law; the law seems to be a "truth without truth" that "guards itself without guarding" and thus the door-keeper guards nothing, "the door remaining open – and open on nothing." The hiding law is thus, states Derrida, "the guarding itself."[3] Although he speaks of literature, Derrida's lines easily apply to theatre, where the space of the given story is highly performative and allows us to draw a link between the text and its potential spatial expression. Just like Kafka's door, theatre as such is always already open for the spectator. The laws of the theatre keep themselves open without keeping themselves. The laws of the theatre coincide with themselves only.

Door

A door is not simply a door, but a threshold through which we enter into another continuum. The act of stepping through a door is a prophetic gesture. A simple step through the opening of a door is a step from the familiarity of the known to the strange and the threatening unknown. The archetypal image of a man on a threshold is found in Oedipus, who arrives at a similar door at the gate of Thebes and "wrestles" with the Sphinx in order to gain access to the city. He shocks the bloodthirsty Sphinx to death by solving the riddle she gives him. He then enters the gate like a hero, unknowingly heading towards his immanent doom. Stepping through the city gate is a gesture that brings him closer to the moment in which the truth about his terrible mistake unveils the full dimension of the catastrophe. By killing his father and sleeping with his mother, he has already unwittingly crossed the invisible threshold of the prohibited and the denied. In the cathartic moment of unconcealment (*aletheia*), the bitter truth is unearthed that had been awaiting its potential emergence, hidden in the very depths of his mind. The door with a man on its threshold is an image of scandal and crisis.

As a physical phenomenon, a door literally consists of a panel and a surrounding frame; but metaphorically a door is also a kind of symbolic edge and the space perceived and experienced behind it can become a very different realm. In theatre, this other space could be simply another room next door, or it could be another continuum, as constructed in films. The doors can be human size or monstrously huge like those in Orson Welles' film based on Kafka's *The Trial*, itself a labyrinth of doors. The doors are there to be opened and closed. The invention of a simple door seems to have profoundly and irreversibly transformed our consciousness. Kafka's door is a primal image of a door; it is an archetype and an icon; it does not come with any kind of detailed description. What characterizes the door in Kafka's tale is the fact that it is already open. To the man from the country, the open door constitutes an ontological impossibility because of the very fact that it is already open, and he spends his lifetime being too petrified to amend the unbearable state of affairs. It seems that in order to enter or leave through the opening frame of a door, a man needs to have an invitation, to solve a riddle or use magic of some kind.

Arnold Aronson argues that in mythology as well as in theatre, a door constitutes a kind of screen, which at the same time separates and unites. In theatre, the door is a metaphorical opening into the abyss and on to infinity: "the door is a threshold, a liminal space that marks a boundary between two spaces yet belongs to neither."[4] He continues that "a passage between two spaces – two worlds – that the door signifies is a dangerous one."[5] Aronson makes a distinction between a metaphoric stage door and a metonymic screen door, saying that, "on the stage, a door is a sign of the liminal, the unknown, the potential, the terrifying, the endless. On the screen, a door is a sign of a door."[6] He speaks here of television comedy, yet, in film, too, a door can become more than just a door, it can become a Door. The camera eye can penetrate a keyhole and quite

147

painlessly bring us to the next room behind the door, but it can also bring us anxiety and fear. The film door is the one we can enter, but which also fills us with awe. In manipulating a film door, the Bachelardian "dialectics of inside and outside" can push the spectator into a drugged consciousness that resembles a dream.[7]

In the film version of the *The Trial* (1962) in which the story *Before the Law* is narrated, Orson Welles uses a mesmerising technique by offering a dream-scape to the spectator: "The logic of this story is the logic of a ... nightmare,"[8] he states in a voiceover sequence. Such is the state of mind while watching a film, which along with being seen is somehow seeing itself. Horror films bring doors into focus as passages to the uncanny, the appalling, and the threatening. Screen frames themselves form a kind of door, gate, or interface into another universe. Behind the "screen door" there are other doors inside the doors inside the doors, and so to infinity, forming the *mise en abîme* of theatre and cinema. To Mark Pizzato the Symbolic frame of the screen both "magnetizes images near it" and emphasizes "the tension between onscreen images and offstage emptiness which stimulates the diegesis (the extension of the screen world) in spectators' minds."[9] The man from the country sees the series of proliferating doors emerging in his mind's eye; for him the opening of the door has become a screen which plays back the phantoms created by his own imagination. He does not seem to doubt that these phantoms truly exist, otherwise he would not be staying; the potential hollowness of the off-screen space does not concern him for a moment. Just as in theatre or cinema, his illusion is dictated by a desire that all spectators share and what Pizzato calls "wanting being a Real hollowness."[10]

The door is an archetypal image that Gaston Bachelard calls "an entire cosmos of the half-open."[11] It operates within the realm of a mysterious game of hide-and-seek, dealing with things that we see and that we do not see at the same time. A metaphor of the world that always comes with the blind spot of non-knowledge: a door that literally opens and closes can be aligned to the *fort/da* (here/there) game of a child, as described by Freud and as restaged by Lacan, helping "to further trace the painful pleasure of the stage edge in theatrical mimesis."[12]

In *Poetics*, Aristotle argues that the origin of pleasure in witnessing painful and tragic poetry derives from childhood. In our insatiable desire to imitate, we tend to "enjoy imitations of all kinds, even of dead bodies."[13] Pizzato's analysis of how theatre takes place in the mind refers to Lacan's description of the mirror stage as the mimetic structuring of identity throughout a lifetime, leading to the assertion that one's desire is actually the desire of the Other. He argues that "the mirror sets up shop within the mind, mirroring identity and staging performance for an internal as well as external Other as audience."[14]

The door thus constitutes a certain cutting "stage edge" that, always, has created a spatial division between spectators and performers in theatre. Here, a comparison of the door edge with a mirror is not totally out of place. As Pizzato has put it, "that edge, crucial to theatre consciousness, is not simply a line. It is the mirror between player and watcher, reflecting to each a crack in the psyche, a fissure between self and other within the mind."[15] That edge can emerge in multiple different ways and derives from the needs of the particular performance. Facing the stage edge, which Pizzato relates to the Lacanian 'drama' of the mirror stage and its associated paradox of a fragmented body, we find "a Self glimpsed – and shattered – through the focal point of the Other's desire, which in later life leads to the nostalgic unity in a lost 'womb' behind the mirror, prior to such split subjectivity."[16] What Kafka's character encounters winking before him reminds us of a restricted visual field of the theatrical space and a spectator with a sideview as opposed to the one with a central position. "Through the stage edge mirror between them," writes Pizzato, "actor and spectator perceive the ecstasy of a separate character onstage and consanguinity of audience communion – despite the hollowness of both mimetic illusions. But why are the hollow illusions of character and communion so compelling at the stage edge?"[17] Pizzato's question brings us back to that of the audience and the pleasure experienced while watching painful acts in a performance. What is perceived behind the stage edge is the constructed consciousness of theatre. Thus what is hidden off stage, behind the proscenium opening and inaccessible to immediate perception, can be treated in this light as unconscious (subconscious). Metaphorically, the edge of the door also reminds us of the cutting edge of a knife that separates what is bonded. Just like a knife, the door cuts us off from the space into which we have already projected our desires, for which we are yearning – our utmost desire to meet the Other. Like an Artaudian knife,

149

it cuts through the perception of the Real and leaves us to contemplate the monsters of our own imagination.

In his analysis of consciousness in a theatrical space, Pizzato introduces *chora*, a term mentioned by Plato in *Timaeus*. For Plato, *chora* is a cosmological space of becoming and he takes pains in describing a full list of its elements as a complex poetry of geometrical and numeric signs which constitute the universe. What seems to be inscribed in Plato, and later reread by Kristeva in linguistic and psychic terms, is that the *chora* is of maternal and feminine origin, a primal space of a long lost mother that is regained in theatre and cinema. Pizzato argues that cinema and television screens "bear an 'uncanny *chora*' in their photographic depth of field – and in the cut of their frames." He argues that *chora* is actually "a shared theatrical womb at the stage edge giving birth to performance onstage."[18] As an acoustic "maternal ghost" *chora* can have a topology, but can never be defined in (per)formative terms. Pizzato takes the argument a step further by saying that the proscenium arch frame surrounding *chora* manifests a "structure of a patriarchal control" which becomes apparent in theatre architecture by "cutting out and embellishing a specific visual field for mirror-stage play."[19] The performative spaces of theatre and cinema consist of a highly amorphous feminine choral space controlled by a stiff masculine frame. Yet, it is not just a physical borderline, but a psychic stage edge relating to "all edges of theatrical perception."[20]

The similarity between the theatre frame and Kafka's door is obvious. The open door, framing what seems to represent the Law of the Patriarchs, is emphasized by the hairy door-keeper with a long pointed nose and a black coat who stands for the Name-of-the-Father, while at the same time mocking "the one that is absent." The space inside the frame of the opening (and behind) is opaque, deep, feminine, abundant, and infinite, one image giving birth to another. Lacan speaks of a triumverate of the Symbolic, the Imaginary and the Real orders (laws), notions that can be easily applied to a performative space. Theatre and cinema both set up an Imaginary space inside a Symbolic frame that operates as a mask for the Real, the object and subject of all the desires. In order to regain access to the Real, the passage through Symbolic and Imaginary has to be made. As Pizzato has written, "this redefinition of stage space by Symbolic frames (blocking and signifying the view, as with Lacan's "No" and "Name" of the Father) stimulates the Imaginary mirror of the *mise en scène*, while repressing a Real absence."[21]

Kafka's man from the country, waiting spellbound before the half open door, resembles a man in a dream state. It is as if he is under a spell or a drug of some kind. His inability to enter a door encapsulates a primal fear of losing one's identity, losing one's self in an act of self-transcendence; a refusal to become enlightened, to become aware of what Aldous Huxley has called the "total reality in its immanent otherness."[22] An understanding of the Other presumes an awareness of what Huxley calls the "is-ness" (*Istigkeit*) or "Suchness" of reality. He suggests that in order to understand one's place and role within the world, it is necessary to open up the doors of perception and place oneself inside and outside at the same time. Huxley argues that "the urge to escape from selfhood and the environment is in almost everyone almost all the time."[23] As an intrinsic feature of human nature, this "urge to transcend the self-conscious selfhood is … a principal appetite of the soul."[24] Summing up the use of mescaline, Huxley writes that "the man who comes back through the door will never be quite the same as the man who went out."[25]

The door holds the greatest potentiality, combining the possible with the impossible. It refers to the "open," described by Heidegger as a moment of illuminating truth. In the falling darkness, the man from the country sees a glimpse of light emanating from the depth beyond the door before it is slammed shut before him. The man has been sitting in front of the door just like the prisoners in Plato's allegory of the cave who see nothing but shadows, and are thus unable to understand the Real.[26] The man dies, and as Derrida has put it, "the man comes to his end without reaching his end. The entrance is destined for and awaits him alone; he arrives there but cannot arrive at entering; he cannot arrive at arriving."[27]

Just like the Sphinx with the cunning riddle, the door-keeper threatens the man by stopping him without entirely denying access. Within the prophetic gesture of crossing the threshold, the performative aspects of hazard and choice are always already included. The man spends his lifetime in front of the door, until his imminent death that finally coincides with the law. Only, the door that was open to him is now to be closed before him.

Other

The man from the country is seeking to meet the Other, embodied within the Law. The other, we understand, is something or someone that comes with a difference and cannot be identified as the same. The other always remains the opposite of the self, often constituting a lower and less valued side of the binary opposition; the other can also mean something foreign, alien, and uncanny. It can be something or someone that is complementary to the man, a principle without which he is unable to exist. In Kafka's fable, the door-keeper and the man from the country look at each other as strangers, but become an inevitable part of each other's life. They become so dependant on each other that the door-keeper's existence has no meaning without the man from the country. The door-keeper, who eclipses the entrance to the law, and the stooping man in front of the door are bonded, as well as 'cut' by the ethical link.

This ethics, though, seems to be asymmetrical; in such a relationship each subject is supposed to be responsible for the other – only through ethics, as Emmanuel Lévinas argues, can the responsibility for another define the nearness of the one to the other. There is always a relation between them, and the one cannot exist without the other. "The same is woken up by the other, as if the other knocked on his walls from within." It is the law he calls "the-other-in-the-same" which presupposes patience and time.[28] Hidden in the complexity of our minds is the uncanny other which "creeps into the tranquility of reason itself" and which "without madness, beauty or faith any more than ethnicity or race, irritate[s] our very being."[29] The other is something genuinely familiar that has been somewhat estranged. Yet, there is the "abyss separating me from the other who shocks me." By facing the stranger "I lose my boundaries, I no longer have a container ... I lose my composure."[30] As Lacan so imaginatively shows us, the discourse of the symbolic other is embedded in our unconscious, while the self is discovered in front of the mirror and dissolved in deep misrecognition (*méconnaissance)* of the haunting specular image through which the ego is constructed. The moment that the man becomes aware of this reflection through the gaze of the other he is another for himself.[31]

The sequence of spaces behind Kafka's door reminds us of Foucault's *heterotopias* (*heterotopoi*), which he sees as "places which are absolutely *other* with respect to all the arrangements that they reflect and of which they speak."[32] A theatrical place is a written literary utopia, which within the performance context emerges as a performative "hetero(u)topia." Kafka's law is nesting in such a complex of alien places, a mental construction in the mind of the man from the country.

What Foucault mentions as one of the principles of heterotopias is their ability to "always presuppose a system of opening and closing that isolates them and makes them penetrable at one and the same time." Theatrical places are heterotopias that we enter deliberately; they often have the "appearance of pure and simple openings," although, as Foucault notes, "they usually conceal curious exclusions." These openings appear to be hardly more than illusion and anyone who enters a heterotopian place is excluded from this place by the "sole (f)act of entering."[33] The entrance into a heterotopia always already includes an exit. This pure and simple opening reminds us of the door in Kafka's story and the peculiar man before it. The impenetrable realm beyond these doors becomes an abysmal space of a mirror (a hetero/utopia) and so does the realm behind the threshold of the stage edge. In order to create a maximum immersion of the spectators' gaze, the scenographic places of theatre are represented in 'real' scale and inhabited by 'real' people who pass through the exits and entrances. Yet, the experience that is expected by the spectator through this spatial and psychic arrangement is exclusively that of the Real.

Seeking to Meet the Other

A man contemplating an open door thus seems to be a parable of a spectator facing the magic opening of a theatrical or cinematic frame. The door-keeper stands for the law, both as a guard and as a representative, and his position reminds us of an artist in the theatre. Like the door-keeper in Kafka's story, the scenographer 'questions' the spectator "about his homeland and many other things" and each time "tells him once more that he cannot let him inside yet." The devoted spectator "spends everything, no matter how valuable, to win over the door-keeper" in order to get closer to the fulfillment of his desires. As Deleuze and Guattari have claimed, the phenomenon of the law "goes hand in

153

hand with power that is operating through the machinal assemblage of desire." To them it seems to be "not a desire-lack, but desire as a plenitude, exercise, and functioning." Yet, it is not "a desire for power," but the "power itself that is desire."[34] The spectators share an immanent machinery of desire; like the man from the country, they "come to know the fleas" in the door-keeper's collar.

The man from the country gives away everything he has brought with him in order to be able to see the law, but does not dare to enter the door. To enter such a door in terms of theatre would mean a leap from the auditorium inhabited by spectators into a performance space where actors move. Although in contemporary forms of theatre the spectator is often included in the actual performance space, merging with the actors and action, it is not simply possible to enter a conventionally framed theatre space without destroying the carefully constructed illusion. Even if the audience is literally incorporated in the performance, there always remains this invisible stage boundary, this cutting edge of a knife, which forms an anamorphic figure or a line that both bonds and slices the performance space from the real, thus keeping the performer and the spectator apart.

Scenographic performative space is a constructed otherness in which scenography operates as an agent, arranging the meeting with the theatrical Other. Anything within this otherness is interrelated in a complex Self/Other (cut/bond) relationship. Places and characters of the scenographic reality of theatre are always already the Other of the spectator. However, through the otherness of places and characters, a nearness of such alien reality is constructed through willing suspension of disbelief. The spectator is always already inside and outside the performance at the same time, yet always displaced – just as the Other is always already exclusively included in the Self. The "other-in-the-same" principle thus seems to be operating in the real world as well as in theatre. Performative space is, therefore, a visualized mental topography, and performance itself is constantly oscillating between the Imaginary, Symbolic and the Real orders, in which the latter is always repressed. In each moment of a theatrical performance, a threefold process of oscillation is in action; theatrical otherness is reconstructed, and the laws of performance are reiterated. As a performative entity, performance space constitutes a fugitive reality and to define it in its complexity seems to be utterly impossible.

The reason one keeps going to theatre or cinema seems to be the desire for the mysterious Other. This intrinsic desire is twofold; first, it is the desire that the spectator always projects onto the abyss of theatrical otherness and, secondly, it is the expectation that this desirable otherness will somehow respond. At the edges of "absence and nonsense," the images thrown on a screen stimulate the stage presence and meaning by "projections from the house as well as the stage, ... extending from the interior mirror/screen of artist's and spectators' minds – to meet at the psychic edge between."[35] It is to be placed in front of the mirror in the Lacanian, the Kafkaean, as well as the Shakespearean sense. Metaphorically speaking, the spectator reaches out a hand, touching his own mirror image, thus hoping to grasp the fugitive Real concealed by the enigmatic laws of the theatre. Just like Kafka's man from the country, the spectator sits and/or stoops over in order to have a better look at what is presented to him only, the world of riddles unfolding before his eyes. As Deleuze and Guattari so persuasively have put it, "where one believed there was law, there is in fact desire and desire alone."[36]

The relationship between spectator and theatre or cinema is an obsessive one. The spectator knows that somewhere beyond the stage frame there is a hidden world that is much more appealing than reality itself. In order to get hold of it, the spectator needs to get beyond the threshold of the imaginary door. Yet, this world reluctantly tends to remain inaccessible, just as there are desires, nomadic and immanent, which can never find satisfaction. The spectator cannot enter the picture frame of the theatre without shattering the image and violating the laws of performance (unless it is inscribed by the law itself). It is impossible to enter the law because one is always already in it, as it is impossible to enter where you already are. Just like the law in Kafka's story, the law of theatre is such that it both offers itself to the spectator and denies access at the same time. As Theodor Adorno maintains, "art makes a gesture-like grab for reality, only to draw back violently as it touches that reality."[37] To enter the space of performance through the stage door is strictly forbidden; it is the space both concealed and repressed, bringing to mind Oedipus at the gates of Thebes and the carnivorous riddling Sphinx. It reveals the imperative of the long lost Father and the everlasting guilt of a misbehaving child. To enter the performance space thus becomes an ontological impossibility for the spectator.

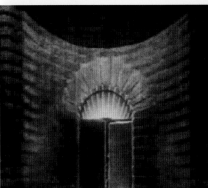

155

Theatre is an abysmal feminine space, an inviting doorway through which access is denied, an opening into somewhere, but this 'where' could mean 'anywhere', 'nowhere', and 'elsewhere' at the same time. The door is the Door, the Eros and the Thanatos, the *jouissance*, and the fulfillment of desire – the framing imaginary line that implicitly or explicitly keeps the performance and the spectator apart. The threshold of a door is a stage edge mirror 'in between'. Just like Kafka's door-keeper and the door he guards, scenographer and scenography manifest their between-ness by separating and uniting the performance and the audience, bonding and cutting both at the same time. The scenographer as a mediator, a witness, and a door-keeper is posited literally and symbolically *in between* the laws of the text and the laws of performance. The enigmatic priest in *The Trial* explains to Josef K: "The Court (Law) wants nothing from you. It receives you when you come and dismisses you when you go."[38] Freedom to make the decision is up to the man from the country, as well as to the spectator in the theatre.

■ ■ ■

"What else do you still want to know?" asks the door-keeper. "You are insatiable," he hereby concludes. "But everybody strives for the law," says the man justifying his still flaming desire. "Nobody else could gain admittance here, this entrance was meant only for you," the door-keeper replies. "I shall now go and close it."

Notes

1 Franz Kafka, *The Trial*, trans. Idris Parry (London: Penguin Modern Classics, 2000), pp. 166-167. *Before the Law* was originally written in 1914, and was later used as a literary metadiegetic supplement to *The Trial* (1925).

2 Ibid. p. 172.

3 See Jacques Derrida, "Before the Law," in *Acts of Literature*, ed. Derek Attridge (London: Routledge, 1992), p. 206.

4 See Arnold Aronson, "Behind the Screen Door," in *Looking into the Abyss: Essays on Scenography* (Ann Arbor: The University of Michigan Press, 2005), p. 59.

5 Ibid., p. 60.

6 Ibid., p. 65.

7 See Gaston Bachelard, "The Dialectics of Outside and Inside," in *The Poetics of Space: The Classic Look at How We Experience Intimate Places* (Boston: Beacon Press, 1994). Bachelard refers to the "first myth of outside and inside," the two terms that come with "alienation and hostility between the two." It is also the dialectics of *here* and *there*, of *being* and *non-being*.

8 See *The Trial* (1962), a film directed by Orson Welles and produced by Miguel and Alexander Salkind.

9 Mark Pizzato, "Edges of Perception in Performance and Audience," in *Performing Arts International* 1.4 (1999), p. 51.

10 Ibid. In this article Pizzato describes desire as the primary mechanism operating in theatre. The hollowness of a cinema screen or TV monitor originates from the proscenium tradition of theatre, and the spectators' drive towards this emptiness in disguise is, therefore, deeply rooted in our psyche, pp. 47-58.

11 Bachelard, *The Poetics of Space*, p. 222.

12 Pizzato, "Edges of Perception," p. 48. Here Pizzato gives an account of the evolution of the "stage edge" between actors and spectators and its impact on theatrical consciousness and its role as "primal psychic edge." Freud has described a scene with a child playing *fort/da* (*here/there*) as a substitute for an absent mother; Lacan's "mirror drama" has restaged it through disappearance and reappearance of self by setting up the mirror "theatre" of the mind. See Lacan's article "The Mirror Stage as Formative of the *I* function," first presented in 1949 in Zürich.

13 See Aristotle, *Poetics* (London: Nick Hern Books, 1999), p. 6.

14 Pizzato, "Edges of Perception," p. 47.

15 Ibid., p. 48.

16 Ibid.

17 Ibid.

18 Ibid., p. 50. On *chora* see Plato's *Timaeus* (Hertfordshire: Wordsworth Classics of World Literature, 1997); see also *Powers of Horror: An Essay on Abjection* (1982), and the article "The True-Real," in *The Kristeva Reader* (1986), both by Julia Kristeva.

19 Ibid., p. 51.

20 Ibid., p. 55.

21 Ibid., p. 51. See a detailed discussion on the theme in Pizzato's *Ghosts of Theatre and Cinema in the Brain* (Basingstoke: Palgrave Macmillan, 2006).

22 Aldous Huxley, *The Doors of Perception & Heaven and Hell* (New York: Perennial Classics, 2004), p. 19.

23 Ibid., p. 15.

24 Ibid., p. 16.

25 Ibid., p. 19.

26 Plato, *Republic* (Hertfordshire: Wordsworth Classics of World Literature, 1997), pp. 513-21. Plato uses the allegory of the cave as a metaphor for the subordination of a layman to the philosopher.

27 Derrida, "Before the Law," p. 210.

28 Emmanuel Lévinas, *God, Death, and Time* (Palo Alto: Stanford University Press, 2000), p. 141. Here Lévinas develops a theory of ethics of the "other-in-the-same" principle. See also Lévinas, *Time and the Other* (Pittsburgh: Duquesne University Press, 2003) and *Humanism of the Other* (Champaign: University of Illinois Press, 2003), both discussing the *self/other* relationship as an ethical entity.

29 Julia Kristeva, *Strangers to Ourselves* (New York: Columbia University Press, 1991), p. 170. Here Kristeva applies a historical dimension to the attitudes towards foreigners and formulates the psychoanalytical basis for these patterns of behavior.

30 Ibid., p. 187.

31 See Jacques Lacan, *Écrits: A Selection* (New York: W.W. Norton & Company, 2002).

32 See Michel Foucault, "Of Other Spaces: Utopias and Heterotopias," in *Rethinking Architecture: A Reader in Cultural Theory*, ed. Neil Leach (New York: Routledge, 1997), p. 353.

33 Ibid.

34 See Gilles Deleuze and Felix Guattari, *Kafka: Toward a Minor Literature* (Minneapolis: University of Minnesota Press, 2003), p. 56.

35 Pizzato, "Edges of Perception," p. 55.

36 Deleuze and Guattari, *Kafka*, p. 49.

37 See Theodor Adorno, *Aesthetic Theory* (London and New York: Continuum, 1984), p. 399.

38 Kafka, *The Trial*, p. 173.

Street Noise

Brandon LaBelle

on the contours and
politics of public sound

Sound provides the most forceful stimulus that human beings experience, and the most evanescent.[1]
Bruce R. Smith

The legacy of spatiality and its design tends to a fixation on the logic of opticality, leaving behind the atmospheric, the haptic, the sonorous, and the sensorial multiplicity intrinsic to life itself and the geographic promise of urban interaction. Against such legacy, the notion of the *performativity* of space reorients an understanding so as to incorporate the often ephemeral and seemingly immaterial occurrences and phenomena that come to influence spatial materiality. Sound, in particular, has led to both an appreciation for the ephemeral and temporal event-nature of spatiality, while also being utilized or incorporated into architectural design. The design of acoustic spaces such as concert halls, radio and sound studios, along with certain public buildings and civic centres, actively features acoustical research and implementation. Material surfaces, dimensional relations, adjustable elements, and related electronic and sound reproduction systems are considered as acoustical features. Acoustics brings forward intuitive and scientific understanding and research into spatiality, and the idea of its design, not only as visual and sculptural effect, but also as sonic materiality and experience. While focusing on specific aspects of space and its auditory shape, acoustics also supports the individual ear as a determining or influential factor in imagining the effect of spaces and their performative natures.

Policies in noise abatement curiously reveal the degree to which acoustic space is also difficult to control. For sound and its spatial influence or effects often challenge the acoustical imagination and understanding, eluding the architectural ability to engineer conductive designs.[2] Yet, such challenges also reveal the degree to which sound, as an experiential feature, opens spatiality up to the peripheries of design, where sonic phenomena allow for unpredictable and generative forms of not only hearing, but also of locating oneself. As Tia De Nora has eloquently argued, sound (and music) allows for flexible participation in re-imagining self-image, and how one might locate points of social contact and participation.[3] Acoustic space, physical as well as emotional and psychological constructions, may create a temporal instant of participatory sharing, a mutuality of space and self, which may also include experiences of annoyance and outrage.

Acoustic Spaces

The demands to introduce increasingly stringent acoustic guidelines for future building and planning, initiated across the European Union since 1998[4] (which includes major noise mapping of all industrialized and metropolitan areas), is a growing indication of governmental consciousness of the noise pollution issues, as well as a general auditory perspective.[5] As an example, London's Ambient Noise Strategy (also referred to as the ANS) being developed by Mayor Ken Livingstone may provide a glimpse into the issues surrounding acoustic space and its status in relation to the modern metropolis. Developed since 1999, the ANS is part of a larger governmental proposal to respond to the current noise problem in cities like London and is structured around three key areas: securing noise-reducing surfaces related to road construction and traffic, securing a night aircraft ban across London, and reducing noise through improved planning and design strategies related to new housing. Notably, questions of transport and traffic stand as essential noises to be dealt with, and can generally be seen also as the key element to consider in most other developed cities.[6] Excessive transport is often seen as degrading to the urban environment on a humanistic level, leading to calls for pedestrianized zones, increased quiet areas, and green spaces, as witnessed, for example, in Copenhagen's pedestrian movement from the 1960s onward.[7] The unbounded nature of sound, though, leads to difficulties in attempts to design spaces and related objects such as vehicles and roadways, forcing the ANS to consider a more overall approach: "However, tackling one noise on its own may not always solve the problem. It can make another, also annoying, noise more audible. So, better ways of coordinating action on noise will be needed. This includes new partnerships at the strategic level, and more resources for action in local areas."[8] A larger tactical strategy is required to combat the problems of noise.

In what way does sound and auditory experience relate to an analysis of spatiality? What kinds of strategies might be utilized in approaching questions of urban design and related experiences of audition? And how might we gain insight into social relations determined by the movements of sound and the city as expressions of performative encounters? As Barry Blesser and Linda-Ruth Salter observe, "The aural architecture of a particular space is a microclimate of auditory spatial awareness."[9]

Edmund Carpenter and Marshall McLuhan propose that acoustic space creates itself from moment to moment according to the forces at play within temporal and interactive participation, for "auditory space has no point of favoured focus. It's a sphere without fixed boundaries, space made by the thing itself, not space containing a thing. It is not a pictorial space, boxed in, but dynamic, always in flux, creating its own dimensions moment by moment."[10] Thus, sound appears in more than one place, through an acoustical flexibility and movement, leading to what Jean-Francois Augoyard has named "the ubiquity effect," which is a sonic effect "that expresses the difficulty or impossibility of locating a sound source."[11] Curiously, he further links this effect to the urban milieu: "because of their particular conditions of propagation favouring the delocalization of sound sources, urban milieus and architectural spaces are the most obvious locations for the emergence of a ubiquity effect."[12] From this perspective, the acoustical proposition of Carpenter and McLuhan seems potently embedded in urban situations. Arising from within the conditions of the city, acoustic spaces as a "sphere without fixed boundaries" find their ultimate material platform in cities.

Following such acoustical thinking I am interested in notating sonic performances that come to supplement or supplant the readability of the city. In doing so, I hope to stage other forms of information outside decibel readings and quality control indicative of acoustic design and urban noise mapping with the ultimate aim of understanding the contours of public sound – to locate the sonic tensions between acoustic design (on an urban scale)[13] and public life, and to recognize how questions of acoustic design butt up against inherent problematics which in themselves are extremely provocative of both a spatial and sonorous imaginary. For auditory cultures not only register the degree to which populations produce and live with noise, but also how culture and society imagine and express the shape of the future, whether in the pedestrian banalities of cross walk signals, which define a set of relational rhythms, or in the occupation of city streets through rioting and parading which may signal instances of social upheaval and celebration. These signals and movements, that either control or distort existing patterns and rhythms of social interaction and structure, may be heard as historical and cultural keynotes sounding the call for change, or as modulations of an existing social and technical architecture bent and sculpted by the agitation of bodies or the unification of timed actions. "Noise, then, can be heard not merely as a symptom of symbolic vulnerability or theoretical disorder, but as the evidence and the occasional catalyst of dynamic cultural change operative across the urban topos."[14] Thus, noise not only signals a lapse in urban design, and an indication of excess traffic, but the sudden movements of a greater social force, one that deserves attention as the acoustical spectrum finds further footing within the urban imagination and its related policies.

By interlacing the ANS with Edmund Carpenter and Marshall McLuhan's version of acoustic space, we arrive at a crucial tension upon which auditory thinking and culture may be articulated. For on one hand, there is no denial as to the intensities with which noise pollution interferes with personal health, undermining ecological growth and resources, and disturbing community safety. On the other hand, noise may be heard as registering a particular vitality within the cultural sphere, signalling the potential for interaction and the sharing of public space. While challenging what we might call the *acoustics of social space*, noise brings with it the expressiveness of freedom, thereby lending significantly to the degree to which social space actually functions. Noise may be said to act as a byproduct to the ongoing interweaving of sharing, which must also include processes of confronting embedded tensions. In its unboundedness noise both fulfils and problematizes the sociality of the built environment by granting it the promise of movement and interaction while also agitating such sharing by adding too much or by deviating from the rigidity of expectation and control, and the evenness of the harmonic. The agitations of noise deliver a deathly blow to a night's sleep, while in turn filling such sleep with the potential to dream, for noise must partially be heard to give form – by being radically formless – to the intensities of diversity, strangeness, and the unfamiliar. Noise may also be heard as a social bond which, while potentially offensive, bespeaks the forms that social identity may take in extreme instances and for extreme purposes.

Riots, Street Fights, and Demonstrations

The city as a topographical condition, as a set of structures and systems, spaces and cultures, bodies and rules and their mixing, is also the site of perennial transformation. The city is a kind of barometer for the confrontations, radicalities and imaginations which may be said to define history: without privileging the urban too much, yet also appreciating it as a special site, it could be said that we read history *through* the city. For the city not only brings together the forces which in their meeting create rich experiences; but it also resounds with their celebrations and arguments. While the historical may be examined through textual records, accounts, written archives and documents, it is equally an audible echo taking shape through material forms, cultural marks, geographic coordinates; sound may then lend a dynamic appeal to the historical imagination to fixate not only on archival pages but to supplement such reading with a sense of the initial vocalizations, frictions and vibrations of social transformation. To read, in turn, might be to hear what lies between the words, inside the white blanks, or over and around the languages that were once scratched onto paper. Yet as Mark M. Smith has commented, the absence of archival sound recordings of particular historical periods does not undermine historical examination of sounds from the past, for these would not necessarily reveal the way a society experienced and received such sounds.[15] How sound comes to circulate, lend meaning, and give shape to social processes and attitudes may still, according to Smith, be found in written documents. The question becomes not so much to seek the original sound, in pure form, but to hear it within history, as a significant phenomenon, medium, and shared experience participating in the movements of history.

The city, then, is also a kind of noise as well as a writing, a culture as well as a map, a reverberant terrain as well as a text full of signs. It is a history surfacing through governments, policy, reporting, appeal and judgements, as well as the sonority and argumentation that envelop everyday spaces. The riot, street fight and demonstration may be understood, then, as instances of conflict and debate, as well as an audible interaction between writing (law) and noise (suspension of law). On one side, the law as a signature of written record, decree, juridical account (*to throw the book at you* or *book him* are expressions revealing law as inherently written), and on the other, a drive toward its overturning, whose momentum relies upon or calls for the development of a separate language, one that stands in opposition, or that brings the law into its own hands.

This other side then resists the written record, the language of the law, and tries to supplant it with its own, one that is often initially shaped by the political speech or revolutionary slogan, and the passing of secret messages, a radical coding, an orality whose power resides in speaking out, rallying, and the very access to having a say. Thus, riots, street fights, and demonstrations produce an audibility that seeks to overturn or disrupt the record, the law, the book and house rule with a meaning that is determined by volume and the promise embedded in making a noise.

A set of examples of rioting, street fighting, and demonstrating may lend to this proposal to listen in while also letting out the nested audibility within history and the tensions intrinsic to acoustic spaces. These could in turn be alternated with more quotidian and everyday instances of sound on the street and within cultural productions that come to occupy urban space or contour it. Appearing as extreme instances of (not only) audibility, the intensities of noise that rioting, street fighting and demonstrating generate allow for an equally extreme recognition of how cities are always at the fore of ideological conflict and debate.

Such perspectives may create a kind of insertion into the current analysis of city spaces and their acoustics. They may speak toward an understanding of the urban topos as a performative matrix animated by the flow of varying forces and their encounters.

Atlanta, Mob Rules

The inconsistencies, disparities, and imbalances at the core of the Atlanta race riots of 1906, as David Fort Godshalk has examined, point toward complicated social and psychological relations amongst blacks and whites at this time. As white mobs brutally sought out and attacked blacks throughout the city, firstly in poorer neighbourhoods and later in more middle-class areas of the city, both black and white civic leaders struggled to give articulation to sets of ideas which in the end were neither for or against, but rather teetered across ideological lines, seeking to understand and articulate the complexity of the situation and all the underlying histories and values embedded therein. Thus, "In Atlanta, public words imperfectly reflected underlying ideologies partly because enormous social and economic disparities dramatically influenced both what blacks and whites could say and how they could say it."[16] As with most riots or demonstrations, the power of the spoken word takes on profound importance, and the ability to capture the public imagination through the use of the voice, language, and related media platforms. The riots in Atlanta were radically marked by such a dynamic, and, more so, by the intensities of those who spoke, lending to the voice and its meaning the presence of skin and colour.

Throughout 1906 in Atlanta, the white imagination of the black threat was emblazoned by the ongoing debate of the racial situation and the endless newspaper reports of attacks by black men on white women, all of which carried threats not only to white society, but specifically to an inherited code of chivalry carried by white southerners based on defending white women. Such social unrest and reporting eventually turned the Atlanta streets into a cacophony of shouted headline reports, gossip, verbal fighting and debate, and finally escalated into mob rule, documented in Thornwell Jacobs' novella *The Law of the White Circle*:

> "Where's the police?" the countryman with the little red moustache on
> the end of his nose asked a young hoodlum who stood by him.
> "Raidin' the dives down on Decatur Street."
> "Listen to that!"
> Again the cry:

"Third assault! Paper, mister?"

"By G_d, there's goin' to be trouble here, and right now, at that! Come on, boys, let's give 'em h__l!"

"I just heard two little white boys was held up and robbed in the suburbs," the hoodlum answered.

"And look a-yonder!" a gamin cried. "Did you see that nigger grab that white woman's pocketbook?"

"Gee-muny-chrismus! They're fightin'!" he yelled, as a white man sprang on the negro and bore him down.

Two other negroes came instantly to the aid of the first, and a rough-and-tumble fight ensued. At last the crowd became noisy, the tension began to give way, the lightning flashed, and the storm broke.[17]

The collectivization of anger, mounting disregard for law and order, and the feverish organization of immediate reaction, form into a radical communicational passing where one voice spurs another, one shout continues from another, ultimately becoming a chorus of embroiled emotion that in this case also crosses and weaves together the tensions of racial conflict in a complicated fabric. The city street as an acoustical partner resounds with aggression, information, pleas and reports, helping to mobilize and provoke, defend and resist according to territorial demarcations – the voice both passes information while defending territorial boundary; from Dark Town to Brownsville, the black neighbourhoods become sites of conflict where the voice is replaced by the sheer force of bodies beating each other, and public squares become the site for attempts at reason. The ideological fact of racial tension, as something mutating through the circulation of values and their expression, may find points of contact through the printed word, as with newspapers, legal documents, and policy making. Still it poignantly presses in on real bodies in acts of vocality, forceful argument and harsh debate. As Judith Butler states, "a statement may be made that, on the basis of a grammatical analysis alone, appears to be no threat. But the threat emerges precisely through the act that the body performs in the speaking act."[18]

London, Suffragette Tactics

While the voice and orality dynamically function within the insurgence of street fighting, a vehicle carrying threat and ideological struggle all in one, the public street also carries with it other potential tactical sonorities. The Suffragette movement in the UK throughout the early twentieth century was a sustained political agitation against established codes of conduct, social mores, and legality, and ultimately aimed to acquire the right for women to vote (which was only fully legalized in the UK in 1928). Throughout their struggle, a variety of tactics were established as the means to give expression to their plight that can be understood to supplement or extend the strict use of vocality to carry the message. One such tactic for the Suffragettes was the method of smashing windowpanes of public buildings, notoriously carried out by Amelia Brown and Alice Paul during the National Anthem at the Lord Mayor's Banquet in 1909.[19] Organized window-smashing became a method of drawing attention to the movement, and to specific protests, by not only vandalizing public property, but by also creating an audible scene: while the voice within public debate is a tool for putting forth alternative views, or generating collective anger through an appeal to reason or emotion, it may also fail to be heard or to find reception – to rise above the established order. Suffragettes smashing windows in public, as well as deploying other tactics such as throwing stones and also burning post boxes, amplifies ideological conflict through another vocabulary. Civic architecture seeks to represent an established system of values, appearing to express the common good through symbolic form. Countering, attacking, searching for a means toward representation, the smashing of windows enacted by the Suffragettes can be heard as exclamation marks underscoring the political view embodied no longer in the voice, or on the skin, but in the gendered body seeking another form of articulation, vocality, and expressivity. Whereas later in the century the afro, the black leather jacket, and the rifle would stand as emblems of the Black Panther movement, formulated into a vocabulary of black resistance, the middle-class English woman smashing windows in 1909 stood out unmistakably against the backdrop of English society, turning the street into an unlikely acoustical partner.

Paris / Bologna, Poetic Politics

The occupation of the Sorbonne in Paris in May 1968 stands as a mythical revolutionary instance whose echoes still seem to resound throughout the contemporary cultural environment, marking the beginning of our current legacy and the ending of a certain Modernist notion of revolution, opposition and subjectivity. The function and usage of media may be seen to shift rapidly at this time, whereby questions of representation, political statements, and debate slide into a slippery space where nomadic identities, metropolitan Indians, radiophonic cacophony, poetic graffiti, and multi-media formats were crafted, hinting at networked collectivities that electrified language. Contoured by the emerging electrified environment of the 1960s, the new stance of revolutionary statements seem sparked by an extensive sonority, whereby words unfolded in multiplied entities, whose reading became a voluptuous act, a promise of subjective becoming.

Following 1968 and the related cultural outpouring, the Autonomia Movement[20] in Italy led to the establishment of various sub-groups, one being Radio Alice, which sought to continue the initial rebellion. For two years the radio broadcasts of Radio Alice functioned as an experiment in political action, identity, and language, operating as an open platform where voices mingled and mutated through call-ins, open broadcasts and open debate, weird reports, noise and music, montages of poetry and newspaper readings, etc.[21] It thus sought to occupy not the streets, or particular institutes and buildings, but an ethereal, electronic space directed at the imagination ensconced within the urban environment: the poetical graffiti scrawled throughout Paris in 1968 was replaced by electrified expressions of total audibility – it was sound on the run, aimed at the heart, targeting not a particular political party or government official, but the very structures of socio-political subjects. Thus, Radio Alice was a kind of demonstration on the airwaves, an ongoing march whose message was difficult to apprehend, and therefore arrest. It remained live, performative, as free media on the air, a sonority spread out across the city.

■ ■ ■

The eruptions in the public streets through modes of rioting, street fighting and demonstrating may help draw the contours and shapes of urban noise. To take to the streets or to seek to disrupt public space has embedded within them a desire or necessity to interfere, through audible agitation, with the established order. Moments of cultural transformation thus often signal, in turn, forms of acoustical sabotage where acoustic space and its design are appropriated to allow other voices to find reception. In contrast, the eruption of revolution- ary noise equally brings with it reactionary attempts to cancel, annul, silence, and over-sound such noise in a battle whose ideological intensities resound in meaningful volumes. The AIDS activist group Act-Up's slogan "silence=death" underscores such perspectives, from the voicing through a language of political struggle to the sheer importance of being heard, on any level, within the sphere where sound is more than just decibels. Silencing as a tactic throughout histori- cal instances of transformative actions may further highlight how auditory his- tory contributes to glimpsing other perspectives.[22] The production of space in this regard can be comprehended and appreciated according to forms of audi- tion as well as readability – to listen to the flows of urban movement in addition to reading its signs. Such notions uncover the performative encounters initiated through the sonic productions which I am pursuing here: to locate the weave of bodies and places as heard in audible frictions.

Marching Bands

The rupturing agitation of rioting, street fighting and demonstrating, with its tumult of related noise and acoustical disruption, gains momentum through the disorganization of bodies contorting under the pressure of arrest. In con- trast, the timed order of military drill (the side of policing and control, law and its composition) necessitates collective subservience to a rehearsed function- ality that folds the individual body into a historical and political time signature. Thus, against the acoustical acts found in taking to the streets or confounding civic order, we might, in turn, hear the keynotes of political order and control resounding as a counter-acoustics throughout the city and history.

As William H. McNeill has elegantly shown, the orientation of military drill functions to secure group cohesion through the initiation and control of group movement. For McNeill, the extreme needs demanded by military order necessitate both an intensification of emotional and muscular potential and expression, fostering the individual ability to do battle, to withstand the radical extremes of war, while participating in an elaborate mechanism of control and command. Thus, the ordering of military drill releases within the individual body a functional relation to emotional investment, enfolding the rapture of embodied expression into a greater choreography of marching, rehearsal, and repetition as a refinement of corporeal organization so as to make the body mechanistic and potently instrumental. Military drill is at the core of battle tactics, war strategies, and philosophies on how to order the inherent chaos of military conflict. Here military actions rely upon and necessitate the total organization of bodies, which includes not only soldiers and commanding personnel, but also factory organization and labor, volunteer help, and the enactment of curfews and rationing onto the movements of daily life. Such mobilization not only expresses an ordered direction but also radically buttresses the individual fighting body: one is able to tackle the demands of the situation by feeling and experiencing a tangible sense of collective motion that is for McNeill primarily muscular, in which "those parts of the nervous system that function subconsciously, maintaining rhythmic heartbeat, digestive peristalsis, and breathing, as well as all the other chemical and physiological balances required for the maintenance of ordinary bodily functions"[23] grant the fighting body necessary support.

The ordering of military drill tapping into the nervous system and the unleashing of muscular and emotional force may in turn find audible expression not only in the passing of information or the signalling of group action, but also, and interestingly, in military marching bands and their inherent musical-muscular functionality.[24] The rioting body on the street breaking shop windows, throwing stones or causing trouble is countered by the drill and dress of military might which produce and are in turn supported by audible intensities.

The marching band, initiated by the military at the end of the seventeenth and eighteenth centuries in Europe and America respectively,[25] stitches the single performing body into the greater order of the marching band through a number of movements. Initially, embodiment is partnered with the musical instrument, extending the individual through this device of auditory expression, which becomes a second voice. Such extension is furthered through participation in the marching band, as an expression of military drill – the rhythmic pulsing of marching in time and collectively, within the framework of a musical work, composes both sound and the body into a larger system. Musical timing and marching embodiment order the self into a radically strict composition which annuls any form of deviation while invigorating the demonstration of victory. Finally, the musical and muscular intensity of such collective organization finds resonance through its occupation of city streets: the reverberant spaces of cities emblazon the marching band with added fervour, granting the expression of territorial occupation an added intensity by making display a public and political act.

The phenomenon of the Buekorps in the city of Bergen in Norway testifies to the weave of music, bodies, and marching bands, formed as public spectacle that still carries with it patterns of competition, battle, and musicalities shaped by the public street and histories of military power. Developed in the 1850s, the original Buekorps emerged from young boys imitating their fathers who formed small battalions or militia to defend local streets and neighbourhoods in Bergen. Wielding wooden rifles, the boys copied their fathers' marching formations, dress and manner, in turn replacing much of the actual defensive concerns with that of music and display, with the drum becoming the essential instrument. Existing to this day, the Buekorps functions as social units of young boys (with a small number accepting girls) who take to the streets throughout the spring in preparation for Independence Day on May 17, during which time competitions take place and turn the streets into a cacophony of percussive rapture and display.[26] The city reverberates with sudden bursts of drumming with each Buekorps demarcating a part of the city as their own, utilizing the narrow streets and hillsides as acoustical partners with accompanying shouts and verbal signals punctuating their marches. The young boys (and girls) thus continue traditions built on the interweaving of military manoeuvres and drumming.

Drawing upon the tradition of the Buekorps, the artist and composer Jørgen Larsson presented his own version of the march, titled *I Ringen* (*In the Ring*), as part of the Borealis Music Festival held in Bergen in March 2007. Working with four units of Buekorps drummers, the performance started with the drummers marching through different parts of the city, finally meeting in a public square for a musical battle or *slagerkonk*. In addition, the artist had set up microphones on the square connected to a series of speakers mounted on building facades. Utilizing computer treatments (driven by MAX/MSP software), Larsson sampled the live drumming while playing it back through the sound system, transformed and modulated into a series of reverberant rhythms that accentuated the drumming with added atmospheric textures, beats, and electronic touches. While the performance lasted, crowds gathered, mesmerized and entertained by the intermingling of the live and the sampled, and by the recognizable marching body (in its accompanying uniform) and the transformation or supplemental electronic addition echoing over the square. The work seemed to underscore the very performative nature of the marching boys, amplifying their public spectacle into a composite of rhythms that also unravelled the order of their march: the sonic supplement seemed to return to the drummers their own music, doubling it up, and slightly confusing its ordered patterning.

Larsson's appropriation of the drummers as identifiable symbols seemed to accentuate the way in which drum, body and city space interweave in a complex of sonic organization, with reverberation and marching as active components, while disrupting these with an excess of electronic treatment and performative bravado – the boys in their battling seemed to accentuate and break apart the existing parodic component already embedded in the Buekorps as imitators of real soldiers by performing an excess of display and amplification. With their reverberant drumming beating throughout the main square, doubled up and pulled apart electronically, the work staged the very staging already intrinsic to the Buekorps *as* performance that acts to bind young boys into tribal units through forms of ritualized synchronization in which drumming awakens the city to the coming of age of their men. Thus their music, recognizable within a repertoire of marching compositions, is a form of agency given its annual freedom at a specified time of year, bringing the body in line with certain orders that are musical as well as social and historical. For in this act of coming out, the Buekorps also functions as a means of granting the public access to the ongoing lineage of male order, which in this sublimated and parodic form may entertain while hinting at a deeper foundation of national values.

The marching band thus forms a nexus or nucleus around which numerous meanings circulate, interweaving music with place and sound with the body in a way that amplifies the inherent sociality and power of music and its related sonics. The marching band, as a collective organizing of bodies and sounds, in rhythmic timing occupying or traversing city streets in legal or illegal fashion, delivers music drummed out in stride with footsteps, stamping out a message through its sonics that aims for the public heart. As an instrument the drum plays a radically vital role within marching bands, and it is the drum which best exemplifies the power that marching bands wield. The drum most readily delivers us back to military history and the acts of drill and dress mentioned earlier, for the drum is both the key timing instrument to marching as well as a sonorously active force that beats an announcement of military force. The history of the drum is interlocked with military history, either by direct involvement or as a rhythmic parallel in which keeping time, unifying single units into collective signatures, and organizing the individual body as an instrument acted to cultivate a machinic potential. As John Mowitt's engaging study of drumming shows, the interplay of percussion, skins (of drums and bodies), and the beat interlock power with the corporeal intensities of cultural expressions found through music. Lingering over Foucault's study of what he calls a "political anatomy" in his *Discipline and Punish*, Mowitt further suggests links between the disciplinary refinement of the timed body, ordered through a regiment of reasoned movement, and drumming as a signalling of the military machine. Drumming and combat, rhythms and fighting, and timing and obedience interweave in the military body and find echoes in currents of public music, as with the Buekorps, where the street functions as an acoustical space in which social meanings rely upon rhythmic display and reverberation.

The marching band, military and otherwise, can be understood to both perform and distort the presentation of aggression through an excess of musicalized timing, forming a radical means for establishing as well as countering order. We might then recognize this weave of marches and music as the very intersection of varying forces in whose performance bodies and cities meet in order to articulate polymorphous intensities that both topple and reinforce tradition. Marching bands carry the historical weight of military might by staging a disruption of public space. Taking over streets, marching bands territorialize through a muscular-musical mechanization, reinforcing notions of public order. From Mardi Gras to funeral marches, and military occupation to high school parades,

the ambulatory movements of a musical message criss-cross the lines of propaganda and protest, radicality and reaction, resounding through the public with
a movement that uses sound to occupy, overturn, or reinforce, lending a sonorous support to the dynamics of both change and stability.[27]

Exit

As the European agency for noise abatement seeks to initiate policies throughout the Union with the intention of minimizing noise levels, and also promoting
future developments with sensitivity to the needs and urgencies surrounding
noise and sound in general, questions as to the relations of sound, self, and collective expressions seem to take on weight. Noise pollution is finding an intensified level of attention, and governmental initiatives that look to the future
acoustic horizon in the hopes of setting a more humane sound level must be
understood to raise the volume on auditory consciousness and debate. That the
self and sound are in a sense uneasily balanced, with the scales easily tipped
from pleasure to pain, and from enjoyment to annoyance, may testify to the
degree to which audition and sound environments contribute to defining selfhood. In turn, such sensitivity makes it difficult to argue *for* noise as a condition
of social and cultural environments. While regulation is important, the total patterning of the soundscape and audible environment would no doubt turn into
a nightmare of homogenized signalling, acoustically softening a city and thus
minimizing any form of personalized or collective noise. To quiet the city may
in turn quiet the movements of historical and cultural transformation, which
always seem to seek an intensification of volume, pitch and sharing, turning
communicational clarity into a political struggle and poetical potential. Acoustic
design may thus register the movements of ideological conflict even while trying to guarantee a night's rest.

Jørgen Larsson, *I Ringen* (*In the Ring*), 2007. Photo: Thor Brødreskift.

Notes

1 Bruce R. Smith, "Coda: Talking Sound History," in *Hearing History: A Reader*, ed. Mark M. Smith (Athens and London: University of Georgia Press, 2004), p. 389.

2 A recent case in point was the State Museum in Copenhagen whose contemporary sculpture hall (designed by the architects Anna Maria Indrio and Mads Møller) inadvertently created an incredible reverberation time of over ten seconds. This led to continual problems, as the hall was also used for public speeches, music performances, and social gatherings. Only recently was this solved with some acoustical fittings and adjustments, reducing the reverberation time to a reported three seconds.

3 See Tia DeNora, *Music in Everyday Life* (Cambridge: Cambridge University Press, 2000).

4 This was initially developed from a 1996 Green Paper drafted by the EU, and was followed in 1998 by the creation of a Noise Expert Network which is to provide assistance to the development of European Noise policies.

5 From a summary of the ANS outline found on the Mayor of London's website <http://www.london.gov.uk/mayor/strategies/noise/index.jsp>.

6 For a study on the effects of noise pollution linked to traffic see *Urban Traffic Pollution*, ed. Dietrich Schwela and Olivier Zali (London: E & FN Spon, 1999).

7 Of note here is the work of Danish urban planner Jan Gehl, whose influential work on cities and human experience has led to increased demand for open and public space in Copenhagen, as well as other cities, such as Melbourne where he has also been an urban consultant. Interestingly, upon meeting Jan Gehl and informally asking him about sound and questions of noise pollution, he mentioned that he has yet to focus adequately on the issue.

8 From a summary of the ANS outline found on the Mayor of London's website <http://www.london.gov.uk/mayor/strategies/noise/index.jsp>.

9 Barry Blesser and Linda-Ruth Salter, *Spaces Speak, Are You Listening?: Experiencing Aural Architecture* (Cambridge, Mass.: MIT Press, 2007), p. 311.

10 Edmund Carpenter and Marshall McLuhan, "Acoustic Space," in *Explorations in Communication: An Anthology*, ed. Edmund Carpenter and Marshall McLuhan, (Boston: Beacon Press, 1960), p. 67.

11 Jean-Francois Augoyard and Henry Torgue, eds., *Sonic Experience: A Guide to Everyday Sounds* (Montreal: McGill-Queen's University Press, 2005), p. 130.

12 Ibid., p. 131.

13 Upon visiting Arup's acoustic studios, which is a state of the art technological tool in examining and designing acoustic spaces, I queried the engineer about its application to larger, more urban environments. In discussing the issue, the engineer revealed that as yet there had been no application of their acoustic tool toward urban design, but he doubted whether it could be useful in such contexts.

14 Eric Wilson, "Plagues, Fairs, and Street Cries: Sounding out Society and Space in Early Modern London," *Modern Language Studies* 25.3 (Summer 1995), p. 12.

15 Mark M. Smith, "Coda: Talking Sound History," in *Hearing History*, ed. Mark M.

Smith (Athens and London: University of Georgia Press, 2004), p. 395.

16 David Fort Godshalk, *Veiled Visions: The 1906 Atlanta Race Riot and the Reshaping of American Race Relations* (Chapel Hill: University of North Carolina Press, 2005), p. 7.

17 Thornwell Jacobs, *The Law of the White Circle* (Athens: The University of Georgia Press, 2006), p. 77.

18 Judith Butler, *Excitable Speech: A Politics of the Performative* (New York: Routledge, 1997), p. 11. Later in this book, Butler explores the ramifications of hate speech and its related legislative debates.

19 Clive Bloom, *Violent London: 2000 Years of Riots, Rebels, and Revolts* (London: Pan Books, 2003), p. 275.

20 The Autonomia Movement emerged in the 1960s in Italy as a leftist platform of ideas and people that attempted to move beyond an established Marxist and Communist party whose legacy for many had failed to deliver the radical transformation of society.

21 See Mikkel Bolt Rasmussen, "Radio Alice," in *Radio Territories*, ed. Erik Granly Jensen and Brandon LaBelle (Copenhagen: Errant Bodies Press, 2007).

22 This can be further glimpsed in the acoustical design of prison cells, where silencing the prisoner, nullifying resonance, and locking out the intermingling of shared voices, allows for an overall policing and arresting of the individual.

23 William H. McNeill, *Keeping Together in Time: Dance and Still in Human History* (Cambridge, Mass.: Harvard University Press, 1995), p. 6.

24 The history and relation of music and marching contains a compelling account of how music is mobilized and incorporated into public display, which in itself spawns an entire oeuvre of marching compositions, from the military to the circus. Compositions from the likes of John Philip Sousa, leader of the US Marine Band from 1880 to 1892, appear as both a backdrop to marching soldiers as well as to the entertainment of circus-goers and high school parades, leading to a general denigration of marching music as pure entertainment. My interest at this stage is to address in what ways the march mobilizes music so as to generate performative displays that come to occupy or define public spaces. Through such a situation, aspects of entertainment, occupation, and military power are interwoven into the formal devices and serve as compositional features.

25 In the US, the tradition of military music (initiated in the Revolutionary War and stemming from European tradition) continues throughout the various branches of the military. The Navy, Air Force, Marines, Army, and the US Coast Guards all maintain extremely active and highly acclaimed orchestras and bands. Performing throughout the year at international and national functions, these bands, and in particular the Marine band, are at the service of the country and the president.

26 Competitions are based on forms of battle whereby each unit attempts to disrupt the other's rhythm.

27 For an interesting study see George McKay, "A Soundtrack to the Insurrection: Street Music, Marching Bands and Popular Protest," *Parallax* 42 (2007).

Encounters with Simple Pleasures

Catherine Bagnall

I climbed Mt Owen in an old white brocade wedding dress with a full circle skirt; it collected the weather and became heavy. I slipped into Lake Constance in my pale pink satin dress, the neckline sparkling with diamantes. On Mount Tongariro in white-out conditions I wore a rich red ball gown that flapped loudly and wildly in the freezing snow wind. On Otarere Crater I wore layers of pale blue and white, and my lumpy silhouette mirrored the black volcanic landscape.

Thinking about the concept of the self in relation to embodied expression, I have decided that feeling is central. Barbara Vinken's suggestion that the division between being and appearance constitutes one of the major conceptual articulations in the discourse of fashion led me to think about what 'being' actually means, looks or feels like. I can't imagine a self without feeling, sensing the elements and enjoying the feeling of feeling. The act of looking, for me as an artist, is an agent for feeling.[1]

Up on Otarere Crater I was dressed in layers of dresses – an old petticoat, a pale blue dancing dress, an old wedding dress into which I had embroidered yellow mountain daises, a pale blue shirt and a cream coloured cardigan that sparkled with sequins. Against the lumpy black volcanic rocks and lichens my lumpy clothed body mirrored the odd shapes. My dresses and boots collected the weather and the red mud. The mist swirled around me and was at times so dense that the blue crater lakes disappeared from sight. Wearing such clothing in the bush heightens the zone around my body - dresses become heavy and wet and brush against my legs.

My fine arts practice draws on the convergence of fashion and performance. Over the last few years I have set off tramping (hiking/rambling) in a range of vintage ball gowns, designer dresses and outfits that I have made in order to explore a heightened intensity of being in the wilderness landscape. Documenting myself dressed up in a range of clothes from old wedding gowns and, more recently, animal suits, I am exploring (as a mature woman) how female pleasure in feeling might appear and how I can represent these experiences.

For Vinken, fashion is a poetological activity that thematises itself and has performative power, representing a relationship between the designer and those who wear the clothes. I am interested in the performative power of fashion to shift and question how we see ourselves – or what we can become. There are many direct and explicit connections between art, fashion and performance and the most interesting for me is the role the 19th-century dandy played in modern life. Like the dandy, I am interested in performing the pleasurable love and use of clothes. As he moves self-consciously through the metropolis, the dandy's focus is on his external sartorial appearance, but I aim to *feel* something. By differencing and feminising the role of the dandy I perform for myself. The wilderness of the New Zealand bush is my stage. I feel pleasure in my clothed body, not reflected from the arcade windows and mirrors of the dandy's urban setting but in the documentation I make of myself looking at myself in the act of sitting, walking or twirling amongst the trees, rivers and craggy ranges.

I favour solitude and my own gaze. In retrospect I have come to see that these performances are about encounters with simple pleasures and the problems of representing the transforming, ecstatic female body.[2]

Notes

1 Barbara Vinken, *Fashion Zeitgeist: Trends and Cycles in the Fashion System* (New York, Oxford: Berg Publishers, 2005).

2 Linda Jane Sayle and Catherine Bagnall, "Simple Pleasures: Scripting the Paradise Valley Project." Conference paper given at the Fashion and Fiction Conference, 26-27 May 2007, University of Technology, Sydney, Australia.

Credits

All images: Catherine Bagnall (2004)

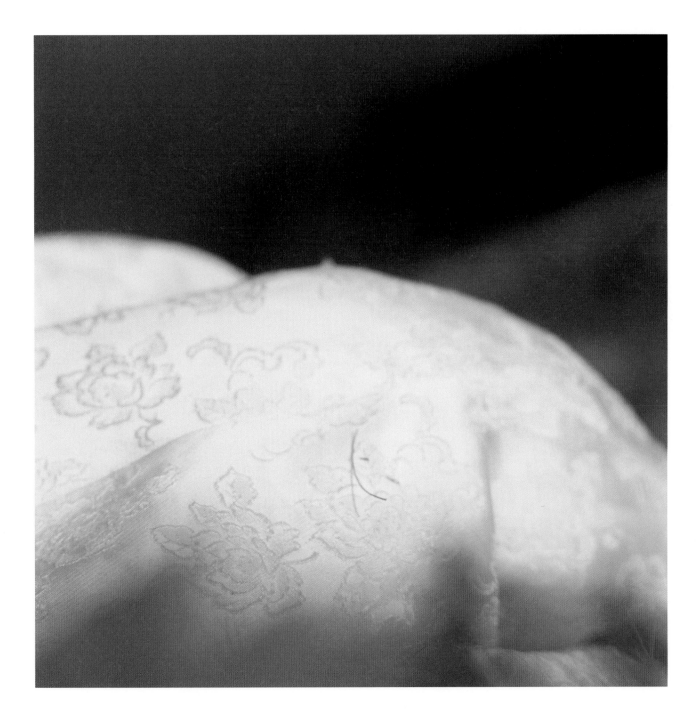

The Memory Project

Luca Ruzza

Reorganising the visible

The Memory Project developed out of *The Reading Projects*, a "hypertext opera" created by the Berlin composer Arnold Dreyblatt between 1991 and 1997. The libretto was originally formed out of thousands of biographical fragments sourced from a 1933 edition of the *Who's Who in Central and East Europe*. This grew into the idea of creating a living archive for the storage of historical data through a production that toured European cities and drew upon the inhabitants to read selections from the archival holdings. In 1998 I designed a temporary three-week installation in the hall of Amsterdam's Felix Meritis, a 200-year-old classicist building that operates as a centre for arts and sciences. The goal of the project was to display archived digital data and collect incoming biographical data specific to Amsterdam. This was presented as a performance event through the live readings of historical and contemporary material which was maintained by a staff of 18 archivists/performers directed by Toni Cots.

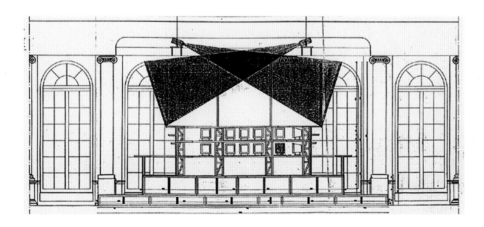

The installation consisted of a monumental form on a wooden platform, central-ised in the space, with reading tables and inclined black plexiglass screens stream-ing archival text from the databases. The structure operated as a digital brain housing 15 computers and the network's central server. Nine freestanding plasma units surrounded the structure on three sides. They displayed animated texts cho-sen from the 1933 *Who's Who*, statements on memory and the nature of archiving, biographical fragments from the Amsterdam contributors, and the accumulat-ing data in the T-Mail Communication Database. These texts provided a dynamic medium that continually composed, decomposed, and transformed during the opening hours of the exhibition. Guided tours to the interior of the brain were held at appointed times that were announced beforehand. Illuminated by a diffuse blue light that was repeated on the black PVC floor, the installation deliberately worked between chaos and control to unsettle and challlenge the participants.

Arnold Dreyblatt's score was composed for 600 voices, meticulously creat-ing harmony from the aural chaos we encounter when in such places as airports, railway stations, or shopping malls. He organised the voices in a manner that was logical yet non-linear. It was based on individuals from the past who have all invariably disappeared, yet their voices and stories live on, continuing to exist in our midst. It was my task as designer to delve into the memory of these sto-ries and find the "image" that remained, designing everything that was visible: the light, the characters, the structures, and the projection system; I selected the materials, the costumes, and the colors. My role was to stubbornly reorgan-ise a vision through retrieving the creatively volatile image.

"Imago"

The term "image" comes from "imago" – the death mask that was created in ancient Greece at the moment of passing away. Theatre productions are not unlike memories of the departed. Just as flesh fills the hollow masks of the dead, they present impressions that wait to be transformed by our imaginations into something definite. The image can only be completed through performance. Designing for theatrical events therefore involves a reorganisation of the visible within a magical space – a space of incarnation.

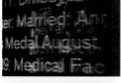

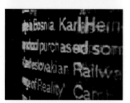

of
party
FREKIC
J,   *Ures Krulj   the
st election

Bosnia Herzogow
known
Sweden,
councillor with
ue-Bubenec. *In 1917
Affairs of the Ukrainian Gover
Zionist Provincial Governmen
party "La   de Fer"
of
KUGLER,   the province
of   home city.   Durgenian
and Agricultural Chamber.
as
Clara Schumann;
HUBERMANN,   *When he
3 months   Isidor Lotto.
telus -> At 6   sh
at the age
had to
*Wrote
years, when   w
there is no
FREKIC
of
and
J,   *Ures Krulj   the
st election

Bosnia Herzogow
known
Sweden,
councillor with
ue-Bubenec. *In 1917
Affairs of the Ukrainian Gover
Zionist Provincial Governmen
party "La   de Fer"
of
KUGLER,   the province
of   home city.   Durgenian
and Agricultural Chamber.
as
Clara Schumann;
HUBERMANN,   *When he

The Reorganisation of the Visible

The word "design" means planning, and not simply drawing. Design is a complete and articulate process that involves the compilation of knowledge, actions, methodologies, and means – all aiming to realise a specific objective, which begins in the early exploratory stages when ideas are conceptually generated and continues until the design reaches its fruition in performance. Design emerged as a professional discipline at the beginning of the 20th century and can be seen in the work of European architects such as Peter Behrens who, working for the AEG company, planned just about everything: the factory buildings, the industrial products, and even the public relations material. Behrens labelled this a "reorganisation of the visible." By the time "design" succeeded as the commonly used term, it had multiplied exponentially to encompass architecture, products, graphics, fashion, lighting, typography, transport, furniture, exhibition, systems, media, and scenography. All these design fields are united by a single purpose: the reorganisation of the visible through which the designer constructs an image in the mind of the observer/spectator/user. This establishes an unstable and volatile situation.

Instability

Instability presents radical conditions that are unpredictable, variable, and challenging. It requires the acceptance of an absence of truth, which entails the tendency of not judging, or of judging from a distance. This means accepting above all the idea of self-destruction – where everything is created with the knowledge that it will eventually be destroyed. You live knowing that you will die, that nothing is stable. Nothing is absolute, not even stainless steel is completely stainless. I am mindful of life's instability when I design and that buried beneath the necessary requirements of modesty, calm, and patience is always the notion that I cannot ever touch the truth. This was evident in *The Memory Project* where stories, histories, and identities were fragmented and fated to remain ephemeral, ineffable and in perpetual motion.

Credits

Design and Technical Direction:
Luca Ruzza
Concept and Sound Composition:
Arnold Dreyblatt
Data Projection and Database:
Alexandr Krestovskij
Producer and Dramaturg:
Toni Cots

Translated by
Nina Heine and Dorita Hannah

194

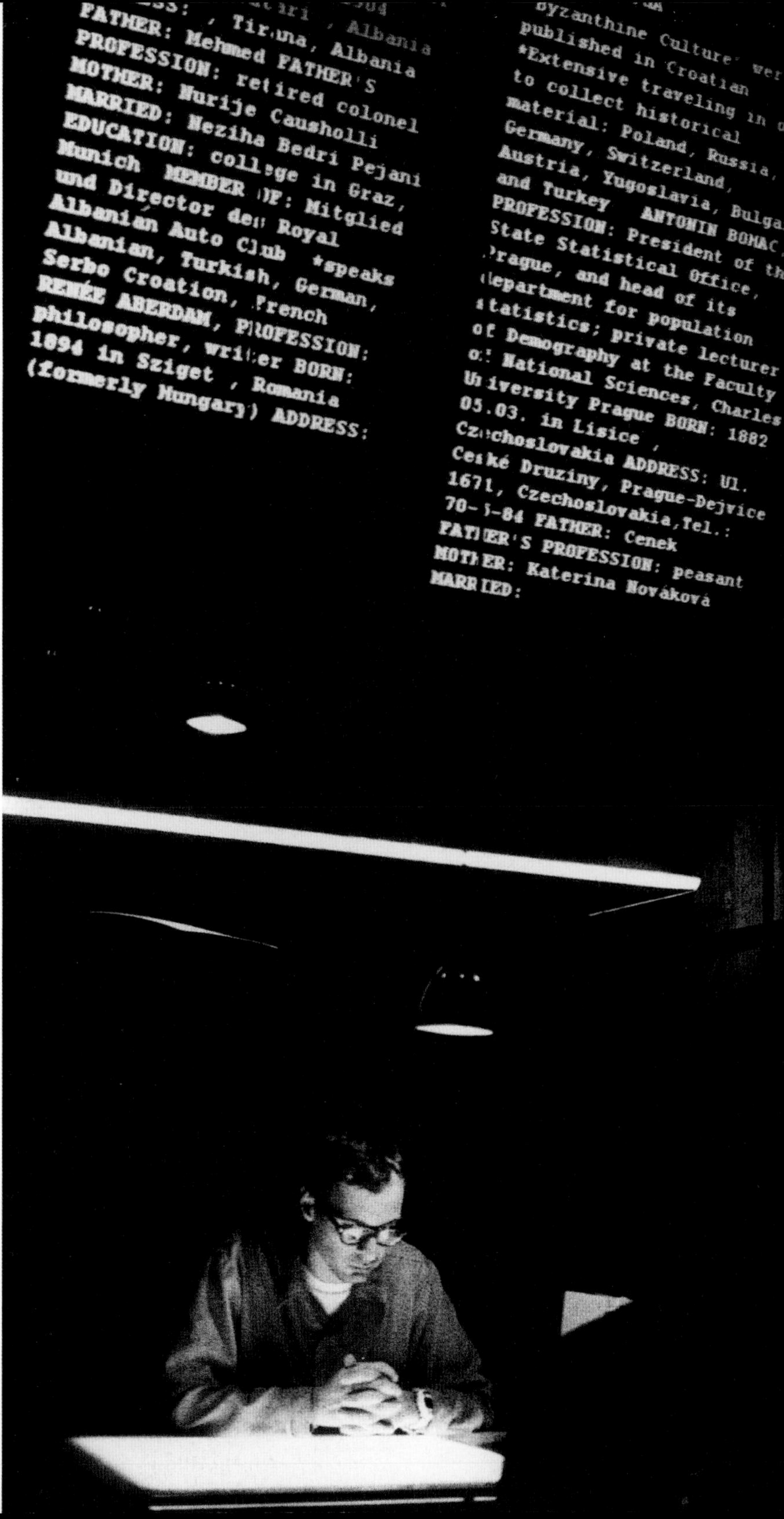

ESS: , Tirana, Albania
FATHER: Mehmed FATHER'S
PROFESSION: retired colonel
MOTHER: Nurije Causholli
MARRIED: Neziha Bedri Pejani
EDUCATION: college in Graz,
Munich MEMBER OP: Mitglied
und Director des Royal
Albanian Auto Club *speaks
Albanian, Turkish, German,
Serbo Croation, French
RENÉE ABERDAM, PROFESSION:
philosopher, writer BORN:
1894 in Sziget , Romania
(formerly Hungary) ADDRESS:

Byzanthine Culture wer
published in Croatian
*Extensive traveling in o
to collect historical
material: Poland, Russia,
Germany, Switzerland,
Austria, Yugoslavia, Bulga
and Turkey ANTONIN BOHAC
PROFESSION: President of th
State Statistical Office,
Prague, and head of its
department for population
statistics; private lecturer
of Demography at the Faculty
o: National Sciences, Charles
University Prague BORN: 1882
05.03. in Lisice ,
Czechoslovakia ADDRESS: Ul.
Ceské Druziny, Prague-Dejvice
1671, Czechoslovakia,Tel.:
70-5-84 FATHER: Cenek
FATHER'S PROFESSION: peasant
MOTHER: Katerina Nováková
MARRIED:

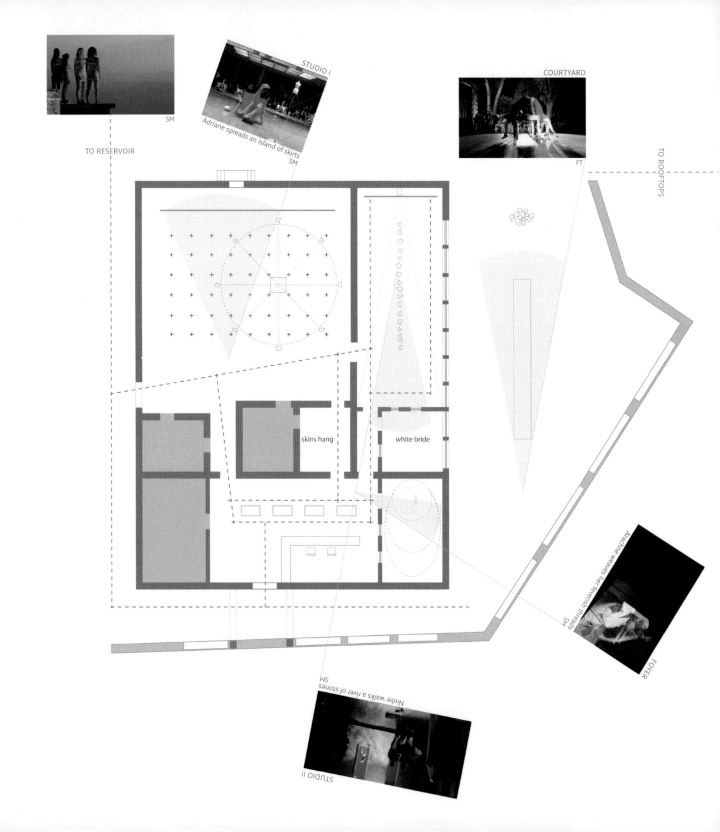

SM

STUDIO I

Adriane spreads an island of skirts
SM

COURTYARD

TO RESERVOIR

TO ROOFTOPS

skins hang

white bride

Adriane weaves her feverish threads
SM

FOYER

Niobe walks a river of stones
SM

STUDIO II

Her Topia | Dorita Hannah
A Dance-Architecture Event
Athens, October 2005

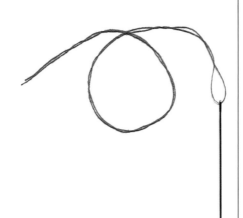

JN

Her Topia is a project in-motion questioning the relationship between the fleeting events of performance and architecture's monumental stasis through themes of mourning, memory and ecstatic release. It began in Athens (October 2005) at the Isadora and Raymond Duncan Dance Research Centre where designer and choreographer were commissioned to create a performance with multi-media artists and 14 dancers. As the first in a proposed series of site-sensitive works it takes Isadora Duncan's notion of dance as an expression of freedom and asks: what is it to dance freedom at a time when wars are being waged in its name?

In 1903 'Clan Duncan' arrived in Greece, a country whose ancient arts held symbolic value for their emerging dance ideology. Dancing ecstatically in the Parthenon's Temple of Dionysus, they resolved "to remain in Athens eternally and there build a temple that should be characteristic of us."[1] As Americans in self-imposed exile they began to construct a hilltop sanctuary that faced the Parthenon on the outskirts of the city. Modelled on the Temple of Agamemnon, their rough stone structure was an attempt to create a utopian elsewhere, drawing on mythology and history, whilst oblivious to the political, cultural and economic realities of the place it occupied. Within a year Isadora was forced to acknowledge the end of her "beautiful illusion," writing "we were not nor ever could be anything other than moderns."[2] She resumed her peripatetic career, leaving the construction to her brother Raymond who completed neither the building nor the utopian dream. In 1980 the ruined structure, now surrounded by apartment buildings in the suburb of Byron, was transformed into the Isadora and Raymond Duncan Dance Research Centre. Although by no means an architectural masterpiece, it represents the first attempt to build a space specifically for modern dance and is today a working centre for contemporary choreographic research in the Duncans' name.

The project investigated what happens when the slow performance of ancient rock and architecture coheres with the fluctuating temporalities of observing and dancing bodies. Stones became linking elements across time, holding memory in their inscrutable objectality.[3] Body-site relationships were explored and established through connections between Isadora and mortal women from Greek mythology such as Arachne and Niobe who, defying the Gods, were punished by them through tragic events and brutal metamorphoses. (This equated with moral judgement on the tragedies that befell the dancer – considered too thoroughly modern in her ways – who lost her children to drowning and was strangled by her own red scarf caught in the wheel of a sports car.) Ariadne is acknowledged as the first architect providing the thread to negotiate the labyrinth. This is seen in the use of the red stitch, a recurring trope in costumes and setting, operating as performative seam, ephemeral architecture, and way-finding mechanism. The ubiquitous dance studio mirror becomes a means of invoking and replicating a virtual Other through smaller reflective units that reconfigure bodies and space.

Over a two-week period in autumn 2005, designer and choreographer utilized embodied research to explore the building, its adjoining site and the surrounding neighbourhood. Combining ancient and contemporary images, stitched into a fluctuating temporal continuum, they wove the audience through interior and exterior spaces in which bodies were fragmented, multiplied and dematerialised in an orchestration of sound, light, video, mirrors and movement that eventually projected the performance out into the cityscape of Athens. Rather than a utopian site, the Duncans' temple is rendered a *heterotopia* – a place of "other" spaces.[4] As such it proposes a performative monumentality where dance as movement veiled in immobility reveals architecture as stasis veiled in movement.[5]

EP

199

Reservoir

As the sun sets on the urban backdrop, a chorus of women carry stones into the industrial landscape of a subterranean reservoir accessed from a concrete structure embellished with graffiti. Like an ancient *skene* this sloping platform faces a circular *orchesis* around which the audience gathers. The performers' bodies are bound in sheer flexible skins of cream-coloured netting with a red running-stitch that can be manipulated by the dancers who adopt poses from Duncan's revolutionary Russian choreographies, antique friezes and contemporary popular culture. Simultaneously ancient and modern, they enact ritualized gestures as caryatids, furies, messengers, activists, mannequins and athletes.

FT   FT   SM

Foyer

In the Centre's foyer the audience gathers around horizontal monitors that form pools of moving images manipulated in real-time by media artists seated behind the reception desk. The images include fragmented viewpoints of Arachne who occupies the glass room, sitting at a treadle sewing machine and stitching her huge dress that spreads out and fills the space. In the adjoining locker room frayed red dresses hang like carapaces from hooks and a dancer stitches herself into the floor with red tape.

FT

SM

Studio I

Ariadne, who provided Theseus with the thread with which he could navigate through the labyrinth, is seen in the figure of a woman whose phantom skirts are anchored by smooth white stones that resemble the egg-sacks of a spider. She is Arachne's spectral Other. This performance is apprehended indirectly through the mirror wall faced by the spectators, between which dancers move carving up their bodies, space and the audience with smaller planes of mirror.

FT

SM (top) FT (bottom)

Studio II

Turned to rock, Niobe slowly walks a river of stones between the spectators – in deep glacial mourning for her 14 dead children. Sheathed in a gown of Fortuny 'Delphos' Pleats and a sheer red veil, she resembles Isadora who compared herself to Niobe after the drowning of her own children. Through the windows of a glazed room that faces a wall of fractured mirrors moves her bridal double, shrouded in white. The space is dematerialised by a constant play of multiple reflections and projections.

FT

JN

FT

Courtyard

Audience and dancers reunite around a long mirror-topped table in the outdoor plaza surrounded by apartment buildings. This is the space of the bacchanal into which Arachne enters dragging her giant dress and weaving gestures across her body and the courtyard. The performance concludes with calls from the rooftops upon which dancers move ecstatically, extending the performance out into the city.

FT   FT   JN

FT

Notes

1 Isadora Duncan, *My Life* (New York: Garden City Pub. Co., *c.*1927), p. 123.

2 Ibid., p. 134.

3 This refers to Henri Lefebvre's notion of *objectality* as a brutal and resistant force in *The Production of Space*, trans. Donald Nicholson-Smith (Oxford: Blackwell, 1991), p. 57.

4 Michel Foucault established the notion of *heterotopia* as a site that is both mythic and real in contrast to the fundamentally unreal spaces of projected utopias, outlined and discussed in his essay "Of Other Spaces" reproduced in *Rethinking Architecture: Reader in Cultural Theory*, ed. Neil Leach (London: Routledge, 1997), pp. 350–355.

5 This is a reworking of Sandra Horton Fraleigh's contention that "dance is movement veiled in immobility." Sandra Horton Fraleigh, *Dance and the Lived Body: A Descriptive Aesthetics* (Pittsburgh: University of Pittsburgh Press), p. 93.

Credits

Project: *Her Topia*: A Dance-Architecture Event

Location: Isadora and Raymond Duncan Dance Research Centre, Athens, Greece

Dates: October 7-8 2005

Concept: Carol Brown and Dorita Hannah

Producer: Penelope Iliaskou

Designer: Dorita Hannah

Choreographer: Carol Brown

Lighting Designer: Thomas Economacos

Video Artists: Christos Hasapis, Jennifer Nelson, and Yannis Nikolaou

Multi-media Artist: Makis Faros

Research Assistants: Efrosini Protopapa and Hannah Davies

Dancers: Frosso Voutsina, Anna Daskalou, Delphine Gaborit, Anneta Kouvelioti, Irida Kyriakopoulou, Atalanti Mouzouri, Gogo Petrali, Marilena Petridou, Evridiki Samara, Takako Segawa, Vanesa Spinasa, Ioanna Toumpakari, Giota Tsagri and Anastasia Tsonou

Sponsored by the British Council and the Municipality of Byronas

Assistance with Image and Chapter Layout: Lauren Skogstad

Photography:
SM: Serge Montval
JN: Jennifer Nelson
EP: Efrosini Protopapa
FT: Fotis Traganoudakis of Public Eye

SM

Geneva – Newcastle 2003

Quarantine Theatre Company Simon Banham

Coming and Going
Images for a production in process

Quarantine Theatre Company was founded in 1998 by directors Richard Gregory, Renny O'Shea and scenographer Simon Banham. Quarantine makes theatre with, and arising from, the histories of the people with whom it works – often using shared rituals, meals or parties, to explore a dramaturgy of reality that breaches the divide between the audience and performer. These familiar social gatherings with their own codes of behaviour allow and encourage an interaction that may range from the intimate to the public and as such can be extended and broadcast within the peculiarities of the theatrical context. It is in that space between the actual and the enacted that the scenography situates itself, tinkering with the reality of the familiar, managing the areas of ambiguity and tension between what we expect to happen and what might happen.

At the point of writing this, *Coming and Going* has not happened.
At the point of reading this, *Coming and Going* may have finished.

Coming and Going may never happen.

This is one of Quarantine's next projects:

For *Coming and Going*, beginning with the notion of the 'outsider', we have visited Liverpool, Napoli, Istanbul, Gdansk and Marseille. Five cities that have been shaped by coming and going, immigration and migration, five cities always *becoming* and therefore in flow; where a sense of place is relational to *placement* and *displacement*, and where a sense of self always shifts somewhere between *coming and going*. (And those strangers now within the gates of the city – what words must they first learn in the new languages to be understood? Home? Fear? Loss? Death? Famine? Hope? Sorry? Or Community?)

Five cities that are on the edge of their 'land'
Five ports
Five doorways ...

Quarantine are at the beginning of the process, the start of our journey of *Coming and Going*, a point of not knowing: seeking traces of maps of the city, maps that might locate those who have arrived and those who remain, and also those *out-with* the gates, for they too are present and must be acknowledged here – and there – within the city.

From our previous body of work, those architectures and landscapes of encounter, what survives? Well, we have the memory of the journey, the sites visited captured here as paper images: moments, questions and possible answers now detached from their original context; memories for those that visited, a piquant note to say *wish you were here* for those who didn't. These cards can now have a new context, other interpretations, and perhaps another purpose. Treat them as souvenirs, or objects, and allow them to bear another message, moving across borders, fugitives from other travels to extend our collective experiences beyond *Coming and Going* in search of each other and new answers.

So, as a traveller in a foreign city sending messages home, I would like to include you in the exchange.

Quarantine presents: Eight Postcards to continue the conversation.

Beyond these pages.

Which scenographic structures can exchange or even remove the distinction between spectator and performer in order to extend the repercussions of the experience beyond the moment of performance itself, extending forward into a social space?

Rantsoen
Gent 2004

Rantsoen – Gent 2004
A performance event with food by Quarantine
www.qtine.com

Photo: Simon Banham

Food and stories from around the world
are served on and around the table.

Rantsoen – Gent 2004
A performance event with food by Quarantine
www.qtine.com

Photo: Simon Banham

Hidden by a red wall – a large round table –
the centre swollen with rice.

How might sceno-
graphic structures be
employed to enable
people to make
discoveries for and
about themselves
– performers and
spectators alike?

White Trash
Manchester 2004

White Trash – Manchester 2004
A piece of theatre made by Quarantine
www.qtine.com

Photo: Renny O'Shea

You choose to sit within the wall, to 'join in', or to stand outside and observe.

White Trash – Manchester 2004
A piece of theatre made by Quarantine
www.qtine.com

Photo: Renny O'Shea

A mundane space: the linoleum floor scarred with cigarette ends, an arena for confrontation and companionship.

Which scenographic
environments might be
created that encourage
interactions between
individuals that can be
variously intimate and
invisible, public and
celebratory?

Susan and Darren
U.K. tour 2006/07

Susan and Darren – U.K. tour 2006/7
An event with dancing by Quarantine
www.qtine.com

Photo: Simon Banham

His father's death, his mother's rape: on the same
piece of land 10 years apart.

Susan and Darren – U.K. tour 2006/7
An event with dancing by Quarantine
www.qtine.com

Photo: Simon Banham

Clearing away: making space for
new guests and another party.

How do we construct
a dramaturgy of
reality, referencing
the mundane whilst
celebrating and
emphasising the poetry
of functional aesthetics?

Butterfly
Glasgow 2004

Butterfly – Glasgow 2004
A performance event with buffet by Quarantine
www.qtine.com

Photo: Simon Banham

Gail retraces her journey to her
grandparents' house.

Butterfly – Glasgow 2004
A performance event with buffet by Quarantine
www.qtine.com

Photo: Simon Banham

Three generations of a family, a public celebration
and an absent brother.

Credits

Performance: *Geneva*
Location: Northern Stage, Newcastle
Company: Quarantine
Date: December 2003
Designer: Simon Banham; lighting design
Mike Brookes
Director: Richard Gregory
Choreographer: Jane Mason

Performance: *Rantsoen*
Location: Gent, Belgium
Company: Quarantine & Victoria
co-production
Date: June 2004
Designer: Simon Banham; lighting design
Mike Brookes; sound design
Ruben Nachtergaele
Director: Renny O'Shea
Choreographer: Anabel Schellekens

Performance: *White trash*
Location: Contact Theatre, Manchester
Company: Quarantine
Date: March 2004
Designer: Simon Banham; lighting design
Mike Brookes; sound design Greg Akehurst
Director: Richard Gregory
Choreographer: Christine Devaney

Performance: *Susan and Darren*
Location: U.K. Touring
Company: Quarantine
Dates: May 2006 – November 2007
Designer: Simon Banham; lighting design
Mike Brookes; video artist Ruth Cross;
sound design Greg Akehurst
Director: Richard Gregory and
Renny O'Shea
Choreographer: Jane Mason

Performance: *Butterfly*
Location: Tramway Theatre, Glasgow
Company: Quarantine
Date: October 2004
Designer: Simon Banham; lighting design
Mike Brookes
Director: Richard Gregory
Choreographer: Vanessa Smith

conSTRUCT

Dancing-Drawing Fields of Presence in *SeaUnSea*

Carol Brown and
Mette Ramsgard Thomsen

Could dancing a drawing be a way to create an ephemeral space? If drawing is a core tool of architectural imagination, the place where space is devised and designed, how can we find ways of thinking drawing as that which is formed through movement, that which follows the flow of presence, continually shifting and forming around the body? What can this drawing suggest? How can we embody the spaces it defines, the territories it creates, the densities it allows?

A performance of drawing might be one way to conSTRUCT an open encounter between audiences, performers and processes of computational design. Unconstrained by the rules of construction as building process, we can imagine drawing as a continuous process of dynamic becomings. In dancing a drawing within both digital and non-digital terrains we deterritorialise, refusing a fixed and stable ground and overcoming the limits of central perspective by manipulating the three-dimensional complexity of the body through multiple dimensions of space. Energy flows through improvisations of swarming, coiling, arcing and pouring streams of data and motional tracings. Traces of embodied and disembodied presence are left as a jagged geometry of lines that slowly fade over time. Sedimented as a mnemonic generated through a dual process of material and immaterial becomings arising from practices of choreography and architecture, this method of design calls for new ways of perceiving and framing performance.

Marina Collard in *SeaUnSea*. Photo: Mattias Ek.

Anna Williams in *SeaUnSea*.
Photo: Mattias Ek.

Practices of Space

Dance and architecture have much in common as both are concerned with practices of space. For a dancer, the act of choreography occurs through the unfolding of spaces by means of gesture and embodied movement, whereas for an architect, space is the medium through which form emerges and habitation is constructed. For both, the first space of experience is the space of the body. This essay is a writing out of the interstices of these two disciplines as they touch and inform each other in the process and production of *SeaUnSea*, an interactive dance installation which premiered at Siobhan Davies Studios as part of Dance Umbrella in London, October 2006. *SeaUnSea* is a collaboration between the authors, choreographer Carol Brown and architect Mette Ramsgard Thomsen, working with programmer Chiron Mottram.

As dance-architecture it explores the practice of live drawing. In the following we will outline how *SeaUnSea* engages the practices of drawing in architecture and dance, and how these processes are linked to spatial production. Seeking to engage the indeterminate spaces of that which is the process of forming, of assembling and dissolving, we will discuss how *SeaUnSea* bridges the different knowledge fields of dance, architecture and computer science.

Drawing-dancing in *SeaUnSea*

SeaUnSea is a dance performance taking place on an interactive stage. A camera is mounted above the stage as an interface for a digital environment. As the dancers move across the stage, their movement becomes input for changes within a digital realm. *SeaUnSea* is an encounter between a physical and a digital realm, between physical and digital agency and presence and asks how we frame such experiences? How do they attain meaning and how can we construct these as part of our collective practices of space?

We conceive *SeaUnSea* as dance-architecture. Dance-architectures can be thought of as hybrid forms emerging at the interface between the disciplines of choreography and architecture through the creation of performance events. Rather than creating dances or constructing buildings as the traditionally privileged domains of our respective practices, we consider dance-architecture as the making and marking of a joint place where space is suggested through its enactment as a live condition, and where boundaries and densities follow the shifting contours of the moving body.

The co-evolution of our joint practice involves inscribing the page and the stage through drawing and dancing, exploring the thinking of a space constructed across temporal and enacted dimensions. Space is the medium for both choreography and architecture and the idea of drawing spaces is common to both. However, we experience the activity of drawing in different ways: For a dancer the act of choreography can be considered a form of movement-writing, as the dancer's body inscribes space through dancing; whereas for the architect, drawing is a place of invention through which the depth of space, its outlines and its place can be probed and discussed. In both architecture and dance, drawing is a primary medium aligned with the processes of invention while simultaneously retaining its role as a place of notation and communication. In both practices the act of drawing engages the two-dimensional plane. Although dancing is always already dealing with the palpably three-dimensional body, the stage, like the page, is conditioned by an inherent awareness of the planar. In *SeaUnSea* we take hold of this shared practice, seeking out manifold ways of reading and drawing space whilst devising new strategies for spatial inscription. By folding and enfolding the lived experiences of drawing and dancing as

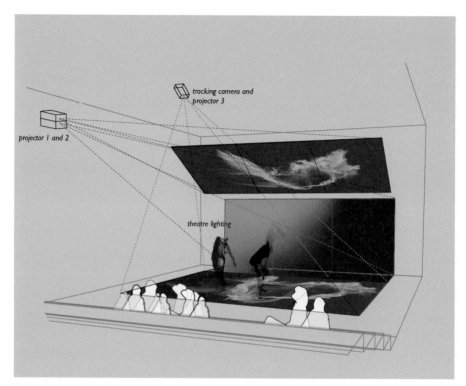

Performance design for *SeaUnSea*.

acts that occur across time and come into being through the sensed immediacy of gravity and the thick dimensionalities of experienced time, we have created a hybrid place where the drawn and the danced take place together. Taking the analogue practices of drawing and dancing and shifting these into a digital terrain, we have found a joint space for interaction in which new geometries, ways of moving and (dis)embodied spaces are created, mutating the two-dimensional practice of drawing through new live dimensions and transforming the theatrical plane.

Liveness of the Drawing Plane

In *SeaUnSea* the drawing evolves as a joint place shared by performers and an ecology of digital agents. Under the camera interface, on the interactive stage, the dancers meet swarms of digital agents drawing live colour trails and crystalline meshes that inscribe the picture plane. The agents can be understood as independent yet co-present small-scale programmes that navigate the flat site of the camera picture plane. The white territory of the dance floor is interrupted by the black contours of the dancers wearing dark costumes. As the agents see this two-dimensional plane and learn to explore, to curiously follow or fluidly avoid their digital shadow, their movement traces create live drawings that are re-projected back into the performance space surrounding the dancers as projections on the floor, wall or a hanging canopy. The dancers are immersed in a fluid space continually acting and reacting to their movement, changing and coming-into-being as they meet and traverse the stage space.

In the digital realm the agents are visualised across time. Their movements across the camera picture plane become the source of fluid particle fields through which crystalline structures take shape. The particles act like plankton evading the body and flowing through a dense digital space. Like traces that follow the agents' movement, the particles form pools and eddies in their wake. In this point space, they create fields of presence that form and de-form with the agents' shifts in behaviour. This immediate interaction is met by the larger time loops of a crystalline mesh structure evolving across the time of the performance. Like a frozen river, the mesh evolves slowly, building up edges and defining territories. The mesh is shaped by the collective behaviour of the agents, weaving a tight skin across the projection surface. The mesh draws a temporal image of the agents' interactions with the environment as well as with each other. Just as water can change imperceptibly in temperature or, at one point, change state and become ice, these changes can be swift and fleeting or protracted and enduring.

The vivid colours, shifting in density and saturation, draw in references to natural and artificial seas. Taking their point of departure from the muted blues, yellows and greens, the space is intensified, becoming alert, as the performance enters the synthetic colourscapes of opal turquoises, harsh pinks and rich golds.

These colours help define spatial tension, shaping its narrative relationship to the dancer and creating a sense of punctuation and flow in the performance.

The drawn is also sketched into a sound space. As the agents move, their clustering and dispersal results in changes in the soundscape of the environment. Developed in collaboration with composer Alistair MacDonald, the sound is thickened and pulled as the agents move across the space following the dancers' movement. Through the use of six speakers surrounding the stage, sonic events pan and cluster as the dancers 'carry' the sounds to different zones. In this way, sound 'weights' the performing environment and heightens the pathways of the dancers. Intensities develop, eroding and dissolving as the dancers find their traces in space. Mixing the aural with the visual, the space becomes multidimensional, surrounding the dancers as a temporal colourscape enriched through sound.

Inscribing Self in Technology

Developing our own software rather than using off the shelf solutions allows us to explore how the body is conceived and held by the technology of the digital. As part of thinking the relationships between body, technology and space, we have created bespoke interfaces for the particular spaces we explore. These interfaces engage the body. The camera sees the body and allows this real-time image to become input for a digital world. This *embodied interface* allows a body-centred sense of presence and agency to engage and enact with the digital. A previous collaboration, *The Changing Room* (2004), involved the development of a camera-tracking interface that saw the body as a white figure against a black background. The camera was mounted upright, creating similarity between the 'eye' of the interface and that of the audience. The data was then mapped in real time onto a digital morphology, creating direct correlations between the movement of the performers and the digital realm. In *SeaUnSea*, we also use a camera interface, but here the relationship is radically different. Firstly, the camera is mounted above the stage so that the dancers reflect themselves in their planometric image, and, secondly, rather than mapping the body on a virtual self, the camera image becomes a merged plane across which the dancers meet a dig-

Matthew Smith, Marina Collard and Anna Williams in *SeaUnSea*. Photo: Mattias Ek.

ital presence, a swarming flow that follows, flows and interjects with the performers. Rather than informing the digital directly through the reconfiguring of tracking data, the interactive stage becomes a joint place shared by performers and digital agents connected through the camera interface.

In *SeaUnSea* the camera also bestows the space with a strange sense of gravity. Mounted above the dance floor, the verticality of the camera looks down at the dancers. As the dancers relate to their digital shadow, they see themselves looking upwards, as if reflecting into a surface above. Like diving in the sea and looking towards the sun from beneath the water surface, gravity seems to surge upwards, drawing light and movement around oneself. It is this planar view that is inscribed in *SeaUnSea*. Informed by the depths of the experienced gravities, and moving below the lightness of air, the drawing finds its dimensions within the aqueous metaphors of the sea.

Carol Brown in *SeaUnSea*. Photo: Anders Ingvartsen

The scenographic design of *SeaUnSea* accommodates this planar view and is conceived as a light box that is filled with movement and colour. Defined by three white surfaces – floor, wall and suspended canopy – the box is understood as a transformative site. Core to its development has been the development of an intuitive interface that allows for connections to be drawn between the different dimensions of the performance, transforming the box into a site of evolving interactions.

Defining drawing in *SeaUnSea*

SeaUnSea is understood as a living drawing, shaped by the movement of the dancers and agents alike. The drawing is indeterminate. Rather than being animate, pointing at its own completion, it is open ended, allowing for the improvised. The notion of indeterminacy in drawing differs from the traditions of architectural production. In architecture, the drawing finds its normative reading in its completion. We see the plan of the drawn building in respect to its entirety; we understand the correlations of rooms, corridors, and exteriors as a set of relationships that need their full description to make sense. As such, the temporal is removed from the drawn. The time of drawing, customarily understood as a tracing of the pencil over the paper in the making of a mark and as that which precedes the artifact of the drawn, is avoided. Choreographically, drawing as a form of notation becomes an artefact and aide-mémoire of the dance. Alternatively, the dance itself can be considered as a live drawing experiment as in Trisha Brown's work *It's a Draw/Live Feed* (2003) where the floor upon which she dances becomes a canvas marked by charcoal placed between her toes.[1] More commonly, dancers refer to 'drawing the space' as a metaphor for the way in which their movement pathways create an invisible ink drawing in the space around their body. In *SeaUnSea* we seek to engage the multiplicitous, the unsure, the open and the indeterminate through processes that find their home within these joint practices of drawing in architecture and choreography. The drawn in *SeaUnSea* is presented as a live interaction, taking place across time, as a process of becoming, continually inscribing and erasing itself, creating its depths and finding its boundaries. This process of becoming is met by the dancers who perform open movement scores; improvisational states that retain an openness towards the drawn and allow the visual landscapes to flow in response to their movement; and, conversely, their movement to be affected and changed by its tracings.

In their computational reality, the agents engage this indeterminate space through their own programmatic liveness. Defined through low-level rules that form their capacity to act and react, they are described through their relational interactions with each other and with their environment. As such they become a new way of drawing. Rather than tracing an outline, or defining a dimension, they draw in respect to a sense of agency. It is this agency, its shifts in agility and intention, that creates depths, densities and boundaries within the space of *SeaUnSea*. And it is this agency that is met by the corresponding motilities and movement languages of the choreography. Unlike previous examples of dancing as drawing, the motional scribing of the dancers in *SeaUnSea* catalyses trails of particle streams and the lacing of digital mesh, embedding movement memories as secretions within a digital scenography.

Drawing in *SeaUnSea* is at once gravitational and temporal; as a lived space it finds its dimensionalities outside the projective geometries of architecture and encoded notations of choreography. In this way, the page and stage become temporal dimensions that find their depth in the experience of a live ecology sinking and rising as movements occur. In our collaboration we have tried to conceptualise this space and to find ways to design and move within it. How could a space be shared between a digital and physical being? What might an understanding of live performance bring to architecture as a means through which to understand a space that flows with the event of time? How can my sense of embodiment yield to the remote touch of a digital being?

The Metaphor of the Sargasso Sea

Conceptually, *SeaUnSea* is shaped through the fluid imagery of water. As swelling strata it finds its dramaturgical place in three parallel images: the deep ecology of the sea, the crystalline structures of ice formations, and the petrified landscape of a hoar frost. Water penetrates and forms through these strata as particulate matter of different densities. The stratification of the work explores temporalised phase shifts between these different images informed by ecological imperatives. Processes of evaporation, crystallisation, vaporisation and decay take shape as evolving structures within the performance.

Through our collaboration we have invented a language of performance in which a shared image repertoire allows us to communicate a sense of motility, emotional resonance and agency. Images such as winter branches, clouds of pollen, entangling seaweeds and the acrid depths of the Aral Sea allow us to

238

Marina Collard in *SeaUnSea*. Photo: Mattias Ek.

imagine a place and a physical ecology for locating the interactive experience, entwining our experience of the event in a narrative at the threshold between the actual and the virtual, the embodied and the disembodied. This ecology evolves over time through processes of interaction, creating patterns, fluid forms and unexpected moments relating to the organic, growing processes of emergence and the co-dependence of ecosystems.

Relating this ecology to an actual seascape, the Sargasso Sea, allowed us to consider how particles of different complexity and density shape the actual environment. In taking inspiration from the Sargasso Sea, *SeaUnSea* is informed by the rhythms and lifeforms of an ever-changing seascape. Situated in the Atlantic, the Sargasso Sea is a sea within a sea; it grows, expands and contracts with the conditions of the environment. The image of the Sargasso thus becomes one of a space in flux, continually in a state of becoming, changing and reforming. In the opening sections of the work, "Green Tide" and "Sargassum," the image of rootless seaweed, drawn by thick gravities, becomes the point of departure for a hybrid form of sonic and visual particles that shape and dissolve as mnemonic traces. The dancers' weighted floor rolls, dives, suspensions hovering between floor and canopy and rotations of tessellating limbs follow and respond to the pull and push of the particles, at times ephemeral, at times crystallising into petrified formations. This hybrid visualisation is projected back into the performance space, generating a state of playful probing and enchantment.

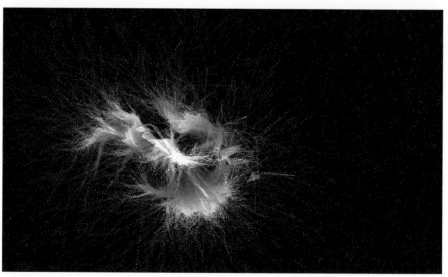

Screen image from performance installation, *SeaUnSea* by Mette Ramsgard Thomsen.

Developing Movement Scores

Imagery from the Sargasso Sea informs behaviour on both sides of the interface and communicates emotional and spatial content for the dancers and design. This shared language has been important for our collaboration in that it allows a sense of freedom for our practices to unfold whilst retaining a common focus. The dramaturgy for *SeaUnSea* considered how the relationships between the plankton of the Sargasso Sea, the growth of sargassum on the surface of the sea and the atmospheric changes affecting cloud formation create an ecosystem of interdependence affecting the weather and air flows.

The time-based as well as spatial nature of these images communicated states of becoming realised through shifts from one condition to another. The growth of the Sargasso Sea as it bathes in lush sunlight or its slow decay as clouds form and water evaporates shape cycles of formation with beginnings and endings. These life-cycles become spaces in which the performer enters as a driving force, at times propelling the evolution of digital spheres, at times settling their collapse.

Dramaturgically, the performance evolves through three cycles reflecting these states: "Sea," "UnSea," and "Frost." Each of these cycles contains micro events based upon movement scores that we describe as "states." These states define differences in the visualisations and movements of the digital agents and dancers alike. In this way the dramaturgical structure follows the rising state changes of water. Beginning with "Sea," the performers follow the flow of a pool, creating eddies and counterflows as particles swarm around them. In "UnSea" this containing environment hardens, crystallising around the body and rising to the surface. Through the image of ice forming, the depth of the computed image is engaged and incorporated. Finally, in "Frost," water fills the air. To give an example of how these states work in practice in "Unfolding Tree," which is part of the "Frost" cycle, the image of a frozen landscape of thick mist accumulating at ground level and becoming frosted branches is embodied and encrypted. The dancer moves with extreme slowness, unfurling brittle movements that twist and rotate. Squatting and standing in an ever-changing pool of light, her movements incorporate the digital agents' motility, creating a tense dialogue with their bursts of growth and slow decay.

Fields of Presence

As the dancer responds to the different layers of time experienced in the work, reacting and triggering the faster motility of the particle streams which draw the space, whilst simultaneously creating the possibility for a sedimented trace of this interaction through building and dissolving the mesh drawings, a polyphonic matting emerges. For an audience, this communication of the space, with its multiple temporalities, creates an opportunity for a transdimensional experience. The multiple strata of the performance ecology encourage a restless energy and a mobile gaze. Freed from a locatable 'ground', audiences follow the movement of the live dancer and 'read' the trail of her pathway in the digital, switching the focal length of viewing between the dancer and screen dimension. Alternatively, the audience may choose to follow the motility of the digital and the points of confluence between dancer and virtual environment as these co-emerge; or they may focus upon the doubled or mirrored image of the dancer as flesh and blood presence and as digital shadow in the screenic dimension. Ideally, we would hope that audiences would journey effortlessly between these layers and levels customised as they can be to a continuity of presence between actual and virtual spaces. Encouraging audiences to switch between floor, canopy and wall, through focusing attention on moments of pooled interactivity, requires negotiating the gaps and spaces between. The moments of movement between floor and screen planes require a tracking gaze, negotiating between different senses of space. In the live performance the audience view the work from the periphery, a space outside the interactive field. However, for the installation event which follows this, small groups of audience are guided onto the stage to 'play' as participants in the environment. This produces a more intimate encounter between audience and digital ecology. As participants in the field, they follow their own desire paths, making connections and intersecting with the environment on a kinaesthetic level. Guided by the performers whom they have previously watched engage the space with directed movement, the audience-participants are encouraged to inhabit the environment and discover their own sense of play within it. This more chaotic, less 'scripted' part of the event, created a tension between our intentions for the work. Whilst we desired to see the ecology made meaningful through a poetic engagement with

Anna Williams in "Unfolding Tree," part of *SeaUnSea*. Photo: Mattias Ek.

the interface, many audience members were more driven by a curiosity to know how it worked and sought to probe the cause and effect aspect of the system. Despite our disappointment with this level of audience interaction, looking 'under the hood' and peering at the agent interface became a part of the performance design and a way of transforming the performer-audience encounter

243

Matthew Smith, Marina Collard and Anna Williams in *SeaUnSea*. Photo: Mattias Ek.

into a shared state of play, removing the illusory aspects of performance and dissolving the separation between performer and audience. In making transparent the process of construction involved in real-time computation, this type of framing foregrounds the liveness of the computation process as co-creator of the space with the live dancers' presence.

Performing the Space

For performer and participant, *SeaUnSea* comes-into-being through an exposure to a digital ecology of intelligent agents. Audience, performer and an intelligent digital dimension search for and create a cross-contaminated place through an evolving choreographic score. As an evolving interactive performance event, the intention is to entangle human presence in a virtual seascape. This work is envisioned as an interactive performance ecology sited within a public building. Performers, audience and intelligent agents cross, converge and create a changing transient state through which emergent behaviours and patterns evolve. Through a camera-based interface, a projection membrane and a multi-dimensional image and soundscape, *SeaUnSea* entangles biological and digital life forms.

This joint space creates new challenges for performers as they move beyond familiar contexts and conventions of performance practice. The question of presence and how the dancer cultivates her awareness of both the material and immaterial elements of the performance is a major challenge as she simultaneously performs with the palpable and the fleshless.

Dancing-drawing through Other Spaces

In creating *SeaUnSea* we have developed an interface environment where digital agents and embodied performers gain a sense of a shared terrain through *dancing-drawing*; the intention being to create a meaningful inter-relation between a digital and a physical sense of agency evolving over time.

Through the creation of embodied interfaces for our projects, *Spawn* (2003), *The Changing Room* (2004) and *SeaUnSea* (2006), we are developing tools for performance spaces that integrate fragments of reality, virtuality and imagination. Dancers involved in these projects are invited to communicate with and through the virtual as well as the material presences on stage within a performance ecology which fuses traditional dance theatre scenography (lights, stage floor) with new technologies (computers, interactive software, camera tracking systems). Dancing on this augmented stage challenges our ideas about liveness and presence.

Our collaborations explore the inhabitation of digital environments and interfaced spaces. As a meeting of bodies and spaces through interactions arising out of the possibilities of digital media, alternative spatio-temporal dimensions and ways of imagining the body are explored. Through this collaborative dialogue we have embraced digital technologies as tools for re-conceiving embodiment and for creating new ways of telling the self.

SeaUnSea creates a palimpsest by overlaying a digital world on the participant's view of the real world so that both 'realities' can be experienced simultaneously, allowing us to *draw* connections between the two. Rather than either/or, this both/and condition of transdimensional space acknowledges the impossibility of a fleshless ontology and the pleasures of presencing in the taking place of a performance that streams digital and physical terrains. Through dancing-drawing agency is inscribed in fluid movements across thresholds that are material and immaterial, physical and virtual, embodied and disembodied.

Notes

1 Trisha Brown's *It's a Draw/Live Feed* premiered at The Fabric Workshop and Museum, Philadelphia, 15-16 March 2003.

Credits

Performance: *SeaUnSea*
Location: Premiered at Siobhan Davies Studios, Dance Umbrella London, UK
Dates: 12-15 October 2006
Concept: Mette Ramsgard Thomsen and Carol Brown
Choreography: Carol Brown in collaboration with the dancers

Architecture and Visualisation: Mette Ramsgard Thomsen
Dancers: Marina Collard, Anna Williams and Matthew Smith
Lighting: Michael Mannion
Computing: Chiron Mottram and Teis Draiby
Sound: Alistair MacDonald

Poul Henningsen in the 1940s. Private photo.

PHantom of the Operas in Sydney and Copenhagen
Interactive performative structures

Olav Harsløf

We know that the various art forms can inspire one another. However, it would seem that they can do more than that. There is every indication that significant but less visible conjunctions in one art form can be illuminated and explained via conjunctions and structures in another art form. Such structures and conjunctions can be termed *performative structures* – as fundamentally shared and interactive structures that are reciprocally creative – and which can include, for our present purposes, spatial/visual art forms and acoustic/musical art forms.

I will endeavour to explain these structures and conjunctions through examples of work by the Danish architects Poul Henningsen (1894-1967), Jørn Utzon (b. 1918), and Henning Larsen (b. 1925), as well as the Danish composers and musicians Bernhard Christensen (1905-2004), Kjeld Bonfils (1918-1984), and Max Brüel (1927-1995). The outcome reveals an improvisational and inter-disciplinary process where architecture, music, and lighting objects spectacularly cohere.

So what are these performative structures in music, architecture, and lighting design? In collaboration with colleagues at the University of Aarhus, and in his book *Improvisation and Thought*, the musician, theoretician, and semiotician Ole Kühl sought to define the mental space of music. He calls it cognitive musicology, and his thesis is that jazz improvisation manifests thought at a very high level. Improvisation is deeply rooted in the body, it takes place in time and in a specific situation, and during the improvisation the musicians listen to the music in the same way as the audience.

With reference to improvisation – and here bebop jazz – Ole Kühl has studied the relationship between time and space in music. A piece of music, a jazz standard, has a certain length – e.g. a chorus consisting of 32 bars – which is played a number of times, determined by the number of joint choruses and, in particular, solos. The length of the individual musicians' solos is not necessarily agreed in advance and none of the musicians can, at the moment of playing, know if a solo will consist of 2, 4, 5, 8 or 14 choruses. During improvisation the melody disappears and the musicians are left working with time (the 32 bar sequence) and the basic chord sequence. This happens corporeally in that the brain is simultaneously carrying out two other tasks: communicating the improvisation being presented, and planning and preparing the next improvisation. Kühl calls this the three-second window. Analyses of jazz solos by Charlie Parker and others show that, while playing, the human brain can plan and store three-second improvisations, corresponding to 2-4 bars, while maintaining the time structure. The brain receives the temporal-rhythmic input together with the tonal input and creates the musical idea that is positioned (i.e. stored), after which it is played and listened to concurrently with the creation and positioning of a new input.

Ole Kühl's thesis shows that music is, in a manner of speaking, three-dimensional – i.e. spatial. It has a timeline, a foreground and a background, a 'before' and a 'now', all of which the brain handles simultaneously. Many architects and sculptors will be all too familiar with this characterisation in view of their own intellectual method: the development of spatial thinking – the capacity to see front and back, depth and surface, all at the same time.

Most of us are familiar with the iconic image of the Sydney Opera House in Australia. And many people know the name of the Danish architect who designed it: Jørn Utzon. Perhaps they have also heard of Henning Larsen, who has designed celebrated buildings all over the world – including the Copenhagen Opera House that opened in the Danish capital in 2005. However, most people are not aware of the fact that Utzon and Larsen each had close friends who were also well-recognised professional jazz musicians – and that they were all profoundly inspired by the Danish architect, lighting designer, revue writer, and "cultural radical"[1] Poul Henningsen. I want to suggest, therefore, that the opera houses on the waterfronts in Sydney and Copenhagen could very well be perceived as two enormous rhythmical, radical lamp performances.

If this is the case, then the two opera houses can be seen as examples of how musical structures can be applied to architecture and thereby corroborate my thesis pertaining to *interactive performative structures*.

Each generation of artists takes its starting point in the preceding generation, either by continuing the line of development or by breaking with it – or by seeking out other sources of inspiration from other neighbourhoods, countries, continents. But the predecessors remain the yardstick – whether covertly or overtly, consciously or unconsciously. As vital sources of inspiration, the most prominent cultural figures of the preceding generation will always remain within the horizon of memory. In this sense, regardless of differing generational views on various matters of form, ideas and politics, all artists have taken their starting point in the artistic or intellectual status of the distinguished forerunner, without, at any given time, compromising their own ambitions or artistic cogency.

In exceptional situations or periods it is customary that a generation of artists is professionally, artistically, culturally, politically and conceptually indebted to the presence of a towering cultural figure, a 'guiding light', even while developing an utterly personal and distinct profile of their own. It is my contention that Poul Henningsen (commonly referred to as PH) was one such guiding light for the Danish architects who trained between 1935 and 1955.

Poul Henningsen developed his aesthetic and analytic theories during the period that witnessed the breakthrough of Danish expressionism and cubism in the years 1917-1920, while he was on the editorial board of the art and literature journal *Klingen* (The Blade). The editorial policy demanded an objective engagement with the genuine elements of art: material, form, colour and space. Henningsen thus proposed a scientific approach in which painting, sculpture, and building structure should have a clear intention – aesthetically, socially, and in terms of form. He applied this combination of expediency and desire for realisation in other societal spheres, seeing the architect as a key figure in the community: the architect as artist – i.e. creating totalities such as optimum housing and the organic town. For Henningsen, the planning of a built environment – towns, transportation, bridges, harbours – was both a social and aesthetic project. He was inspired by the English architect Raymond Unwin and the German engineer Werner Jakstein, with his aesthetic sense informed by the French architect Le Corbusier.

The modern radical artists had a strong and widespread interest in side-stepping naturalism and romanticism while advocating aspects of eighteenth-century rationalism – that which was pure, clarified, and logical: the application of reason. The works of rationalist architects and writers were promoted, composers took up J.S. Bach, and a philosophical superstructure was erected, based on Immanuel Kant's theories through the juxtaposition of Marxist materialism and Kantian humanism. It therefore comes as no surprise that Henningsen's cubism bore a strong air of neoclassicism, while his social and political commitment was one of Neo-Kantianism, which he endeavoured to apply to architecture, often stating that "Humankind as a concept is part of the substance of architecture."

In tandem with developing his artistic ideas, Poul Henningsen designed new forms of lamps and methods of light distribution. During the first half of the 1920s, he became known as an interesting and inventive lamp designer by virtue of his chandeliers with decorated glass trumpet shades, balls of nickel silver or brass rings, drop glass shell wall lights, and table lamps with shades made of silver-plated bronze. He was an official Danish participant in the 1925 Paris Exposition Internationale des Arts Décoratifs et Industriels Modernes, where he was awarded a Gold Medal for his six-shade model in matt nickel silver. By the following year he had developed the final design for what immediately became known as the "PH-lamp" when light from hundreds of the three-copper-shade fittings shone down on a major motor show in Forum exhibition hall in Copenhagen. However, the lamp could still only cast its light downwards.

The design was put into production by the Danish light-fixture manufacturer Louis Poulsen, and an aggressive marketing campaign sold the lamp in various sizes and coatings. In the spring of 1926 Poul Henningsen started using hand-blown and sand-blasted solid opal glass, which dispersed twelve per cent of the light out through the multi-shade, successfully launching the popular PH-lamp.

PH-lamp casting its light upwards and downwards. Model 1926. Photo: Mads Folmer.

On 1 July 1926 the first issue of *Kritisk Revy* (Critical Review), a journal dealing with architecture and urban planning, was published – with Poul Henningsen as editor-in-chief. The early issues blatantly promoted his lamps amid articles about town and tenement housing, bridges, harbour and suburban development, as well as the journal's distinctive architectural criticism; these, however, were soon competing for space with articles on literature, theatre, stage revues, dance, jazz and neoclassicist music.

The brand "Poul Henningsen" was now no longer simply a lamp – it was also a philosophy and a lifestyle. In 1928 Henningsen saw a performance given by the African-American singer and dancer Josephine Baker at one of Copenhagen's popular theatres; she appeared virtually naked, her costume consisting of small briefs and a skirt made from artificial bananas. The reviews considered her performance to be immoral, and a foreign prince even referred to her as "negresse." But for Henningsen she was an overwhelming inspiration; her performance demonstrated to him how crucial the body is to the cultural development of humankind. He wrote of her:

> ... we view her manner and technique as merely a costume that fits around her never-failing naturalness. We, who have witnessed this dance and music in its early stages and have that sense of rhythm within us, probably find it easier to appreciate the beauty of the costume than would many older people. But we consider it to be no more than a cosmetic which animates her vivid face without at any moment concealing it.[2]

> It is ... her finely cultivated personality which conducts her bearing ... Her movements are those of an animal, but not for an instant bestial ... She has all the qualities, both as artist and as human being, to pass safely through life.[3]

Many have since speculated on what it was about Josephine Baker that made such a strong impression on Henningsen. Was it her singing, was it her body, or was it the 'emancipation' she radiated? Although the ideologists of the Danish feminist movement in the 1970s maintained, logically enough, that it was her bare breasts, it was not really that simple. I believe Henningsen experienced her performance as a total coherence of rhythm, resonance, and body. Josephine Baker could breach norms by other means than those at his own command. She taught him that rhythm was the binding agency between body and consciousness, and that the person capable of blending these three entities opened the way to completely new artistic powers and forms of presentation which, until then, had been absent from his own options as a successful lighting designer, art and culture critic and journal editor.

In 1928 Poul Henningsen closed down *Kritisk Revy* and, with a couple of his co-editors, began writing analytic revues for the Copenhagen stage. This led to collaboration with the composer, arranger, pianist and organist Bernhard Christensen. Their partnership was from the outset an extremely close one. From 1931 to Henningsen's death in 1967 they were professionally inseparable. On a number of occasions Henningsen acknowledged that had it not been for Bernhard Christensen's insight, his own cultural-political achievements would not have made the almost revolutionary impact that they did. It was Christensen who opened his eyes to what I have chosen to call *performative structures* – creative structures in one art form which, with intense innovative effect, could be applied to another art form. Having listened to Christensen's explanations and examples taken from jazz and modern neoclassical music, Henningsen applied these new provocative features to his own art form – design.

Bernhard Christensen's vivid account of how the composer and conductor Igor Stravinsky tackled the Danish Royal Theatre's orchestra proved to be especially motivating.[4] In 1934 the theatre had engaged Stravinsky to work on some of his compositions, including *Petrushka*, and during the rehearsals he fought doughtily with an orchestra for which neoclassicism was made of much the same kind of inferior material as jazz. Christensen, who also worked with the orchestra at this time, crept up into one of the balconies to listen in on how it was faring under the baton of the maestro. And, sure enough, things were not going too smoothly. In the middle of the rehearsal, a clarinettist sarcastically remarked: "Oh no, I've just realised that I should have played that movement on a B clarinet, and I've played the whole thing on my A clarinet.

But it doesn't matter, does it?" – "No," replied Stravinsky, "as long as you do it rhythmically!"

That the musician was a note wide was of no importance whatsoever to Stravinsky, who focused on the specified rhythms. This was a revelation to Christensen – and consequently to Poul Henningsen. That rhythm took precedence over sound was quite simply revolutionary.

Poul Henningsen embraced this startling breach of convention and brought it into action as an artistic weapon in all his activities. He first implemented it in 1935 for a documentary and publicity film commissioned by the Ministry of Foreign Affairs entitled *Danmark*, subsequently known as *Danmarksfilmen* (The Film of Denmark). The previous year he had combined his new insights into the human body and jazz music in an article titled "Jazz, hav og elskov" (Jazz, Sea and Love):

> As regards jazz and dance, [they are] more instinctive areas ... The agenda for modern dance is purely that of naturalness, balance, composure – and un-lasciviousness ... Modern dance and music can be said to be a passionless and aesthetically cool composition on the subject: when the two sexes really meet.[5]

This optimistic linking of jazz and sexuality tended to be perceived by the vast majority of the Danish population in an entirely negative light. Jazz was the music of untamed instincts, inciting lasciviousness, immoral living, and lechery. Christensen was well aware of this when Henningsen asked him to compose the score for the *Danmark* propaganda film, cautioning that the nation was not yet ready to set its agricultural and manufacturing exports against a background of music written by a jazz composer. But Henningsen stood firm, insisting that he would not make the film without Christensen.

The composer provided an hour-long score comprising oriental themes, vocal trios, big band, instrumental improvisation and neoclassicism. For example, Christensen and Henningsen used the jazz sound for their description of cement production in Aalborg, a city in the north of Jutland – and by the end of the film they had created a completely new cinematic architecture by letting the camera follow the basic neoclassical rhythmical structure of the music.

The film was met with exactly the reception that Bernhard Christensen had anticipated – the accompanying jazz music being the greatest bone of contention. Moreover, a number of reviewers sensed that Poul Henningsen's visual composition and filming technique had been inspired by Soviet film directors such as Sergei Eisenstein, which certainly did not make the response less hostile. Poul Henningsen was depicted as an internationalist who was trying to smuggle Black jazz, Soviet cinema, and German Bauhaus functionalism into Danish national realism. That the Danish Communist *Arbejder-Bladet* (Workers' Journal) wrote an extremely positive review, and made special mention of the music, would hardly have helped a film about Denmark that was scheduled to be shown in every country other than the Soviet Union (where jazz, incidentally, in 1935, was censured in much the same way as it was in, for example, the Nazi-Fascist countries Germany, Italy, Spain and Portugal). The film was well received in Belgium, for instance, but this, inevitably, had no influence on Danish opinion. The film-musical version of "Jazz, Sea, and Love" – albeit duly wrapped up in butter, bacon, smoked herring, beer and cement – did not represent 'all' of Denmark and was therefore labelled un-Danish. The film was re-edited into smaller segments and garnished with traditional national tunes. This was Poul Henningsen's only foray into the film medium. Twenty years later *Danmark* was hailed as a masterpiece, and today it remains one of the high points of Danish documentary filmmaking.

Poul Henningsen continued to write articles for left-wing journals and songs for polemical revues. All these new social and artistic perspectives enabled him to formulate a specific concept which he called "cultural coherence." He first introduced this concept in 1933 in a book titled *Hvad med kulturen?* (What about Culture?), and he developed it in many articles and lectures during the 1930s. His thesis was that there is a cultural concord between concurrent phenomena and modes of expression – mental as well as material: work, leisure, family, entertainment, art, emotions.

During the German occupation of Denmark in the Second World War, Poul Henningsen wrote a number of cryptic songs for polemical theatre revues, and, following threats from Danish Nazi collaborators in 1944, he had to seek refuge in Sweden like many other artists and intellectuals at the time, where he would continue to write and give lectures.

Young Danish (and Swedish) architects, painters, writers, actors, composers, and musicians in the 1930s and 1940s admired his free-thinking, his critical sense of humour, and his uncompromising opinions on architecture, town planning, and cultural affairs – and, not least, his inventive approach to work with lamps and lighting. This was also the case with two young students who attended the School of Architecture at the Royal Academy of Fine Arts in Copenhagen – Jørn Utzon and Henning Larsen, later to become internationally recognised architects. And in much the same way as Poul Henningsen had been closely affiliated with an innovative jazz composer and musician since his youth, so did Utzon and Larsen each link up with a fellow student in the 1940s with whom they would remain friends for the rest of their lives: the two highly gifted and innovative musicians Kjeld Bonfils (architect, composer and pianist/vibraphonist) and Max Brüel (architect and saxophonist).

Jørn Utzon and Kjeld Bonfils studied together at the School of Architecture from 1937 to 1942. Bonfils was one of Utzon's close friends. He provided a direct link to jazz and modern music, to the liberal – "cultural radical" – lifestyle, as well as to Poul Henningsen. In his architectural designs, Utzon is deeply concerned with basic musical structures. The foundation in his architectural approach is the musical classicism of Johan Sebastian Bach and the Bach sons. But, as happened to the organist Bernhard Christensen, Stravinsky's reconstruction and redesigning of the great Baroque masters was also to be Utzon's destiny. The Sydney Opera House is clearly planned along Russian neoclassical musical lines – an architectural visualisation of Stravinsky's *Petrushka*.

In an interview, Jørn Utzon spoke to me about the influence of music on his architectural work and about his relationship with Poul Henningsen:

> Poul Henningsen was of course an interesting man. In him our generation had a man who was older than us, and with his revues he basically set the tone for the social life of the time. Kjeld Bonfils, who played jazz, was in my study group. There was such an atmosphere of jazz. He was also a highly talented architect. Poul Henningsen's approach to architecture was very different to that of Kay Fisker, Kaare Klint, and

Steen Eiler Rasmussen,[6] etc. They were traditional in some ways. But he, Poul Henningsen, was very inspiring.

Was Poul Henningsen's modern approach a kind of resistance to what you learnt at the Academy?

Some modern things came from him. But it was mostly that strange lifestyle that appealed to our generation.

What kind of music did you listen to apart from jazz?

Different kinds of music, actually – Russian music, for example. The classics, of course. But Shostakovich and Stravinsky too, everything Russian. And folk music! I didn't listen to the music that came along later – although quite a lot of twelve-tone music, Arnold Schoenberg, for example. But when I got further into the work with the Opera House, I entered an absolutely fantastic universe. Music has been good for me – and I was listening to Stravinsky when I was designing the Opera House.

[A design based on the music of] Carl Philipp Emanuel Bach is hanging there. In the Opera House you can see Carl Philipp Emanuel Bach's *Englische Konzerte*. No buildings – apart from churches – have art works telling you what goes on inside them. And so I had to have a picture of the music. And Carl Philipp Emanuel Bach's music provides the precept: the deep notes make for an onward-moving rhythm and the solo instruments play a fluttering sound-picture between and behind. It's the only place that has a music picture hanging on its walls. There aren't any in the new Opera [Copenhagen Opera House].[7]

Throughout his work Utzon has adhered to the connection between musical and architectural structures. In the book documenting his ESPANSIVA building system that was utilised in his many courtyard houses, and with a few pages from a cello tutorial, he insists on the direct structural – and I would say performative – connection between the building blocks of music and those of architecture. "And if you take ESPANSIVA," he explains, "you could almost say that it corresponds to a notation system playing its music."[8]

The idea of an inspirational connection between Poul Henningsen's lamps and Utzon's Sydney Opera House is tempting. And, indeed, Utzon told me that a Spanish architect had illustrated this connection by trying to slice through a PH-lamp on its side. I, too, have long toyed with the idea – and the lamps. Not to demonstrate any dependence – inspiration comes from anywhere and everywhere – but in order to point to a tradition and also to show respect for an admired predecessor. It is precisely in this way that Baroque composers, so highly valued by Utzon, honoured their role models – through hidden sequences, quotations and accent. Kjeld Bonfils composed a piece called "Contrasts" which could very well have been the working title for the Sydney Opera House designs. The illustration below shows Utzon's Sydney Opera House superimposed with a PH-light.

Sydney Opera House with PH-lamp. Photo: Jesper Larsen and Mads Folmer. Montage: Mads Folmer

Ten years later a similar alliance between an architect and a jazz musician occurred. Henning Larsen, who studied at the School of Architecture in the years 1948-52, became close friends with fellow student and saxophonist Max Brüel – and they later became collaborators. Through Brüel he got to know the new bebop-jazz milieu of the time, and through Verner Panton (a student who would later became a renowned architect and lighting designer) he met the circle surrounding Poul Henningsen.

Henning Larsen spoke about these friendships and acquaintances in an interview that outlined the significant role music played in his architectural work:

> I knew Max Brüel very well. Needless to say, we talked about music, but, you know, he was the supreme musician, incredibly dynamic. And he was just as much a musician – if not more – as he was an architect, I would say. And if any musicians came to Copenhagen from abroad – Louis Armstrong, for example – then he'd have to play with them, and they had these splendid jam sessions.

Have you felt inspired by classical composers?

> Yes, indeed. I'm very fond of classical music. Particularly the works I have long appreciated and enjoyed.

What about Stravinsky?

> I remember the first Stravinsky concert I attended at the Academy of Fine Arts in Copenhagen many years ago. It made a deep impression on me. It was the first time I'd ever heard Stravinsky's music. It was in 1949, or something like that. It was quite incredible. I thought it was fantastic and very stimulating and completely different from everything else I'd heard. I was passionate about it from the very moment of that first concert.

Did you have any contact with Poul Henningsen when you were studying at the School of Architecture?

> I knew his son-in-law, Verner Panton. We were good friends and spent a lot of time together. I met PH on many occasions and visited his

home in Usserød [a suburb of Copenhagen], and through Verner I also had a lot of contact with the people around PH.

The cultural radical milieu? Did you go along with that?

Yes, completely. That was PH, after all. And, indeed, the times, too. Architects were very inspired by PH's ideas. And that's what the radical milieu and free-thinkers like himself – and his own daughter – advocated. Verner Panton was very open-minded. Well, we all were!

Have his lamps had any influence on you?

I've greatly admired the lamps, but they particularly influenced Verner Panton, who became a lighting designer himself. He was very taken with PH and his lighting and lamps.[9]

Henning Larsen's considerations of light can be seen put into practice all over the world, and his bond with musical structures is very clear in his Copenhagen Opera House. In the evening and early morning the building resembles a blank page of sheet music. During the day the notes move around the windows and

create visual life and musical movements. And, moreover, he has designed the Opera House as a large expanse of glass that can reflect and be reflected, a glowing form that can be switched on and switched off. A lamp!

The illustration of the Copenhagen Opera House superimposed on a PH-lamp (as with Utzon's Sydney Opera House) illustrates the speculative connection I am making between Henning Larsen and Poul Henningsen, whom he greatly admired and respected.

Poul Henningsen is not very well known outside Denmark – even though millions of his PH-lamps are currently used all around the world. One of them (from the first 1926 series with solid opal glass) is in the collection at the Museum of Modern Art in New York. Throughout his adult life he goaded the elite art establishment and outraged most of the Danish population. For a small but steadily growing group of his compatriots he was a pioneer and role model. But for architects, designers, artists from every discipline, and intellectuals, he was a major figure who introduced the new modern lifestyle in which social criticism and polemical arts were implicit. And it is my contention that for Jørn Utzon and Henning Larsen, Poul Henningsen was The *PH*antom of the Operas in Sydney and Copenhagen.

Translated by Gaye Kynoch

The Copenhagen Opera House with PH-lamp.
"The Cone" model 1958. Day and night.
Photo and montage: Mads Folmer.

Notes

1 "Cultural radicalism" translates the Danish "kulturradikalisme," and designates a historical cultural movement – intellectual and leftist in orientation – which emerged in the Danish inter-war period, and which had Poul Henningsen as one of its leading figures.

2 "Til Josephine Baker" ("To Josephine Baker"), in the newspaper Politiken (26 June 1928).

3 "Pornografiens pædagogiske Værdi" (The Pedagogic Significance of Pornography), in Kritisk Revy 2 (1928).

4 In Denmark, the national opera, ballet and spoken drama companies – relics of the eighteenth-century monarchical form of government – are still gathered under one umbrella institution: the Royal Danish Theatre.

5 Published in the journal Aandehullet (literally: a blowhole; figuratively: a place where one can breathe freely), 3 (1934).

6 Architects and professors at the School of Architecture, Royal Academy of Fine Arts, Copenhagen.

7 A fourteen metre long floor-to-ceiling tapestry designed by Utzon. It was installed in the former Reception Hall re-named the Utzon Room in honour of the architect in 2004. The design was inspired by C.P.E. Bach's Hamburg Symphonies (in the English Concert-style) and Raphael's painting Procession to Calvary. Sourced from the Sydney Opera House's website at <http://sydneyoperahouse.com/about/utzon_room.aspx>.

8 Jørn Utzon, interview by author, 22 January 2005.

9 Henning Larsen, interview by author, 29 January 2005.

You Are Here

John Di Stefano

moving image + documentary paradigm + performativity

1. Evidence

1.1 Amsterdam. September.

It is overcast and windy. I am with my partner. We are walking in the city. We pass the Anne Frank House in the Jordaan district and walk toward Westerkerk church on our way to the adjacent canal. I spontaneously begin recording with my video camera. My partner points out *Homomonument*, the international gay monument, next to Westerkerk. Church bells ring and I suddenly recall Anne Frank's description of Westerkerk's bells from her diaries. She describes the bells as both joyous in their purity and horrific in their ability to remind her of the enclosure she is forced to inhabit. The church bells mark out the passing of time. It is remarkable to me that I am listening to the same bells that Anne Frank had experienced and written about more than fifty years earlier.

My partner finds a plaque that reads:

> HOMOMONUMENT
> Commemorates all men and women ever oppressed and
> Persecuted because of their homosexuality.
> Supports the international gay and lesbian movement in their [sic]
> Struggle against contempt, discrimination and oppression.
> Demonstrates that we are not alone.
> Calls for permanent vigilance.
> Past, present and future are represented by the
> 3 triangles on the square, designed by Karin Daan, 1987.

Homomonument is comprised of three separate pink granite elements:
(a) a tiered triangular pier that juts into the adjacent canal;
(b) a large triangular structure at knee height, suitable for sitting;
(c) a similar sized triangular element, flush at street level inscribed with:
NAAR VRIENDSCHAP ZULK EEN MATELOOS VERLANGEN
(For friendship, such an immeasurable longing).

The three pink granite elements are configured to form a larger triangular zone superimposed over the square situated between Westerkerk and the adjoining canal. These three separate granite elements are linked together by a continuous line of granite embedded into the street's cobblestones. People walk across the monument, and cars drive over the monument where it overlaps with the street. I trace the periphery of the monument with my video camera.

1.2 Filming the area surrounding *Homomonument*, I stop moving and frame the pier of the monument with the video camera. There are people on the pier. Two men walk back off the pier, move towards me, notice the camera, and subsequently turn away and exit the frame. A man and a woman stand on the pier for a while; she is animated and he is not. They do not see me. They do not know I am recording them. At the same time, a tourist barge is passing by in the canal. The man and the woman move towards the edge of the pier. In the foreground, a taxi passes across the frame while I focus on the couple. As the man and woman reach the edge of the pier, the man opens a container that he has been holding. He empties its contents – ashes – into the canal. The woman puts her arm around the man. I am at once incredulous and deeply moved by what has just transpired in the viewfinder. I ask my partner if he also witnessed what has just happened. He puts his arms around me and tells me that the man has just spread someone's ashes into the canal. I stop recording.

2. Spatial Considerations

2.1 *Homomonument* is grafted into the cobblestones of the city, and is thus physically and figuratively imbedded in its everyday activities. Due to the nature of its

268

on street-level design, the monument might be thought of as an urban space at which temporal activities unfold. It is a dynamic urban space that is activated by the actions, meetings, coincidences, etc., which occur there, such as the event that I was able to capture on video. We might thus think of *Homomonument* as a type of node or hub of experience. This implies a future potentiality since it embodies perpetuating actions in the everyday. It is not the physical space *per se* that constitutes *Homomonument*, but rather the events that 'take place' there that demarcate and delineate it as a site of intersections, arrivals and departures. This also evokes the image of a palimpsest since it puts into play 'something that was (t)here'. In this way, we might think of temporality and duration as constituting elements of *Homomonument*.

While recording, I was moved by the events unfolding in front of me, but also by the way in which the act itself of recording seemed to concentrate the intensity and accumulation of experiential elements – past and present, subjective and objective – at that place, at that time, *through* the camera. The convergence of such fragmentary events within the complexity of the everyday movement of the city was astonishing to me, but perhaps not so rare given the nature of a city like Amsterdam with its numerous inhabitants and visitors, and with the city's historical past. However, these seemingly unrelated occurrences might have been ignored, overlooked or never perceived at all were it not for the video camera's presence. My own subjective position outside of the frame – behind the camera – connected my memory of reading about the chiming church bells of Westerkerk in Anne Frank's diaries (enacting a connection to the historical extermination of Jews and gays in World War II) with the unfolding act of mourning and commemoration of the spreading of ashes, occurring in the present. Past and present converge idiosyncratically.

My complicity in the events at *Homomonument* involved my embodiment as a witness of the spreading of ashes *through* the act of recording. This witnessing was given a particular resonance by my memory of reading about the trauma of the Holocaust. Place, time and machine were aligned in such a way as to offer me a fleeting glimpse into the complexities of interwoven present human actions and the lingering residues of a historical past. The act of recording became the site (sight) in which a singular temporality was written over, eclipsed, by a multiple and personal 'history-in-the-making', a 'becoming-

269

history' involving memory, commemoration and witnessing within the every-day of the city. The camera and the act of recording created an opening up of a tangible 'space' for such a convergence to occur and thus 'mark the spot' at *Homomonument*. You might say that I was at the right place and the right time, conjointly at *Homomonument* and behind the camera.

2.2 Critical theorist Sue Golding offers some useful observations that might shed more light on the events at *Homomonument*. In her own attempt at radicalizing notions of space, time and belonging, Golding introduces the concept of *not-space* to describe a state that oscillates between a conceptual, non-physical articulation of place, a discussion of concrete space, and notions of fluid identities.[1] She refers to the city as the site of possibilities and potentialities – of multiple, overlapping and simultaneous identities that appear and re-appear continually – much as I experienced and recorded them at *Homomonument*.

She puts forth the concept of *space-time* as a kind of imaginary but never-theless real and dynamic fourth-dimension where the body (both symbolic and real) manifests itself along the city's many trajectories. The diversity of experi-ences in the city leads to different discourses for different audiences, and sug-gests that a historical imagination seems to be annihilating the geographical as we have known it. The visual quality itself of the city has important signifi-cance for providing clarity, or legibility of the cityscape, and we must thus look beyond the city as an object in itself to the city as perceived/perceivable by those who traverse it.

We might thus consider the city of Amsterdam as made up of a series of nodes or synapses in a larger global network of diasporic movement rather than as an imagined, fixed multicultural community that seeks to impose unity upon difference within a sanctioned nation-state (in this case the Netherlands). Arjun Appadurai would call this *trans-city*,[2] a notion of the city that turns away from the sphere of fixed, even nationalist, types of definitions and (self)imaginings. Here, cities become open spaces of potential (and thus infinite) crossings. Out of these notions of the city emerges a view of identities that places the diasporic flows of people who constitute the city's cultural diversity in the context of con-temporary transnational movements of information, cultures, commodities and capital. In other words, Amsterdam emerges as what postcolonial theorist Avtar

270

Brah describes as *diaspora space*,[3] a space in which the genealogies of cultural dispersion become entangled with those of 'staying put'. These modalities can, and indeed do, happen and exist in a type of simultaneity. Brah suggests adopting a framework of multilocationality by which diasporic communities, in their myriad configurations, sustain an ideology of 'return' without buying into a discourse of fixed origins. The complex form of dispersion described by the concept of diaspora leads to a multi-placedness of 'home' which allows people to feel at home without declaring a particular, singular and fixed place *as* home (or abode). *Homomonument* might thus represent one type of home for gays – a place where one person's ashes might return home.

2.3 Although situated in Amsterdam, *Homomonument* could be anywhere, and, indeed, there exist many similar places of commemoration dispersed throughout the world. In this sense, we can consider *Homomonument* a type of *trans-locality* or a place that is characterized by Brah's idea of *multilocationality*. This highlights the way in which this space/place can be simultaneously part of the Amsterdam city/Dutch nation-state and also separated from it. Due to the flow of people-events through it and the mobility and diversity of the population, we might argue that *Homomonument* can be situated as both a peripheral enclave determined by notions of sexual orientation within a dominantly non-queer Amsterdam, and a global space/place reflecting changes in the international arena. Not least among the diasporic movements that constitute and activate the space of *Homomonument* in this way are the comings and goings of the gay-lesbian-queer community and the relations of exchange (in the form of leaving flowers, spreading ashes, videotaping, etc.) they maintain with their localized gay-lesbian-queer communities in their countries of origin.

The 'queer nation' is indeed a type of diasporic community if we are to understand Brah's notion of diasporic movement in the context of the transnational flows associated with globalization, both because these flows accelerate and augment the possibilities for the mobility of people, and because they facilitate enhanced modes of contact and exchange within and between diasporic communities. Notions of time and space as concurrent elements of an ever-changing configuration might thus better reflect the diversity and multiplicity of people's experience across physical and symbolic borders.

271

3. Objectivity/Performativity

3.1 In his reflections on the filmic, Andrei Tarkovsky proposes that moving images are the taking of an impression of time, and that the currency of cinema exists principally in its ability to embody time "lost or spent or not yet had."[4] According to Tarkovsky, cinema concentrates the experience of time and in so doing enhances experience by making it more memorable since it allows the viewer to experience time as a type of 'memory-happening-now'; that is, it re-presents the past as an experience in the present. The filmic apparatus is built around the ability to suture the viewer into a type of spatio-temporal system of representation that is experiential as much as it is representational. This sutur-ing covers over the absence of the viewer at the 'original' event by creating a representational experience of that event within a durational realm.

Within documentary discourse, suturing is key in the viewer's ability to engage with the image. Susan Scheibler states that

> [the] desire to represent the unnameable, to name the other, to organ-ize the past and memory into a discourse and to furnish that discourse with referentiality, often seeks to find an articulation through the doc-umentary image. The notion of documentary attempts to legitimize its discourse by means of a claim to a privileged relationship to the real ... [suggesting that the spectator be] an omnipotent and omniscient observer, able to traverse the gap between signifier and signified by means of various codes of authenticity and veracity. These codes, in turn, act to guarantee a position of unity and mastery, a suturing over of a lost plenitude and coherence.[5]

In documentary discourse there has been a tendency to regard the objective recording of events as maintaining a rhetoric that keeps the self behind the camera, officially absent or invisible from what happens in front of the lens. This notion has been challenged for well over half a century by generations of doc-umentary makers who have rethought the language that seeks 'objectivity' by creating a gap between subject or self and the object or other. Filmmakers have evolved various modes of documentary practice that acknowledge (and indeed

272

foreground) their position behind the camera.[6] This suggests that there is more than simply factual information that goes into our understanding of the world. Bill Nichols proposes that for some documentary makers this knowledge might be best described as being concrete and embodied. Nichols coins the term *performative* documentary to describe a mode that emphasizes the subjective and affective dimensions of the world within the documentary paradigm.[7] This suggests a revised thinking about visible evidence as something aligned along the axis of private rather than singularly public realities, as something that moves towards the 'truthful' rather than simply 'factual'.

In his discussions on photography, Roland Barthes posits that the photographic image establishes a unique relationship between appearance and reality by forming a binding interface between representation and object.[8] Unlike other means of representation, photography does not 'invent' but rather engages with a type of authentification since its referent is necessarily real. This is based on a belief that at some time an object has been present in front of the camera, thus providing the photograph with an inherent referentiality. The photography is thus defined by its ability to bind the referent to itself. This apparent convergence of truth and reality has been the foundation of our ability to believe the documentary image.

Annette Kuhn suggests that the importance of on-the-spot observation and the centrality of the camera operator serve as the defining characteristics of a filmic practice which renders visible the already observable.[9] Scheilber continues:

> The "having-been-there" of the image provides the groundwork for the belief that what is seen is what would have been there had not the photographer ... been present ... The sense of immediacy, in turn, guarantees that the referent that adheres to the image is able to certify the existence of what it represents. By pointing out and pointing to the object, observation and description emerge as legitimate enterprises entailed by the photographic image which documents the existence of the real even as it certifies its own authenticity.[10]

273

Scheibler provides useful distinctions between the constative and the performative as they relate to the authenticity and authority of the documentary's interrogation of the object.[11] She characterizes the constative as a modality that (a) promises consistency and resemblance of sign (signifier) to referent (signified); (b) depends on the principle of equivalence which promises that an image equals a representation of its referent, thus understanding the referent as a nameable, knowable and mastered actuality; (c) understands filmic language as being able to transmit truth and provide a means of knowing and mastering reality, allowing for meaning to last and remain stable and coherent. The *performative* is understood to (a) examine the breaks and ruptures in the constative as well as in the discursive apparatus itself; (b) reveal the *desire* for referentiality rather than actually constructing it; (c) not inform or describe, but rather accomplishes an act through the very process of its enunciation (i.e. it *does* something rather than *says* something); (d) confront the constative with its own assumptions of authority, authenticity, veracity, and the ability to be verified.

3.2 The acknowledgment of the camera operator certainly serves to authenticate the 'having-been-there' of the constative. Too often, however, the camera operator's presence in the mechanism of gathering visible evidence is reduced merely to that of a technician. I would suggest that in certain instances – as in the case of the *Homomonument* footage – there is more at play. The subjectivity of the camera operator (i.e. myself, the filmmaker) might suggest ways in which we might understand a documentary practice of observational recording as providing an expanded spatial understanding of belonging,

We might consider this foregrounding of the filmic apparatus as a performative move in its self-reflexive attitude within the constative aspect of the documentary image. The self-reflexivity implicit in the performative can be considered the motivating factor that might transform a mere observer into an engaged witness. Here I am suggesting that there exists an important distinction between observing and witnessing. To witness implies that one assumes the position of an external observer: that is, someone not directly involved in enacting the event being observed. However, witnessing also implies an empathetic stance that somehow 'binds' witnesses to what they see unfolding before them, whereas observing lacks that subjective positioning. Jill Bennett suggests that the filmmaker who witnesses in this way partakes in a larger system of meaning. By recording, the filmmaker acts as a type of facilitator who enables the subjects to articulate their experience, allowing them to come into view.[12] A complicity is implied here since the facilitator, by default, is invested in the process of something coming to view. Some have even gone as far as to suggest that this complicity is crucial to a genuine engagement with any documentary image.[13] We might consider the observing and recording of visible evidence at *Homomonument* to be akin to a fluid, subjective performative act within a specifically localized environment *through* the act of witnessing.

As a witness, I inhabit a space of *betweeness* with regards to the event transpiring (spreading of ashes) and with regards to the documentary object being produced (video recording of the spreading of ashes). There is both a connection to the event and a separation from it. This entails the ability to *feel* or empathize as well as the sense of not fully embodying the event due to my position away from it (behind the camera and in the realm of the anonymous). This gap can only be bridged if we understand my position *between* as one that is constituted in the performative. Here the performative is not concerned with describing in a constative manner, but rather accomplishes an act through the very physicality of my 'being-there'. My being-there is constituted not only in my role as camera operator, but also as a human witness with subjectivity that provides the potential to *feel* without being directly involved in the events transpiring before the camera. In this way my *betweeness* might also be described as a *doubling*, where an affective encounter creates meaning and engages with the performative.

Bennett elaborates on the nature of encounter by turning to Gilles Deleuze's notion of the *encountered sign*. An encountered sign is physical and can only convey meaning via what is felt through the body, propelling "us into a form of intellectual inquiry through its assault on our senses, emotions and bodies."[14] Encountered signs do not rely on the mimetic shock value of an image, but rather on the ability the image has to evoke the duration of trauma in memory: "Our bodies take us into this place, not as witnesses overshadowing the primary subjects of this pain, but in a manner that demonstrates, at the same time, the limited possibilities of either containing or translating pain."[15]

I would posit that the physical realm that Deleuze identifies in his formulation of the *encountered sign* is linked to the performative. As a particular

kind of witness to the spreading of ashes at *Homomonument*, my role encompasses more than merely being a camera operator. I am also a gay man who has come to this particular site on my *own* trajectory through the city. I too come to *Homomonument* to seek a space of belonging. The convergence of the ringing of Westerkerk's bells and the spreading of ashes is a remarkable coincidence to be sure, but it is the *physical* (aural) chiming of the church bells that triggered a particular memory in my mind (Holocaust), which then converged with, and superimposed itself over, the spreading of ashes. This convergence could not be fully recorded on video however. It was only fully manifest through my physical presence at that place and at that time. It was *through* the act of recording that I was able to embody the realm of the performative. The camera acts as a mediating device in its ability to make a referential image, but also in its ability to create an activity (i.e. recording) within which I could insert myself as subjective witness. The video camera was able only to focus on and record the sound of the church bells amidst the cacophony of the city, followed by the visible act of ashes being spread in the canal. The link between the two – their relation – could only be manifested in my physical presence there as *witness*.

If we return to Susan Scheibler's description of the performative, we might say that my subjective, physical self does not inform or describe but rather accomplishes an act of *betweeness* or *doubling* through the very process of its enunciation, thus confronting the constative (the video recording) with its own *limited* assumptions of authority, authenticity, veracity, and verifiability. Here we might reconsider the referential aspect as one that is not necessarily viewed as an entity to be captured but rather as a discourse that expresses its referential knowledge as an act within and through the performative. This reminds us that the performative involves an opening up of the experiential field of desire. The desire here involves my role not only as a type of facilitator *between* an event and its recording, but also as embodiment of a *doubling* of the past (Anne Frank) and the present (spreading ashes). I would posit that in this performative realm of betweeness and doubling, I engage in my own subjective form of belonging and *return* through the *performance* of witnessing and commemoration.

3.3 In his writing on film, Pier Paolo Pasolini proposed a provocative way of thinking about the relationship between the documentary image and death.[16]

276

He believed that for every event that could be documented, multiple perspectives exist, all of which potentially impart valuable information about the event. No singular vantage point of any event could be privileged over another, and all vantage points are inherently subjective. If we had documentary footage of an event recorded from every possible vantage point, we might say that we possessed a collection of multiple subjectivities of a singular event. In this way we would have a multiplication of present moments. Consequently, these multiple 'presents' have the effect of emptying out our notion of a singular definitive present since the existence of multiple (filmic) presents reveals the unreliability and ambiguity of a singular definitive truth. Each of these representations of reality (which we might call fragments) is impoverished when we consider that each one is only one among many.

Pasolini continues by stating that, despite the uncertainty elicited by multiple vantage points, each of the documentary fragments does express reality, albeit in a limited, partial way. They each speak their own language, which is one of action. Each fragment is a sign that is firmly engaged with the *present* act of witnessing a given event. What is important for Pasolini is that *presentness* (i.e. action) is the language of such a documentary object, and is therefore a non-symbolic sign. The non-symbolic sign can only make sense, however, if it is contexualized. For it to have meaning, the non-symbolic sign must be related to other languages of action. This contextualization (in the form of editing) requires each non-symbolic sign, or fragment, to find a relation to another in order to render the present of each fragment as past. It is in this way that the various fragments acquire meaning. Pasolini states that in this process of contextualization (editing), there is a potential for the emergence of a "real order" – understood to be a way of relating significant parts of the various fragments in a sequence so that the differing points of view dissolve and subjectivity gives way to objectivity. Editing thus transforms the present into the past:

> The substance of cinema is therefore an endlessly long take, as is reality to our senses for as long as we are able to feel (a long take that ends with the end of our lives); and this long take is nothing but the reproduction of the language of reality. In other words, it is the reproduction of the present.[17]

Pasolini insists that reality has its own language and that indeed reality *is* a language. This language coincides with human action since it represents our ability to modify and imprint ourselves on reality. Like the multiple documentary fragments, action lacks unity as long as it remains incomplete. Put another way, as long as there is a future (i.e. as long as someone is still alive) the language of one's actions remains open to change and thus cannot be defined. Until a person is dead (i.e. ceases to have action), they cannot be known because their actions are still unfolding and thus have the potential to recontextualize all preceding actions. Pasolini asserts that it is necessary to die "because while living we lack meaning, and the language of our lives ... is untranslatable: a chaos of possibilities, a search for relations among discontinuous meanings."[18] Death is akin to the editing process he describes above, where the various fragments dissolve and subjectivity gives way to objectivity (i.e. closure). Here, the significant moments of one's life (no longer changeable) become sequenced and thus convene our uncertain present into a definitive and describable past. In this way, it is only through death that life becomes expressive.

4. Coda

4.1 If knowledge arises in large part from subjective, embodied experience as Deleuze suggests, to what extent can it be represented by the impersonal and disembodied language of the observational recorder? I have made an initial attempt at trying to theorize away from the dominant notions of visible evidence that privilege a disembodied stance over feeling and the corporeal. I have suggested that some documentary/observational practice insists on the acknowledgment and representation of experience and, therefore, the body itself as a subjective witness to what it observes.

If we are to consider the events that I witnessed/recorded at *Homomonument* as an example, we can identify a potential schism between the apparently objective position I occupied as camera operator and the simultaneous subjective experience I embodied (as a gay man) as a witness at this queer site. But this apparent schism only emerges if a singular, constative position is privileged. To understand this event as constituted by multiple positions, and thus "unnameable" by necessity, is to begin to move towards a more complex and nuanced understanding of the real. The expressivity that is implied by such a shift is central to understanding representation that breaks with documentary conventions of authenticity by resorting to the performative.

The performative play in and around the constative claims of the documentary image might now be understood as necessary to an expanded relationship between actuality and 'non-fictional' representation. In other words, the space of the camera, and the space behind the camera, might become integral to the understanding of events in front of the camera. In the case at *Homomonument*, not only do the ashes find a home to which they may return; I, too, as a witness and a documenter, find a space in which I might enact a return. The camera becomes a nodal means providing a space of meeting between subject and observer, and also a space of interface, both technically and conceptually, where various articulations of home meet. The articulation of home is doubled in a particular way here. It is embodied by the spreading of ashes and by having the event witnessed, but also – and crucial to our discussion here – this act of witnessing takes place *through* the act of recording. Ironically, the end of a life is preserved and able to live on in various forms through the flux of moving images.

Notes

1 Sue Golding, "Quantum Philosophy, Impossible Geographies and a Few Small Points about Life, Liberty and the Pursuit of Sex (All in the Name of Democracy)," in *Place and the Politics of Identity*, ed. Michael Keith and Steven Pile (London: Routledge, 1993).

2 Arjun Appadurai, *Modernity at Large: Cultural Dimensions of Globalization* (Minneapolis: University of Minnesota Press, 1996).

3 Avtar Brah, *Cartographies of Diaspora: Contesting Identities* (London: Routledge, 1996).

4 Andrei Tarkovsky, *Sculpting in Time: Reflections on the Cinema* (Austin: University of Texas Press, 1989).

5 Susan Scheibler, "Constantly Performing the Documentary: The Seductive Promise of *Lightning Over Water*," in *Theorizing Documentary*, ed. Michael Renov (New York: Routledge, 1993), p. 136.

6 Bill Nichols identifies some of these as the *participatory* mode, the *reflexive* mode and the *performative* mode. See Bill Nichols, *Blurred Boundaries: Questions of Meaning in Contemporary Culture* (Bloomington: Indiana University Press, 1994).

7 Bill Nichols, *Introduction to Documentary* (Bloomington: Indiana University Press, 2001), p. 131.

8 Roland Barthes, *Camera Lucida: Reflections on Photography* (New York: Hill and Wang, 1981).

9 Annette Kuhn, "The Camera I: Observations on Documentary," *Screen* 19.2 (1978), as cited by Susan Scheibler in "Constantly Performing the Documentary," in *Theorizing Documentary*, ed. Michael Renov, pp. 141-142.

10 Susan Scheibler, "Constantly Performing the Documentary," p. 142.

11 Ibid., pp. 139-140.

12 Jill Bennett, *Empathic Vision: Affect, Trauma and Contemporary Art* (Stanford: Stanford University Press, 2005).

13 E. Ann Kaplan, *Trauma Culture: The Politics of Terror and Loss in Media and Literature* (New Brunswick: Rutgers University Press, 2005), p. 124.

14 Jill Bennett, *Empathic Vision: Affect, Trauma and Contemporary Art*, p. 64.

15 Ibid., p. 65.

16 Pier Paolo Pasolini, "Osservazioni sul piano-sequenza," in *Empirismo Eretico* (Milan: Garzanti Editore, 1972), pp. 237-241.

17 Ibid., p. 240.

18 Ibid., p. 241.

Credits

All images: John Di Stefano

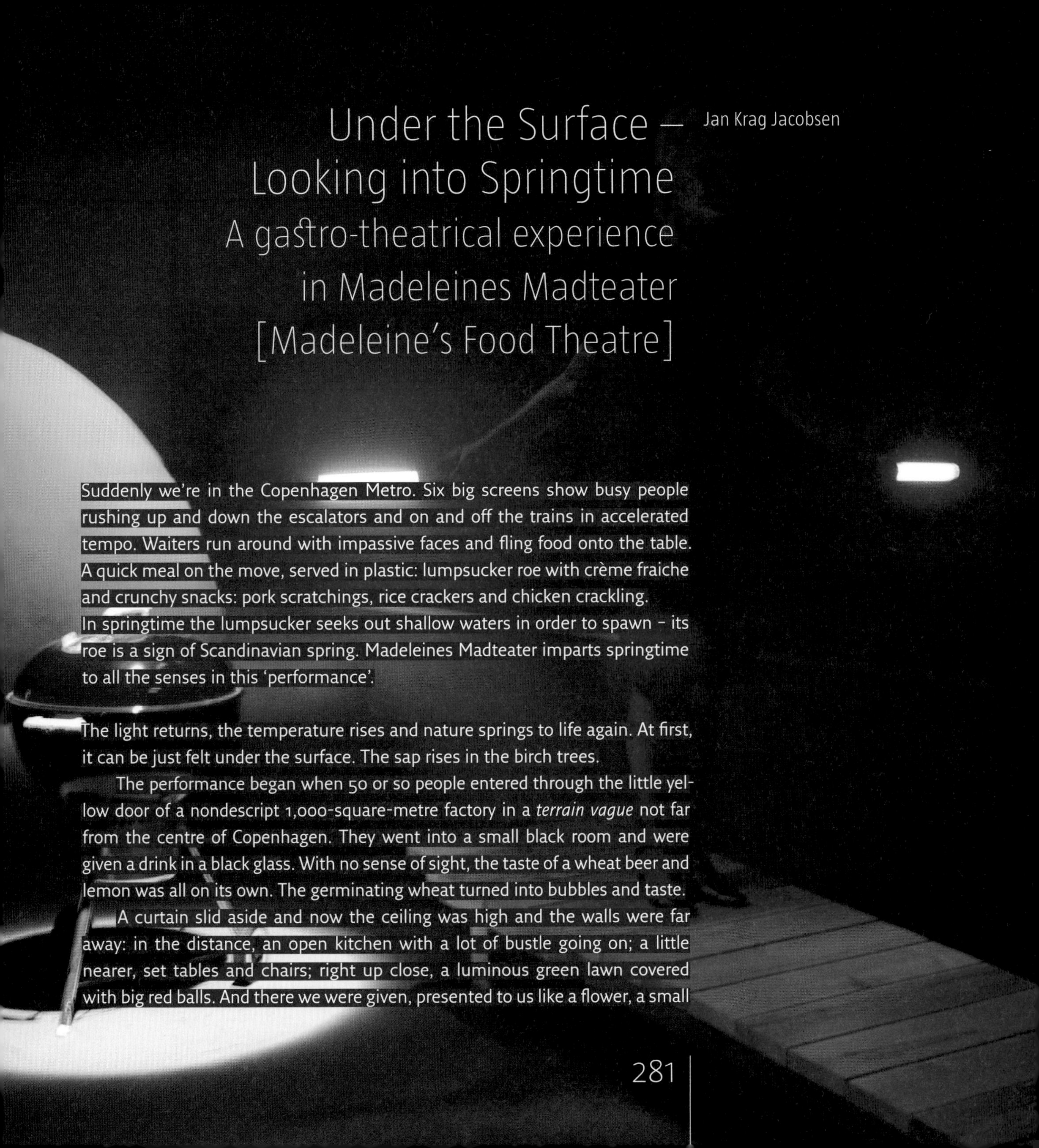

Under the Surface — Looking into Springtime

Jan Krag Jacobsen

A gastro-theatrical experience in Madeleines Madteater [Madeleine's Food Theatre]

Suddenly we're in the Copenhagen Metro. Six big screens show busy people rushing up and down the escalators and on and off the trains in accelerated tempo. Waiters run around with impassive faces and fling food onto the table. A quick meal on the move, served in plastic: lumpsucker roe with crème fraiche and crunchy snacks: pork scratchings, rice crackers and chicken crackling. In springtime the lumpsucker seeks out shallow waters in order to spawn – its roe is a sign of Scandinavian spring. Madeleines Madteater imparts springtime to all the senses in this 'performance'.

The light returns, the temperature rises and nature springs to life again. At first, it can be just felt under the surface. The sap rises in the birch trees.

The performance began when 50 or so people entered through the little yellow door of a nondescript 1,000-square-metre factory in a *terrain vague* not far from the centre of Copenhagen. They went into a small black room and were given a drink in a black glass. With no sense of sight, the taste of a wheat beer and lemon was all on its own. The germinating wheat turned into bubbles and taste.

A curtain slid aside and now the ceiling was high and the walls were far away: in the distance, an open kitchen with a lot of bustle going on; a little nearer, set tables and chairs; right up close, a luminous green lawn covered with big red balls. And there we were given, presented to us like a flower, a small

281

bread on a stick, and the waiter straight away blew a little prawn-mint-peanut foam onto it. A lit barbecue with a sparerib added to the garden-party atmosphere. The meat was not to be eaten, just smelt. Suspense hanging in the air. The light vanishes.

A shining bridge emerged. It led us to our dining table, and then we ate spring herring, pickled cumquat, smoked eel foam and calves marrow pesto. There was birch sap and Riesling in the glasses, while naked people moved gracefully through blue water and amid ascending bubbles on the big screens. A spring poem sent words into the air. And the busy people on the kitchen plateau were always in view.

Rush-hour noise in the Metro was abruptly replaced with the sounds of nature. Contrast. The tables were cut off from one another by lengths of white material. The food arrived in airplane trolleys: sous-vide squid with herb bouillon, baked garlic, garlic mayonnaise, potato crisps and rose petals. A hot cloth bag of wheat grains was placed on each persons neck. Solicitude. Birdsong merged into classical Japanese music.

At this point all our senses were stirred and we were on the verge of losing our bearings. But, with perfect timing, a printed menu appeared, looking back and forth in the experience.

The white cloth walls disappeared and the surround film began again. A poem written on a child's naked body. Soft Japanese pop music. Calf's tongue and meat balls with springtime stinging nettles, lovage and broccoli. An aromatic Côtes du Rhône glistened in the glasses.

A child's hand turned into a red tulip, and flower after flower blossomed on the big screens. Sweet things on the plates and plum wine in the glasses. The chefs come in and hang little cakes of various colours on a gnarled tree in the middle of the room. The light dims, small paper flowers tumble down from the ceiling over the tree. The light becomes stronger, the show is over.

Finally, we go into Madeleine's tea salon, where we drink tea. Lounging on sand-coloured divans we enjoy a *petite madeleine* with a nod to Marcel Proust's *Remembrance of Things Past* which is triggered by a cake dipped in linden tea.

Credits

Performance: *Under the Surface – Looking into Springtime*
Location: Drechselsgade 10, 2300 Copenhagen S, Denmark
Date: spring 2007
Chef: Mette Sia Martinussen
Designer: Nikolaj Danielsen
Photographer: Annick Boel

Translated by Gaye Kynoch

SEEN Fruits of our Labor is an interactive installation that invigorates a public plaza through an alternative form of communication. It was installed in front of the San Jose Museum of Art facing Cesar Chavez Park during the ZeroOne San Jose Festival 2006. The 'monolith' is a communication device modeled after the ubiquitous obelisks, plaques and sculptures that populate public squares. Such traditional monuments carry messages that memorialize founding principles or historical events. However, this monument presents a seemingly inscrutable object to the public that, through interaction, broadcasts a variety of unshared principles from the mouths of everyday people. These deal with their projected hopes and the American Dream in light of globalization.

The project asks members of three communities that make up San Jose's labor needs – Silicon Valley's technology workers, undocumented service workers and outsourced call center workers – one question: What is the fruit of your labor? Their responses are displayed back to San Jose's general public on a 4' × 8' infrared LED screen that can only be viewed using digital capture devices like cell phone cameras, digital cameras, DVcams, etc. This is because the image capture technologies on these digital devices are sensitive to infrared wavelengths that are invisible to the naked eye. Our interest in using this alternative communication spectrum was in response to the evermore spectacular media that constantly accost our attention. By presenting the public with a 'visibly' silent screen, the audience is solicited to consciously participate or labor to interact with the information.

SEEN Fruits of our Labor | Omar Khan

The relationship that binds these disparate communities is economics. Through the globalization of networked communication an unprecedented population is now able to engage in the market place with results that are both exploitative and liberating. Silicon Valley is a key global player whose products are consumed the world over. Whilst the workers' reliance on its economy is clear, their understanding of mutual participation in it is less obvious. For instance, the outsourced call center workers are physically remote from the valley while the undocumented service workers maintain a necessary invisibility so as not to be deported. *SEEN Fruits of our Labor* attempts to make this globally dispersed group of people more perceptible to one another as a coherent community. The traditional role of the public plaza as the means through which people and institutions communicate with one another has long been superseded by mass communication – what Marshall McLuhan called the electronic agora. *SEEN* looks at the potential confluence of these two divergent technologies, public space and mass communication, to reanimate conversations between communities. During its installation *SEEN* instigated vibrant interactions between people who shared their viewing devices with total strangers, discussed its streaming messages and telematically communicated their viewing experience with others in their phonebook. It also brought voices, like the badly stigmatized undocumented workers, into the public arena.

Credits

Performance: *SEEN Fruits of our Labor*
Location: San Jose, California
Date: August 2006
Producers: Omar Khan and Osman Khan through an awarded commission by the ZeroOne San Jose Festival 2006
Designers: Omar Khan and Osman Khan with Alice Ko, Drura Parish and Dustin Ohara assisting in the fabrication of the screen and César Cedano and Matthew Zinski assisting in the surveys, media production and installation of the screen
Directors: Omar Khan and Osman Khan

Black Box

Black boxes hide their workings. We know what they do but not how. They record everything and in the event of a catastrophe can be relied upon to divulge secrets of which even we who participated were unaware. The monolith is an 8' tall, 4' wide, 1'6" deep black acrylic screen embedded with infrared LEDs. To the naked eye it is a blank surface waiting for information to be carved into it. However, when viewed through any CCD device (digital, digital video or phone cameras) its messages magically appear on the user's screen. What was previously hidden from view, the fruits of others' labors are revealed to them to be photographed and shared.

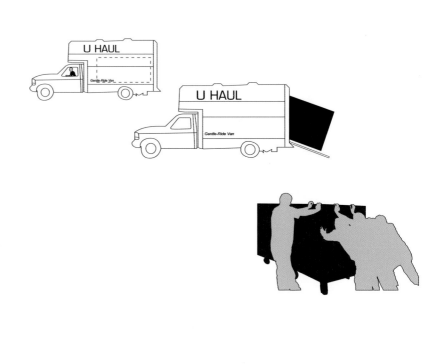

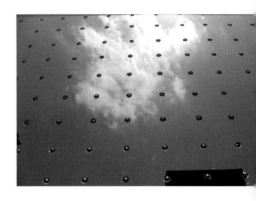

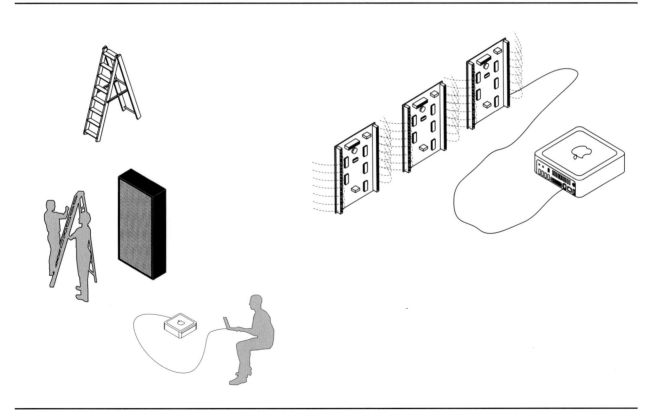

The Local Neighborhood-
Silicon Valley

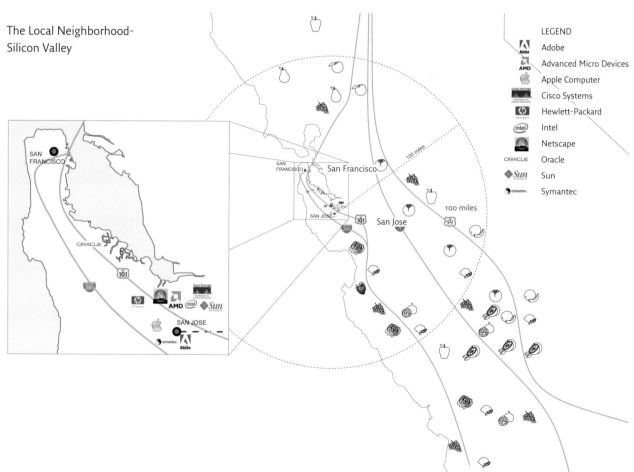

LEGEND

Adobe
Advanced Micro Devices
Apple Computer
Cisco Systems
Hewlett-Packard
Intel
Netscape
Oracle
Sun
Symantec

The Global Neighborhood-
The migration of fruit and labor

Shanghai
Hangzhou

Hsinchu

Guangzhou

New Delhi

Mumbai
Hyderabad
Chennai
Bangalore

Davao City

San Jose

Mexico
57% undocumented immigration

Latin America
24% undocumented immigration

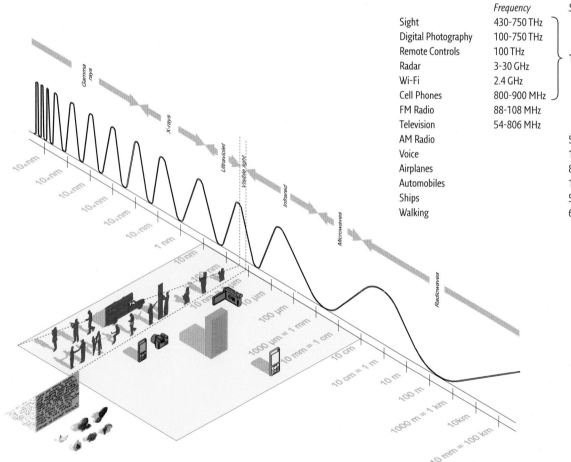

	Frequency	Speed
Sight	430-750 THz	
Digital Photography	100-750 THz	
Remote Controls	100 THz	
Radar	3-30 GHz	1,079,252,848.8 km/h
Wi-Fi	2.4 GHz	
Cell Phones	800-900 MHz	
FM Radio	88-108 MHz	
Television	54-806 MHz	
AM Radio	530 kHz-1.7 MHz	
Voice		1238 km/h
Airplanes		885 km/h
Automobiles		100 km/h
Ships		52 km/h
Walking		6 km/h

The **American Dream** is a foundational myth, which says that through hard work and determination one can achieve prosperity. For citizens as well as immigrants it is an enduring hallmark of the United States. However, continuing uncertainties about the future have made many skeptical of achieving this potential.

62% say it is harder to achieve the American Dream compared to their parents' generation while 24% say it is easier.

Reasons

76% personal debt
69% expectation of a good life handed to them
69% lost touch with important values
68% harder to make ends meet
61% materialistic culture
58% government has wrong priorities
54% society favors the rich
51% low wages

Impediments

81% high cost of healthcare
66% high cost of housing
66% outsourcing of jobs
63% taxes
61% government spending
42% say they will not be able to achieve their idea of the American Dream while 22% are unsure.

[Source: 2004 poll conducted by Widmeyer Communications for the Center for a New American Dream]

corridor 1

empty room

shadows

candle

sweeping paper + dolls

puppet family

puppet baby

baby birds

waiting

puppet murder

skirt dance

Laundry

feeding mother

corridor 2

Homesick storyboard:
Joslin McKinney.

Homesick
The scenographic exchange

Joslin McKinney

This visual essay explores the nature of the communication between scenography and its audiences by engaging with the notion of performance design as construction. For Caspar Neher design was emphatically a construction and not a picture. This called attention to the physical interaction between the stage space and the performer but also emphasised scenography as essential in the meaning-making process of theatre and a vehicle for ideas in parallel with, but separate from, the actor and the text.[1] Creating meaning through the apparatus of scenography originates with the scenographer, but during the performance the audience become complicit in this process. An engagement with the interactive elements of scenography – space, bodies, objects, movement, and the images that are subsequently created – affords a means of revealing the world.[2]

Homesick was a piece of performance-as-research that engaged audiences directly through a sensory immersion in scenography. The performance evoked images of childhood memory, homely routine and domestic tension. The design heightened the audience's awareness of space, scale and objects and the way they themselves were enfolded within the scenographic environment. I intended to produce a visual narrative which was evocative yet open-ended, triggering sensations and inviting further reflections from each of the spectators.

Afterwards, participants were invited to process their experience through making and discussing their own images. These images reflect, elaborate, and reinterpret the scenography as originally conceived. They also point to some key characteristics which might be more universally applied to scenography.

"...an impression of whiteness, diffused light, traces of things happening beyond the light, things in the past, like a brass rubbing."

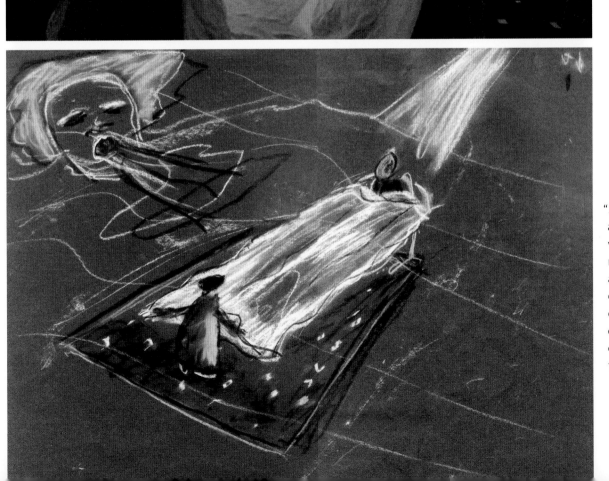

Photo: Paul Davies

"... a drawing of a face blowing wind like on old maps ... wind and generation of air ... a sensory experience ... the double cloth ... the cloth got bigger and took over the space."

"...a figure with one arm raised, the top hand much larger and distorted, like a goblin with long fingers in a book from my childhood... the lower hand is smaller, like a child's... It was an unnerving image which reoccurred as female puppet wiped hands after murder."

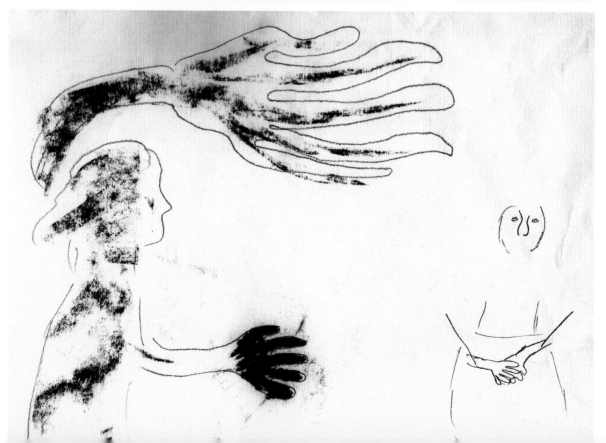

Photo: Paul Davies

"...a small figure in a very large house, a lonely person trapped in one room in what could have been endless possibilities in huge house, but stuck in one room."

"I drew an eye to show a sense of being watched by other audience and by the performers. It is an old eye, an experienced eye."

Audience responses show that scenography can be experienced through several senses simultaneously. Although vision is the principle means of perception, this is complemented by images being perceived haptically, stimulating embodied understandings of the physical and material world. These sensations are often registered through impressions and fragments rather than in fully-formed images. Details of the composition spark new points of reference, often linked to the spectators' subjective feelings and their private experiences from the past. Their own scenographic imaginations are set to work. They extend the designed visio-spatial realm by projecting and transforming the scenography of the performance into significant images and spaces of their own. Through this research, I am in the privileged position of being able to see how the original images multiply and mutate, returning to be folded back into my subsequent work.

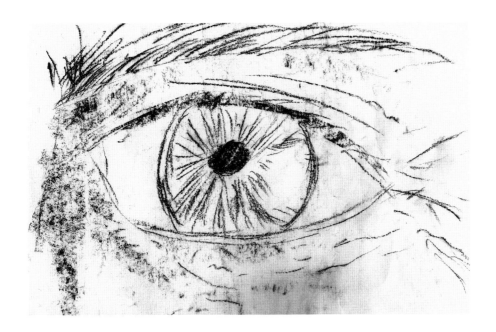

Homesick was a site for exchange where the process of experiencing and making sense of scenography became a mutual imaginative construction containing multiple refractions and perspectives. The spatial dimension of the performance offered a modality of experience and thought where alternative ways of seeing could be activated. In this way, performance design can be considered as a communal, even collaborative, experience of image construction.

Notes

1 Neher developed his theories on performance design while working with Bertolt Brecht. For further discussion see Christopher Baugh, "Brecht and Stage Design: The Bühnenbildner and the Bühnenbauer," in *The Cambridge Companion to Brecht*, ed. Peter Thomson and Glendyr Sacks (Cambridge: Cambridge University Press, 1994), and Christopher Baugh, *Theatre, Performance and Technology: The Development of Scenography in the Twentieth Century* (Basingstoke and New York: Palgrave Macmillan, 2005), pp. 74-79.

2 Heidegger's exploration of *techné* and its definition as a means of revealing through engagement with the material world offers a perspective on scenography as a process of thinking or a provocation to think in new ways. See Martin Heidegger, *The Question Concerning Technology and Other Essays* (New York: Harper and Row, 1977), pp. 3-35. See also Paul Crowther's exploration of Heidegger's theories in relation to the work of art and the viewer and the notion of the "sensuous manifold" in Paul Crowther, *Art and Embodiment: From Aesthetics to Self-Consciousness* (Oxford and New York: Oxford University Press, 1993).

Credits

Performance: *Homesick*
Location: University of Leeds, UK
Date: 28 and 29 April 2005
Designer and Director: Joslin McKinney
Design Assistants: Aram Park, Helen Smith and Rebecca Walker
Research Assistants: Jenniefer Gadsby and Gillian Parker
Performers: Matthew Davidson, Jonathan White and Kathleen Yore

Probably, you were not there. Probably, when the shutter snapped (upon 1/60, 1/125, 1/500 of a second) you were not there. Had you been, chances are you were looking the other way – perhaps at something more interesting. And then, had you been there, had your head even been poised upon the photographer's shoulder, your view, still, would not (quite) have been his. Furthermore, these brilliant lenses – what else had they been cast upon that day/life/lunchtime? We blink our shutters upon a unique viewpoint moment by moment and even then the inner screen upon which we throw the picture is constantly ghosted by the trace of every preceding, unique image...

And so, perhaps, that's where the work finally 'is'. Perhaps the destiny of 'display', the fate of 'encounter', is simply to invite and assist another's 'construct' – 'If we come, they will build it', so to speak. At least this was the way of *The Water Banquet*: a field of activity delivering a series of 'dishes' (object/sound/image) assembled as 'courses' (beginnings/middles/ends) according to the menu selections of eighteen strangers gathered at a table of water. Whilst precise in preparation and service, 'consumption' was prized as another's business. For example, you order the Kinder Piñata (beginnings). By a great and circuitous route and within a mesh of juxtaposed activity, a young girl, finally, delivers you a duck egg which, cracked into a silver-rimmed glass, produces a cascade of blue liquid and a tiny photograph of an elderly man summoning courage before the camera. On the reverse is written, 'I first picked up the violin when I was five...' What will you *make* of it? I couldn't say. Nor, when, thirty minutes later (middles), you see an elderly gentleman playing a violin at the table's head whilst a waitress meticulously plants 116 forks into the table in a steady downpour of rain. I can only guess at what it is you see... I don't know the correct way to assimilate these things any more than I know the correct way to

The Water Banquet | Richard Downing

taste honey, or hear Mozart. But I do know this. You really had to be there. And you had to be you. And had you been there, amongst eighteen unique 'others', the thing itself would, in turn, have become a different display/encounter/construct. With The Water Banquet we referred not to the *spectator*, but to the *guest* – this has much to do with the necessity of co-presence, but even more with recognition of another's imagination as the real site of completion.

But what to do now, now that the 'work' has been invited into a book (a strange invitation – like inviting a butterfly to pin itself to the board)? How to display traces for the constructive encounter of a guest present only after the fact, and how to embody that invitation towards creative completion? Well, maybe a problem's only an opportunity in jackboots... So I spent some time cutting and folding paper, printing onto acetates and shining torches through these onto blank pages. I made some 'pop-up' experiments; tried the images in sealed sleeves of water, etc. I toyed with navigable VRML environments, and flirted with the interactive possibilities of the digital. And then, at last, I did something simple and had one of those 'voila' moments that sometimes await simplicity – I turned the pictures upside down. The quality of 'mirror', or, better, 'window' to an imaginative elsewhere seemed to come forward again. And this, now, was something that the new viewer had never missed because it was only ever available, thus. In a sense, fresh bites from the table (not the 'show') are served, displayed, for further creative making. And what is seen through these windows is personal to the new guest, to be blinked, in addition, onto that unique, ghosted, screen because... probably, you were not there. But dammit, you're here now.

Bon appetit.

Credits

Performance/Installation:
The Water Banquet
Location and Dates: Aberystwyth Arts Centre (19-21 October 2001 and 16-23 November 2002); City Hall, Porsgrunn, Norway (15-16 December 2001); Tactile Bosch, Cardiff (16-19 April 2003)
Production Company: U-Man Zoo
Concept/Design/Direction: Richard Downing
Images: Richard Downing, except pp. 320 and 325: Daniel Buxton.

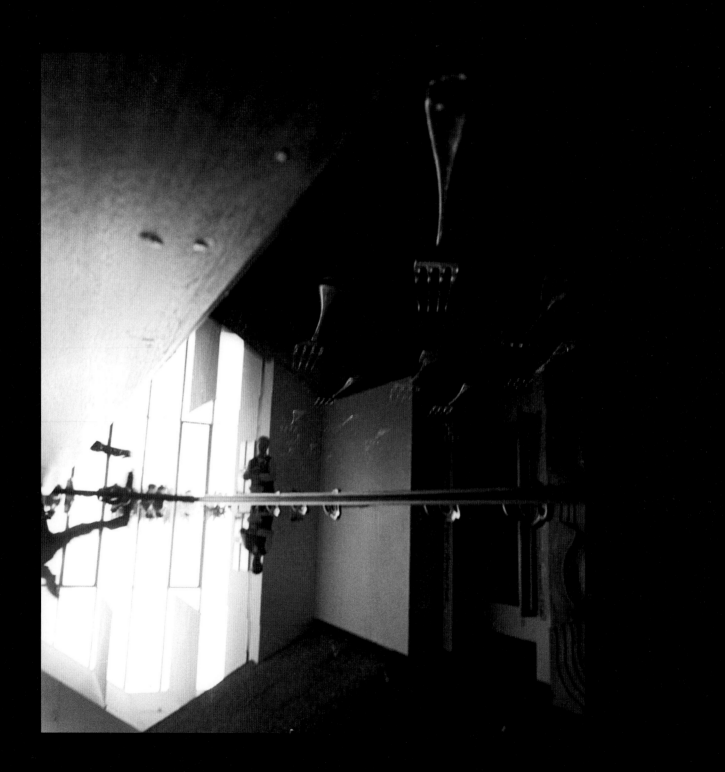

Contributors

ARNOLD ARONSON is Professor of Theatre at Columbia University in New York. He has written numerous books and articles on scenography, including *American Set Design* (1985), *American Avant-Garde Theatre: A History* (2001), and *Looking into the Abyss: Essays on Scenography* (2005). He has been an active member of OISTAT (International Organization of Scenographers, Theatre Architects and Technicians), chairing the Commission for History and Theory, and in 2007 he served as General Commissioner of the Prague Quadrennial, a four-yearly international exposition on theatre architecture and design.

THE ART DESIGN COLLECTIVE is an interdisciplinary team based at Massey University's College of Creative Arts in Wellington, New Zealand, which was formed to research the intersection between art and design. The collective consists of artist Anne Noble, who is Professor of Fine Arts (Research) and a noted international photographer, designer Sven Mehzoud, who lectures in Spatial Design and focuses on performance and exhibition design, and graphic designer Lee Jensen, who lectures in Visual Communication Design.

CATHERINE BAGNALL lectures in the Fashion program at Massey University's College of Creative Arts in New Zealand. Her practice as an artist positions itself between fashion and performance, exploring clothing's ability to transform and transcend the wearer. Current work focuses on how clothing can offer revelatory experiences in feminine ways of being and becoming through representations of the clothed female body.

SIMON BANHAM is Lecturer in Scenography at Aberystwyth University in Wales. He is a founder member of Quarantine Theatre Company. At the core of his work is the renegotiation of the relationship between performers and spectators, exploring a "reality" of encounter that couples the immediacy and comprehension of the mundane with the intensity and heightened awareness of a theatrical event.

LILJA BLUMENFELD is Professor of Scenography at the Estonian Academy of Arts in Tallinn. As a scenographer she has designed extensively in many theatres in Estonia and recently in London. She is a guest lecturer at London College of Fashion, Wimbledon

College of Art, and Zurich University of Applied Arts, as well as a researcher at ELO, University of Art and Design, Helsinki, where her focus is on the visual constructions of consciousness in the theatre and on the screen.

CAROL BROWN is a choreographer, performer and writer whose company, Carol Brown Dances, is based in London and tours nationally and internationally. Formed in 1996 with the composer Russell Scoones, the company is renowned for collaborations with visual artists, photographers, film makers, architects and sound designers. The dances arise from an ongoing investigation into bodies, their histories and inventions, and the mediation of these through writings, film, digitization, buildings and sounds. Carol Brown is Reader in Choreography at Roehampton University.

FABRIZIO CRISAFULLI is Professor at the Academy of Fine Arts in Florence, Italy, and also a theatre director and visual artist. He is the leader of the Rome-based theatre company Il Pudore Bene in Vista. A major part of his theatre and installation works are site-specific events. His special contribution to performance design lies in the use of light as a structural and poetic device of the piece. Crisafulli has written books and essays on theatre and design.

KIRSTEN DEHLHOLM is the founder and artistic director of Hotel Pro Forma (1985-). As a visual artist she directs performances that combine the visual arts with architecture, sound, language, light design and digital media. She regards each production as a new experiment that contains a double staging: the contents and the space. Hotel Pro Forma has performed in Europe, Asia, Australia, Russia and the USA. Dehlholm's work has been acknowledged through many awards from important Danish Arts Institutions.

RICHARD DOWNING is Artistic Director of installation/performance company *U-Man Zoo* and lectures in Scenography at Aberystwyth University, Wales. As a writer of texts once dismissed as "theatrically unreasonable" by a commissioning theatre in London, his creative practice and teaching nonetheless continue to approach scenography as a holistic form of authorship; one often inspired by location and object and capable of affording extraordinary encounters in unorthodox places.

DORITA HANNAH is Associate Professor at Massey University's College of Creative Arts in New Zealand. As architect and scenographer her focus is on the intersection between space and performance, allowing her to operate as an interdisciplinarian on a variety of research projects and publications, ranging from designing performances through to buildings, exhibitions, fashion and installations.

OLAV HARSLØF is Professor at Roskilde University's Department of Performance Design in Denmark. He has written many books, essays and articles on design, architecture, theatre, music, sound, art, cultural history and cultural politics. He has previously headed the Danish National Schools of Theatre and Dance, as well as the Rhythmic Music Conservatory and has curated exhibitions at the Royal Danish Library.

KATHLEEN IRWIN is Associate Professor in the Theatre Department, University of Regina, Canada. She is Co-Artistic Director of Knowhere Productions Inc. In her community-based, site-specific practice, she explores the performative and generative nature of found space to unlock memory and to redevelop abandoned institutional and industrial space into vibrant cultural environments.

JAN KRAG JACOBSEN is Senior Lecturer in Performance Design at Roskilde University, Denmark, where he has lectured extensively in the departments of Communication and Journalism. He has a background in natural science (chemistry) and is an experienced producer of radio and television programmes. He was president of The Danish Gastronomic Academy for many years and remains active in researching and disseminating knowledge centred on gastronomy and food culture.

OMAR KHAN is Assistant Professor at the University at Buffalo, USA. He is an architect, educator and researcher whose work spans the disciplines of architecture, installation/performance art and digital media. His work and teaching explores the intersection of architecture and pervasive computing for designing increasingly responsive and performative environments. He is Co-Director of the Center for Virtual Architecture and researcher in the Situated Technologies Research Group.

BRANDON LABELLE is an artist and writer working with sounds, places, bodies, and cultural frictions. He is the author of *Background Noise: Perspectives on Sound Art* and co-editor of the "Surface Tension" series published by Errant Bodies Press, which focuses on forms of spatial practice and related issues. He teaches at the University of Copenhagen, and is currently developing projects on auditory design, emotional geographies and street cultures.

JON MCKENZIE teaches courses in performance, new media, and civil disobedience at the University of Wisconsin. He is author of *Perform or Else: From Discipline to Performance* (2001). His current research examines modes of performative power operative in contemporary American imperialism, ranging from executive speech acts to theatres of torture to the mining of data for "actionable intelligence."

JOSLIN MCKINNEY is Lecturer in Scenography in the School of Performance and Cultural Industries at the University of Leeds. She utilises her practice as a means of researching the nature of the communication between scenography and its audiences and is interested in the ways in which design for performance can offer a space for re-interpreting the world.

LISA MUNNELLY lectures at Massey University's College of Creative Arts in New Zealand. Her fine arts practice explores the production and reception of art, with a particular interest in the intimate and unfolding nature of the conversation that occurs between the artist and her work, and how such a dialogue links into ideas of transience, immanence, materiality, immateriality and time. Her work was most recently exhibited in China.

LUCA RUZZA is an architect, set designer and researcher at Sapienza University of Rome. Integrating performance and architecture using high technology systems is the main focus of interest in his creative work. He has been collaborating with national and international theatres and festivals on the creation of multi-media projects dedicated to examining the relationship between images and spaces of varying identities.

JOHN DI STEFANO is Associate Professor and Director of Postgraduate Studies at Massey University's School of Fine Arts in New Zealand. He is an interdisciplinary visual artist, videomaker, writer and curator whose present research examines the relationship between identity, displacement and transnationalism by examining how concepts and perceptions of memory, space/place, and time shape the articulation of subjectivities.

METTE RAMSGARD THOMSEN is Associate Professor at the Royal Danish Academy of Fine Arts, School of Architecture, where she leads the research facility Centre for Information Technology and Architecture (CITA). Her research centres on the design of spaces that are defined by physical as well as digital dimensions. Through a focus on intelligent programming and ideas of emergence, her performance projects explore how computational logics can lead to the design and realisation of behavioural space.

RODRIGO TISI teaches architecture and design at Universidad Católica, Universidad Nacional Andrés Bello and at Universidad Diego Portales in Santiago, Chile. He has written articles on architecture, design, visual arts and performance, taking part in different exhibitions located at the intersection of these disciplines, in Chile and abroad. Recently, he founded MESS, a design studio focusing on the production of space within the constraints of contemporary culture.

Bibliography

Adorno, Theodor. *Aesthetic Theory* (London and New York: Continuum, 1984).

Appadurai, Arjun. *Modernity at Large: Cultural Dimensions of Globalization* (Minneapolis: University of Minnesota Press, 1996).

Appia, Adolphe. *Essays, Scenarios, and Designs.* Edited by Richard C. Beacham. Translated by Walther R. Volbach (Ann Arbor: UMI Research Press, 1989).

Aronson, Arnold. *The History and Theory of Environmental Scenography* (Ann Arbor: UMI Research Press, 1981).

Aronson, Arnold. *Looking into the Abyss: Essays on Scenography* (Ann Arbor: The University of Michigan Press, 2005).

Aronson, Arnold. "Avant-Garde Scenography and the Frames of Theatre." In *Against Theatre: Creative Destructions on the Modernist Stage.* Edited by Alan Ackerman and Martin Puchner (New York: Palgrave, 2006).

Artaud, Antonin. *The Theatre and Its Double.* Translated by Victor Corti (London: Calder and Boyars, 1970).

Augoyard, Jean-Francois and Henry Torgue, eds. *Sonic Experience: A Guide to Everyday Sounds* (Montreal: McGill-Queen's University Press, 2005).

Auslander, Philip. *Liveness: Performance in a Mediatized Culture* (London: Routledge, 1999).

Austin, J.L. *How to Do Things with Words* (Cambridge, Mass.: Harvard University Press, 1975).

Bachelard, Gaston. *The Poetics of Space: The Classic Look at How We Experience Intimate Places* (Boston: Beacon Press, 1994).

Badiou, Alain. "The Event in Deleuze." *Parrhesia* 2 (2007).

Barish, Jonas. *The Antitheatrical Prejudice* (Berkeley: University of California Press, 1981).

Banes, Sally and André Lepecki, eds. *The Senses in Performance* (New York and London: Routledge, 2006).

Barthes, Roland. *Camera Lucida: Reflections on Photography* (New York: Hill and Wang, 1981).

Baugh, Christopher. "Brecht and Stage Design: The Bühnenbildner and the Bühnenbauer." In *The Cambridge Companion to Brecht.* Edited by Peter Thomson and Glendyr Sacks (Cambridge: Cambridge University Press, 1994).

Baugh, Christopher. *Theatre, Performance and Technology: The Development of Scenography in the Twentieth Century* (Basingstoke and New York: Palgrave Macmillan, 2005).

Benjamin, Andrew. *Art, Mimesis and the Avant-Garde: Aspects of a Philosophy of Difference* (London and New York: Routledge, 1991).

Benjamin, Walter. "The Work of Art in the Age of Mechanical Reproduction." In *Illuminations* (London: Jonathon Cape, 1970).

Bennett, Jill. *Empathic Vision: Affect, Trauma and Contemporary Art* (Stanford: Stanford University Press, 2005).

Bhabha, Homi K. *The Location of Culture* (London and New York: Routledge, 1994).

Blesser, Barry and Linda-Ruth Salter. *Spaces Speak, Are You Listening?: Experiencing Aural Architecture* (Cambridge, Mass.: The MIT Press, 2007).

Bloom, Clive. *Violent London: 2000 Years of Riots, Rebels, and Revolts* (London: Pan Books, 2003).

Boyer, Christine. *The City of Collective Memory: Its Historical Imagery and Architectural Entertainments* (Cambridge, Mass.: The MIT Press, 1996)

Brah, Avtar. *Cartographies of Diaspora: Contesting Identities* (London: Routledge, 1996).

Broadhurst, Susan. *Liminal Acts: A Critical Overview of Contemporary Performance and Theory* (New York: Cassell Academic, 1999).

Butler, Cornelia H. *AfterImage: Drawing Through Process* (Los Angeles: Museum of Contemporary Art; Cambridge, Mass.: The MIT Press, 1999).

Butler, Judith. "Performative Acts and Gender Constitution: An Essay in Phenomenology and Feminist Theory." In *Performing Feminisms: Feminist Critical Theory and Theatre.* Edited by Sue-Ellen Case (Baltimore: Johns Hopkins University Press, 1990).

Butler, Judith. *Bodies that Matter: On the Discursive Limits of "Sex"* (New York: Routledge, 1993).

Butler, Judith. *Excitable Speech: A Politics of the Performative* (New York: Routledge, 1997).

Calinescu, Matei. *Five Faces of Modernity: Modernism, Avant-Garde, Decadence, Kitsch, Postmodernism* (Durham: Duke University Press, 1987).

Carlson, Marvin. *Performance: A Critical Introduction* (London and New York: Routledge, 1996).

Case, Sue-Ellen. *Performing Feminisms: Feminist Critical Theory and Theatre* (Baltimore: Johns Hopkins University Press, 1990).

Chapple, Freda and Chiel Kattenbelt, eds. *Intermediality in Theatre and Performance* (Amsterdam and New York: IFTR, 2006).

Chaudhuri, Una. *Staging Place: The Geography of Modern Drama* (Ann Arbor: University of Michigan Press, 1997).

Crary, Jonathan. *Suspensions of Perception: Attention, Spectacle, and Modern Culture* (Cambridge, Mass.: The MIT Press, 1999).

Cresswell, Tim. *In Place / Out of Place: Geography, Ideology and Transgression* (Minneapolis and London: University of Minnesota Press, 1996).

Crowther, Paul. *Art and Embodiment: From Aesthetics to Self-Consciousness* (Oxford and New York: Oxford University Press, 1993).

Csikszentmihalyi, Mihaly and Rick E. Robinson. *The Art of Seeing: An Interpretation of the Aesthetic Encounter* (California: Getty Trust Collections, 1990).

Debord, Guy. *Society of the Spectacle* (Detroit: Black & Red, 1977).

DeNora, Tia. *Music in Everyday Life* (Cambridge: Cambridge University Press, 2000).

Derrida, Jacques. *Writing and Difference*. Translated by Alan Bass (Chicago: University of Chicago Press, 1978).

Derrida, Jacques. *Positions*. Translated by Alan Bass (Chicago: University of Chicago Press, 1981).

Derrida, Jacques. *The Truth in Painting*. Translated by Geoff Bennington and Ian McLeod (Chicago: University of Chicago Press, 1987).

Derrida, Jacques. "Before the Law." In *Acts of Literature*. Edited by Derek Attridge (London: Routledge, 1992).

Diamond, Elin, ed. *Performance and Cultural Politics* (London and New York: Routledge, 1996).

Docherty, Thomas, ed. *Postmodernism: A Reader* (New York: Columbia University Press, 1993).

Elam, Keir. *The Semiotics of Theatre and Drama* (London and New York: Routledge, 1980).

Foucault, Michel. "Of Other Spaces: Utopias and Heterotopias." In *Rethinking Architecture: Reader in Cultural Theory*. Edited by Neil Leach (London: Routledge, 1997).

Fraleigh, Sandra Horton. *Dance and the Lived Body: A Descriptive Aesthetics* (Pittsburgh: University of Pittsburgh Press, 1987).

Fuchs, Elinor and Una Chaudhuri, eds. *Land/Scape/Theater* (Ann Arbor: University of Michigan Press, 2002).

Gade, Rune and Anne Jerslev, eds. *Performative Realism: Interdisciplinary Studies in Art and Media* (Copenhagen: Museum Tusculanum Press, 2005).

Giedion, Sigfried. *Mechanization Takes Command: A Contribution to Anonymous History* (New York: Oxford University Press, 1948).

Grosz, Elizabeth. *Architecture from the Outside: Essays on Virtual and Real Space* (Cambridge, Mass.: The MIT Press, 2001).

Hannah, Dorita. "Body Space: Mining the Limits between Architecture and Dance." In *Sasha Waltz: Cluster* (Berlin: Henschel Verlag, 2007).

Hardt, Michael and Antonio Negri. *Multitude: War and Democracy in the Age of Empire* (New York: The Penguin Press, 2004).

Hartoonian, Gevork. *Crisis of the Object: The Architecture of Theatricality* (London: Routledge, 2006).

Harvey, David. *The Condition of Postmodernity: An Enquiry into the Origins of Cultural Change* (London and Cambridge, Mass.: Blackwell, 1989).

Hays, Michael. *The Public and Performance: Essays in the History of French and German Theatre, 1871–1900* (Ann Arbor: UMI Research Press, 1981).

Heathfield, Adrian, ed. *Live: Art and Performance* (New York: Routledge, 2004).

Heidegger, Martin. *The Question Concerning Technology* (New York: Harper and Row, 1977).

Hoffman, Jens and Joan Jonas. *Art Works Perform* (London: Thames and Hudson, 2005).

Houston, Andrew. "Postmodernism: A Construction of Reality and the Limit of Representation" (Diss., University of Kent, Canterbury, 1994).

Howard, Pamela. *What is Scenography?* (London and New York: Routledge, 2002).

Innes, Christopher. *Avant Garde Theatre 1892–1992* (London: Routledge, 1993).

Jameson, Frederic. *Postmodernism, or, The Cultural Logic of Late Capitalism* (Durham, N.C.: Duke University Press, 1991).

Jay, Martin. *Downcast Eyes: The Denigration of Vision in Twentieth-Century French Thought* (Berkeley and Los Angeles: University of California Press, 1993).

Jones, Amelia and Andrew Stephenson, eds. *Performing the Body/Performing the Text* (London and New York: Routledge, 1999).

Juergensmeyer, Mark. *Terror in the Mind of God: The Global Rise of Religious Violence* (Berkeley: University of California Press, 2000).

Kafka, Franz. *The Trial*. Translated by Idris Parry (London: Penguin Modern Classics, 2000).

Khan, Omar and Dorita Hannah, eds. "PERFORMANCE / ARCHITECTURE." Theme Issue of *JAE: Journal of Architectural Education* 61.4 (2008).

Kantor, Tadeusz. *A Journey Through Other Spaces: Essays and Manifestos, 1944–1990* (Berkeley: University of California Press, 1993).

Kaplan, E. Ann. *Trauma Culture: The Politics of Terror and Loss in Media and Literature* (New Brunswick: Rutgers University Press, 2005).

Kaprow, Allan. *Essays on the Blurring of Art and Life*. Edited by Jeff Kelley (Berkeley and London: University of California Press, 1993).

Kaye, Nick. *Site-Specific Art: Performance, Place and Documentation* (London: Routledge, 2000).

Kern, Stephen. *The Culture of Time and Space: 1880–1918* (Cambridge, Mass.: Harvard University Press, 1982).

Kingston, Angela et al. *What is drawing?* (London and New York: Black Dog Publishing, 2003).

Kipnis, Jeffrey. "Nolo Contendere." *Assemblage* 11 (1990).

Kirshenblatt-Gimblett, Barbara. "Performance Studies." In *The Performance Studies Reader*. Edited by Henry Bial (London and New York: Routledge, 2004).

Kolarevic, Branko and Ali M. Malkawi. *Performative Architecture: Beyond Instrumentality* (New York and London: Spon Press, 2005).

Kristeva, Julia. *Powers of Horror: An Essay on Abjection* (New York: Columbia University Press, 1982).

Kristeva, Julia. *Strangers to Ourselves* (New York: Columbia University Press, 1991).

Kuhn, Annette. "The Camera I: Observations on Documentary." *Screen* 19.2 (1978).

Kwinter, Sanford. *Architectures of Time: Toward a Theory of the Event in Modernist Culture* (Cambridge, MA: The MIT Press, 2001).

Kwon, Miwon. *One Place After Another: Site-Specific Art and Locational Identity* (Cambridge, Mass. and London: The MIT Press, 2004).

Lacan, Jacques. *The Four Fundamental Concepts of Psycho-Analysis*. Edited by Jacques-Alain Miller. Translated by Alan Sheridan (New York: W.W. Norton & Company, 1981).

Lacan, Jacques. *Écrits: A Selection* (New York: W.W. Norton & Company, 2002).

Lacy, Suzanne, ed. *Mapping the Terrain: New Genre Public Art* (Seattle: Bay Press, 1995).

Laurel, Brenda. *Computers as Theatre* (Reading, Mass.: Addison-Wesley, 1993).

Lefebvre, Henri. *The Production of Space*. Translated by Donald Nicholson-Smith (Oxford and Cambridge: Blackwell, 1991).

Lehmann, Hans-Thies. *Postdramatic Theatre*. Translated by Karen Jürs-Munby (London and New York: Routledge, 2006).

Lepecki, André. *Of the Presence of the Body: Essays on Dance and Performance Theory* (Middletown, Conn.: Wesleyan University Press, 2004).

Lepecki, André. *Exhausting Dance: Performance and the Politics of Movement* (New York and London: Routledge, 2006).

Lévinas, Emmanuel. *Time and the Other* (Pittsburgh: Duquesne University Press, 2003).

Lévinas, Emmanuel. *Humanism of the Other* (Champaign: University of Illinois Press, 2003).

Lippard, Lucy R. *The Lure of the Local: Senses of Place in a Multicentered Society* (New York: New Press, 1997).

Lyotard, Jean-Francois. "The Sublime and the Avant-Garde." In *The Continental Aesthetics Reader*. Edited by Clive Cazeaux (London and New York: Routledge, 2000).

McAuley, Gay. *Space in Performance: Making Meaning in the Theatre* (Ann Arbor: University of Michigan Press, 2000).

McHale, Brian. *Constructing Postmodernism* (London and New York: Routledge, 1992).

McKenzie, Jon. "Genre Trouble: (The) Butler Did It." In *The Ends of Performance*. Edited by Peggy Phelan and Jill Lane (New York and London: New York University Press, 1998).

McKenzie, Jon. *Perform or Else: From Discipline to Performance* (London: Routledge, 2001).

McLuhan, Marshall. *Understanding Media: The Extensions of Man* (London and New York: Routledge 1995).

McNeill, William H. *Keeping Together in Time: Dance and Still in Human History* (Cambridge, Mass.: Harvard University Press, 1995).

Marcuse, Herbert. *Towards a Critical Theory of Society* (London: Routledge, 2001).

Massey, Doreen. *Space, Place and Gender* (Minneapolis: University of Minnesota Press, 1994).

Massumi, Brian. *Parables for the Virtual: Movement, Affect, Sensation* (London: Duke University Press, 2002).

Mau, Bruce. *Massive Change: A Manifesto for the Future Global Design Culture* (Phaidon Press, 2004).

Munnelly, Lisa. *The Aesthetics of Immersion: Time Process and Performance in Practice* (MFA Thesis, Wellington: Massey University School of Fine Arts, 2003).

Murray, Chris, ed. *Key Writers on Art: The Twentieth Century* (London and New York: Routledge, 2003).

Murray, Timothy, ed. *Mimesis, Masochism and Mimesis: The Politics of Theatricality in Contemporary French Thought* (Ann Arbor: University of Michigan Press, 1997).

Nichols, Bill. *Blurred Boundaries: Questions of Meaning in Contemporary Culture* (Bloomington: Indiana University Press, 1994).

Nichols, Bill. *Introduction to Documentary* (Bloomington: Indiana University Press, 2001).

Packer, Randall and Ken Jordan, eds. *Multimedia: From Wagner to Virtual Reality* (New York: W.W. Norton & Company, 2002).

Panofsky, Erwin. *Perspective as Symbolic Form*. Translated by Christopher S. Wood (New York: Zone Books, 1991).

Parker, Andrew and Eve Kosofsky Sedgwick, eds. *Performativity and Performance* (New York: Routledge, 1995).

Pasolini, Pier Paolo. "Osservazioni sul piano-sequenza." In *Empirismo Eretico* (Milan: Garzanti Editore, 1972).

Pavis, Patrice. *Dictionary of the Theatre: Terms, Concepts, and Analysis* (Toronto, Buffalo, and London: University of Toronto Press, 1998).

Pavis, Patrice. *Analyzing Performance: Theater, Dance and Film*. Translated by David Williams (Ann Arbor: University of Michigan Press, 2003).

Pearson, Mike and Michael Shanks. *Theatre/Archaeology* (London and New York: Routledge, 2001).

Petroski, Henry. *The Evolution of Useful Things: How Everyday Artifacts-From Forks and Pins to Paper Clips and Zippers-Came to be as They are* (New York: Vintage Books, 1994).

Pine, B. Joseph and James H. Gilmore. *The Experience Economy: Work is Theater & Every Business a Stage* (Cambridge, Mass.: Harvard Business School, 1999).

Pizzato, Mark. "Edges of Perception in Performance and Audience." *Performing Arts International* 1.4 (1999).

Pizzato, Mark. *Ghosts of Theatre and Cinema in the Brain* (Basingstoke: Palgrave Macmillan, 2006).

Rancière, Jacques. *The Future of the Image*. Translated by Gregory Elliott (London: Verso, 2007).

Read, Alan. *Theatre and Everyday Life: An Ethics of Performance* (Routledge: London, 1993).

Robbins, Bruce. *Feeling Global: Internationalism in Distress* (New York: New York University Press, 1999).

Sartre, Jean-Paul. *Being and Nothingness: A Phenomenological Essay on Ontology*. Translated by Hazel E. Barnes (New York: Washington Square Press, 1956).

Schechner, Richard. *By Means of Performance: Intercultural Studies of Theatre and Ritual* (Cambridge: Cambridge University Press, 1990).

Schechner, Richard. *Environmental Theatre* (London and New York: Applause Books, 1994).

Scheer, Edward, ed. *Antonin Artaud: A Critical Reader* (London and New York: Routledge, 2004).

Scheibler, Susan. "Constantly Performing the Documentary: The Seductive Promise of *Lightning Over Water*." In *Theorizing Documentary*. Edited by Michael Renov (New York: Routledge, 1993).

Schneider, Rebecca. "Solo Solo Solo." In *After Criticism: New Responses to Art and Performance*. Edited by Gavin Butt (Malden, Mass.: Blackwell Publishing, 2005).

Schwabsky, Barry. "Painting in the Interrogative Mode." In *Vitamin B: New Perspectives in Painting* (Oxford: Phaidon Press, 2002).

Smith, Bruce R. *The Total Work Of Art: From Bayreuth To Cyberspace* (New York: Routledge, 2007).

Soja, Edward W. "Thirdspace: expanding the scope of the geographical imagination." In *Architecturally Speaking: Practices of Art, Architecture and the Everyday*. Edited by

Alan Read (New York: Routledge, 2000).

Tarkovsky, Andrei. *Sculpting in Time: Reflections on the Cinema* (Austin: University of Texas Press, 1989).

Turner, Victor. "Frame, Flow and Reflection: Ritual and Drama as Public Liminality." In *Performance in Postmodern Culture*. Edited by Michel Benamou and Charles Caramello (Madison, Wisconsin: Coda Press, 1977).

Veltrusky, Jiri. "Man and Object in the Theater." In *A Prague School Reader on Esthetics, Literary Structure, and Style*. Edited and translated by Paul Garvin (Washington: Georgetown Press, 1964).

Vidler, Anthony, ed. *Architecture Between Spectacle and Use* (Yale University Press, 2008).

Vinken, Barbara. *Fashion Zeitgeist: Trends and Cycles in the Fashion System* (New York and Oxford: Berg Publishers, 2005).

Virilio, Paul. *The Aesthetics of Disappearance* (New York: Semiotext(e), 1991).

Warr, Tracey, ed. *The Artist's Body* (London: Phaidon, 2000).

Weiss, Allen S. *Feast and Folly: Cuisine, Intoxication, and the Poetics of the Sublime* (Albany: State University of New York Press, 2002).

Wiles, David. *A Short History of Western Performance Space* (Cambridge: Cambridge University Press, 2003).

Wilson, Eric. "Plagues, Fairs, and Street Cries: Sounding out Society and Space in Early Modern London." *Modern Language Studies* 25.3 (Summer 1995).